iPad®
SECRETS

iPad®
SECRETS

DO WHAT YOU NEVER THOUGHT POSSIBLE WITH YOUR IPAD

Darren Murph

WILEY

John Wiley & Sons, Inc.

ACQUISITIONS EDITOR: Mary James

PROJECT EDITOR: Katherine Burt

TECHNICAL EDITOR: Todd Davis

PRODUCTION EDITOR: Kathleen Wisor

COPY EDITOR: Charlotte Kughen, The Wordsmithery LLC

EDITORIAL MANAGER: Mary Beth Wakefield

FREELANCER EDITORIAL MANAGER: Rosemarie Graham

ASSOCIATE DIRECTOR OF MARKETING: David Mayhew

MARKETING MANAGER: Ashley Zurcher

BUSINESS MANAGER: Amy Knies

PRODUCTION MANAGER: Tim Tate

VICE PRESIDENT AND EXECUTIVE GROUP PUBLISHER: Richard Swadley

VICE PRESIDENT AND EXECUTIVE PUBLISHER: Neil Edde

ASSOCIATE PUBLISHER: Jim Minatel

PROJECT COORDINATOR, COVER: Katie Crocker

COMPOSITOR: Craig Woods, Happenstance Type-O-Rama

PROOFREADER: Nancy Carassco

INDEXER: John Sleeva

COVER DESIGNER: Ryan Sneed

COVER IMAGE: © Chad Baker / Lifesize / Getty Images

iPad® Secrets

Published by

John Wiley & Sons, Inc.

10475 Crosspoint Boulevard

Indianapolis, IN 46256

www.wiley.com

Copyright © 2012 by John Wiley & Sons, Inc., Indianapolis, Indiana

Published simultaneously in Canada

ISBN: 978-1-118-24736-5

ISBN: 978-1-118-28709-5 (ebk)

ISBN: 978-1-118-28320-2 (ebk)

ISBN: 978-1-118-28435-3 (ebk)

Manufactured in the United States of America

10 9 8 7 6 5 4 3 2 1

For general information on our other products and services please contact our Customer Care Department within the United States at (877) 762-2974, outside the United States at (317) 572-3993 or fax (317) 572-4002.

Wiley publishes in a variety of print and electronic formats and by print-on-demand. Some material included with standard print versions of this book may not be included in e-books or in print-on-demand. If this book refers to media such as a CD or DVD that is not included in the version you purchased, you may download this material at http://booksupport.wiley.com. For more information about Wiley products, visit www.wiley.com.

Library of Congress Control Number: 2012933405

This book is dedicated to Dana Murph, who keeps me grounded, invigorated, and passionate; my heaven-sent parents; and my late Uncle Jr., who proved to me that life was nothing without love, laughter, dogs, and travel.

About The Author

Darren Murph is the managing editor of Engadget, a respected publication in the wide world of consumer electronics. He's written nearly 20,000 posts—enough to earn him a Guinness World Record as the planet's most prolific professional blogger—on everything from speech synthesis to gadget dissection. He's a gadget critic, reviewer, and author, and he splits his time between breaking news, covering new launches at trade shows around the world, and reviewing new consumer gadgets.

He has also been a keynote speaker at NEXT Aarhus (an innovation conference in Denmark) and contributes how-to and hacker guides to Bonnier Corporation's *Popular Science* publication. When not immersed in technology, he's a freelancer travel writer for Gadling, where he has covered such extremes as Alaska in the winter and conducted an interview with The Travel Channel's own "Bert the Conqueror."

Darren received a B.S. in Supply Chain Management in 2006 from North Carolina State University and an MBA from Campbell University in 2008. In a former life, he troubleshot a Mac lab at NC State University's D.H. Hill Library, shopped for chemicals at DuPont, and watched Nortel sink into oblivion. He's driven a motorized vehicle in all 50 U.S. states, attempted a FaceTime call with the Queen of England, and has an utterly innocent dog named Gangster.

About the Technical Editor

 Todd Davis is the Media and Communications Director and a licensed minister at Hope Chapel in Apex, North Carolina, near the state's capital. He grew up on the Outer Banks and received a B.S. in Communications & Media Production from East Carolina University.

Todd specializes in video production, web design, and graphic design. As founder of Shorewire Productions, he has created web video and graphic arts for clients ranging from local bands to the regional YMCA.

When he isn't developing iOS apps, creating music, or crafting custom furniture and cornhole boards, Todd enjoys spending time with his wife and two sons.

Acknowledgments

To say the writing of this book was a journey would be an understatement of epic proportions. That said, I couldn't be more thrilled to have taken it, and I have to start by thanking Mary James, my acquisitions editor. Without her taking notice, this project would've never gotten off of the ground. I'm also grateful to Ryan Block and Peter Rojas, the two men that took a chance by starting Engadget, and soon after, hiring me as a freelance editor. It's been an honor to devote my career to covering the world of consumer electronics.

I owe a great deal to editors that have come before me, my teachers, and my mentors. Each former and current Engadget colleague is dear to my heart, and without learning from all of you, I would've been in no position to tackle this book. Thanks to my rivals for keeping me sharp, and thanks to the readers for keeping me accurate.

On a more personal note, I'm hugely grateful to my dearest wife, Dana, for not only agreeing to let me sink countless hours into the construction of this book, but for encouraging me all the while. My mother, Alice, and father, Larry, have been instrumental in keeping me focused, and I'm forever indebted to them both for their unwavering support and love. To the rest of my family: Thank you for believing in me, despite not ever fully understanding what it is that I do.

Special thanks to my technical editor and best friend, Todd Davis, for jumping in headfirst on this endeavor. Writing a guide such as this can be a daunting task, and having a pal and confidante as amazing as Todd enabled me to never truly feel alone. He managed to devote his full attention to this project even after welcoming his second child into the world as we were just getting started, and for that I'm monumentally thankful. To Sam and Ethan, thanks for letting me borrow your pops.

I want to thank Apple for proving me wrong. I wasn't convinced that the iPad had staying power upon its release, and I've never been happier to eat crow. In time, I've come to understand just how important the company's efforts in the mobile realm have become, and I cannot close this section without a tip of the hat to the late Steve Jobs. Our world will be forever less interesting without his genius, but I'm genuinely appreciative for being able to cover and enjoy his final—and most substantial—inventions.

Finally, I want to thank my late Uncle Jr., who taught me that love, perseverance, laughter, and aimless wandering were vital to fulfillment. He's the freest soul I ever knew, and if there are iPads in heaven, I'm sure he'll get a kick out of reading this.

Contents at a Glance

Contents

Introduction

Welcome to iPad Secrets and the universe of iOS. Regardless of whether you're brand new to Apple, iOS, tablets, or computing in general, this book will prove to be the perfect partner in wading through the joys that lie ahead. If you're a seasoned iPad user, the chapters ahead peel back the proverbial onion in order to enrich what's undoubtedly already a rewarding experience.

The pages that follow describe how to slip into the nooks and crannies that are scattered about the iPad world. From little-known tips about tweaking iOS for productivity, to advice on how to make iTunes work *for* you instead of *against* you, it's all here. This book was dreamed up after Apple's iPad had already made an indelible mark on the computing world; in the realm of tablets, there's the iPad and then there's everything else.

In typical Apple fashion, the iPad is drop-dead simple to use, but, perhaps troublingly, there's almost no information handed over in the box as to how to make the most of it. The iPad has carved out an entire new product category, and there are plenty of misconceptions about how to best use the planet's most popular tablet. This book covers in detail everything from advanced setup procedures to workflow strategies, with the excruciating technobabble omitted in order to make the most of your time.

I even dive into the wide and overwhelming world of apps and accessories, pointing out the best and brightest in order to make your iPad the tool you'd always dreamed that it would be. Having issues? There's an entire chapter on troubleshooting, so feel free to get your hands dirty.

I've segmented this book in a way that flows logically for those just picking up an iPad, but if you're an existing owner, I meet you right where you stand. The iPad's easy to use, but it's a tough device to master. iOS 5 has introduced a great many new wrinkles to the equation, and even if you feel comfortable navigating iOS 4, this book provides plenty of new morsels to educate you on all that's new in Apple's latest mobile operating system.

More than anything, I hope this book inspires you to see the iPad as more than just a tabletop accessory, or a content consumption device. It's a powerful tool, but only if you possess the knowledge to uncover its deepest secrets. As you might expect, that's where this book comes in. I should also note that prices provided in the book were accurate at the time of writing but are subject to change.

What You'll Learn from This Book

iPad Secrets shows you more than you ever thought possible about the iPad, a device that you may assume you're already intimately familiar with. Moreover, the book takes a deep dive into all the areas that round off a complete iPad experience, showing you how to master iTunes, the cloud, and all of Apple's related cloud services.

You learn how to tweak your home panes for maximum efficiency, which apps are deserving of your attention, which accessories are worth splurging on, and how to keep your digital life in order. You also gain a greater understanding about iTunes, while also recognizing the incredible streaming power in tools such as AirPrint and AirPlay. You begin to understand how the iPad can become the center of your multimedia-filled life and how it can potentially take the place of numerous gadgets within the home.

After you've digested this book, you'll be able to fully *grok* the intricacies of iOS 5, and you'll know how to fix any issues that you might run into while pushing the iPad to its extremes. You also learn a great deal about yourself, and how you can take the advice that lies ahead and apply it to your specific usage patterns and needs.

Who Should Read This Book

Anyone who is even remotely interested in Apple's iPad family, or iOS 5 on the whole, stands to learn something from this book. Even if you've been an avid iPad user from the start, there's plenty in this book to educate you. This book focuses on iOS 5, Apple's newest mobile OS. It's without question the company's most substantial overhaul yet of iOS, and I've devoted the majority of the pages ahead to breaking down (and digging into) the subtleties of this new build.

Even if you're familiar with the cloud, you can supplement your existing know-how with the tips and tricks explained here. One's iPad experience is largely limited by what one has come into contact with. I introduce you to new apps, techniques, and accessories that you've probably never heard of, all of which are handpicked in order to advance your overall iPad experience. If you think you know it all, or have yourself convinced that you know nothing at all, there's plenty here for you. And you. And *you*.

How This Book Is Structured

The fact that this book is many, many times thicker than the actual iPad says a lot. There's a serious amount of content here and ample avenues to explore. I engineered the layout so that you can read it cover-to-cover and glean plenty, but it's worth taking a more detailed look at how things are segmented. I recommend sticking *loosely* to how the chapters are laid out sequentially, but those with reduced interest in select portions can skip over and return without any loss in understanding. Plow through the first four chapters, and from there, feel free to choose your own adventure.

The opening chapters revolve around the iPad selection process, setting things up initially and getting grounded when it comes to iTunes and iOS interactions. Here, you also learn how to arrange your icons and establish an efficient and productive e-mail management system; in my mind, these are cornerstones to enjoying the iPad.

The middle is where the technophiles will truly find their groove. If there's a nook or cranny within the iPad universe to be explored, you find it here. These chapters dive deep into advanced functionality and accessories, providing an in-depth look at oft-overlooked settings and scenarios to make the most of your iPad purchase.

The closing chapters are meant mostly for those who aren't afraid of serious tinkering, and also, for those who bundled in a budget to snap up a few accessories. Many extensions of the iPad require external purchases, and if you're willing to splurge, the best of the best are listed here. I close with a full chapter dedicated to troubleshooting; if you run into issues at any point, feel free to flip to the end and dig in.

Features and Icons Used in This Book

The following features and icons are used in this book to help draw your attention to some of the most important or useful information in the book, some of the most valuable tips, insights, and advice that can help you unlock the secrets of the iPad.

Watch for margin notes like this one that highlight some key piece of information or that discuss some poorly documented or hard to find technique or approach.

SIDEBARS

Sidebars like this one feature additional information about topics related to the nearby text.

TIP The Tip icon indicates a helpful trick or technique.

NOTE The Note icon points out or expands on items of importance or interest.

CROSSREF The Cross-Reference icon points to chapters where additional information can be found.

WARNING The Warning icon warns you about possible negative side effects or precautions you should take before making a change.

PART I

BECOMING AN IPAD SETUP PRO

CHAPTER 1

Selecting and Setting Up Your iPad

IN THIS CHAPTER

- ▶ Deciding which iPad is right for you
- ▶ Understanding the perks (and costs) of 3G/4G-enabled data
- ▶ Dealing with non-expandable storage
- ▶ Configuring Find my iPad
- ▶ Working with wireless networks
- ▶ Updating your iTunes build
- ▶ Organizing your iLife

One of the beautiful things about Apple in general, and the iPad in particular, is the complete simplicity of the buying process. Apple's never been one to offer limitless customization options, which just so happens to be both a blessing and a curse. Tweakers are no doubt flustered by the single screen size option (9.7"), the sole CPU choice, and the inability to order an iPad with more memory, but the limits also serve to curb confusion and fragmentation in the portfolio. This chapter breaks down the options that *do* exist in the blossoming iPad universe, explaining the pros and cons of each so you can decide if you should use your hard-earned greenbacks for an upscale model. I also help you understand how to manage the storage you're dealt, untangle the mystery of wireless connectivity, and ensure that your PC or Mac is ready to work in concert with your freshly birthed tablet. I've found that iPad ownership—much like home, car, and pet ownership—is far more gratifying when things are kept tidy. Hence, a deep dive into the organization of your looming iLife awaits.

NOTE Increasingly, the iPad is becoming a device that's only truly alive when it's connected. Consuming content while offline is a major part of the entertainment aspect, but true power users quickly realize that the iPad—much like any other mobile device, smartphones included—is severely hamstrung without a live connection to the Internet. Much of what you can do is limited to how often you're online, which makes the proposition of a 3G/4G-enabled iPad that much more intriguing. However, those who already own a mobile hotspot (or have a smartphone with a tethering plan) may be able to enjoy the 3G/4G spoils without committing to another mobile data contract.

CHOOSING WHICH IPAD TO BUY

In my introduction, I made it sound like the process of buying an iPad is as easy as choosing between chocolate and cheesecake for breakfast. And it is. *Sort of*. But having relatively few options doesn't mean that you have *no* options whatsoever. Apple's slate, much like a full-on computer, is apt to serve you for years to come, so it's worth overthinking the model selection. Apple provides only two types of wireless (Wi-Fi and Wi-Fi + 3G or 4G), three types of storage (16GB, 32GB, or 64GB), and two carrier options (Verizon Wireless and AT&T). I focus on the most current models—the iPad 2 and 4G LTE-equipped iPad—but by-and-large, most of the options for the iPad 2 were present for the original iPad, if you're looking to buy used.

In other words, you're looking at a grand total of three different model decisions. The screen size (9.7"), processor, internal storage amount, and the front- and rear-facing cameras are set in stone, depending on the model you buy. The original iPad shipped with an A4 processor, while the iPad 2 stepped up to an A5, and the new, 4G LTE-capable version has an A5X; the latter actually has the same CPU as the iPad 2, but the package adds a quad-core graphics processor to handle the increased screen resolution. This "take it or leave it" style has always been a polarizing trademark for Apple, but I'm of the belief that fewer buying options enables a tighter seal between the hardware and software. Apple is unique in its insistence on handcrafting both the physical tablet and the operating system (iOS) that runs beneath it, and the only logical way to guarantee a stellar—or, at the very least, uniform—experience across the entire iPad portfolio is to quell deviation with regard to specifications. Supply chain aficionados might refer to this as "vertical integration." Digressions aside, making the three aforementioned choices may sound easy, but I'd caution you not to make them in haste. Let's dig in to find out what combination would be idyllic for you if you're still situated outside of the iPad Owners Club.

Saving Money the Refurbished Way

It's a common theme, really. Apple introduces a new product. Apple sees massive demand. Apple sees people lined up for hours in order to get their hands on Apple's new product. But eventually, supply catches up with demand, and if you wait even longer, you can even find yesterday's hottest commodity in refurbished form.

If you've ever tried to find an Apple product—particularly an iPad of any description—on "sale," you've probably realized that it's a Herculean task. Apple has notoriously tight controls on pricing, and, unlike products in the PC universe, you won't find typical discount stores selling Apple wares at a discount. Even Walmart is only permitted to shave a few precious cents from its iPhone and iPod touch offerings. So, is there any hope whatsoever to get on the iPad bandwagon on the cheap? You bet.

Apple only ever advertises the MSRP, but I have a tried-and-trusted alternative to paying top dollar—Apple's astonishingly well-stocked refurbished store (store.apple.com/us/browse/home/specialdeals), which is shown in Figure 1-1. It's continually updated as new batches of refurb iPads flow in. I know—you've probably done "the refurb thing" elsewhere, only to get a heavily used device with a warranty that expired before the postal service could even deliver it. But here's the thing: Apple's refurbished products are better than any other refurbished product I've ever come across.

> Generally speaking, Apple only sells refurbished gear through its online store. Don't bother looking in one of its physical retail outlets; the best you can find there is a closeout on an old model, or perhaps a used store demo.

> Refresh Apple's refurbished section early and often; the hottest deals vanish within minutes of appearing, and there's absolutely no way to sign up and be alerted when new stock arrives. It just takes plenty of patience and a little luck.

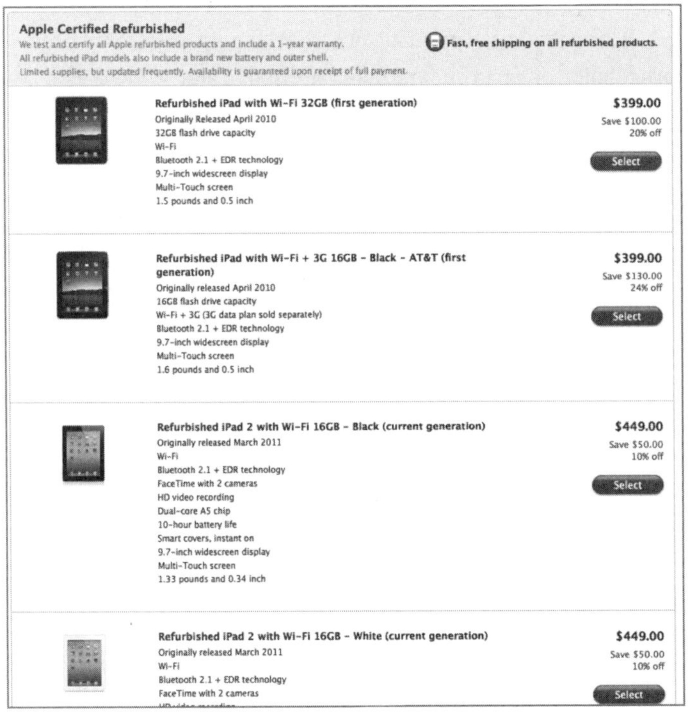

Apple Certified Refurbished
We test and certify all Apple refurbished products and include a 1-year warranty. All refurbished iPad models also include a brand new battery and outer shell. Limited supplies, but updated frequently. Availability is guaranteed upon receipt of full payment.

⊘ Fast, free shipping on all refurbished products.

Refurbished iPad with Wi-Fi 32GB (first generation) — $399.00
Originally Released April 2010 — Save $100.00, 20% off
32GB flash drive capacity
Wi-Fi
Bluetooth 2.1 + EDR technology
9.7-inch widescreen display
Multi-Touch screen
1.5 pounds and 0.5 inch
Select

Refurbished iPad with Wi-Fi + 3G 16GB – Black – AT&T (first generation) — $399.00
Originally released April 2010 — Save $130.00, 24% off
16GB flash drive capacity
Wi-Fi + 3G (3G data plan sold separately)
Bluetooth 2.1 + EDR technology
9.7-inch widescreen display
Multi-Touch screen
1.6 pounds and 0.5 inch
Select

Refurbished iPad 2 with Wi-Fi 16GB – Black (current generation) — $449.00
Originally released March 2011 — Save $50.00, 10% off
Wi-Fi
Bluetooth 2.1 + EDR technology
FaceTime with 2 cameras
HD video recording
Dual-core A5 chip
10-hour battery life
Smart covers, instant on
9.7-inch widescreen display
Multi-Touch screen
1.33 pounds and 0.34 inch
Select

Refurbished iPad 2 with Wi-Fi 16GB – White (current generation) — $449.00
Originally released March 2011 — Save $50.00, 10% off
Wi-Fi
Bluetooth 2.1 + EDR technology
FaceTime with 2 cameras
Select

FIGURE 1-1: See that? Good-as-new iPads for less than retail. Just be quick on the (virtual) trigger.

When I say they're "as good as new," I'm thoroughly downplaying reality. In fact, I rarely recommend that people buy an Apple product new. Refurbished iPads, just like the company's refurbished Macs and iPods, arrive in fresh plastic wrap with polished accessories, a user guide, and the exact same one-year warranty that's affixed to new Apple products. The only difference? A drab cardboard exterior compared to the flashily designed boxes you see in the store. Aside from the packaging, you'd be remarkably hard-pressed to tell an Apple refurb apart from a brand new piece of kit.

Wi-Fi Only or Wi-Fi + 3G/4G: Which, and Why?

▶ On average, you can save anywhere from 8% to 28% by buying refurbished. Considering that you get the same warranty, resting easy on that decision should be... well, easy.

I won't spend too much time detailing what you likely already understand, but it's worth pointing out the basic differences between the Wi-Fi only and the Wi-Fi + 3G/4G models. Both the original iPad and the iPad 2 are offered in Wi-Fi and Wi-Fi + 3G models. The former is the more affordable of the two, offering only a Wi-Fi module for wireless connectivity. The iPad revealed in early 2012, however, ushered in support of LTE, a next-generation 4G network that offers wildly fast transfer rates on the go. In other words, a Wi-Fi iPad can only connect to the Internet (or in turn, the cloud) through Wi-Fi, so it's on you to provide a signal. When you stray too far from a Wi-Fi signal, the iPad drops offline until you come back into range.

The Wi-Fi + 3G/4G variant costs $130 more than the same sized Wi-Fi only model (visual proof is in Figure 1-2), and it's worth pointing out what that up-front surcharge gets you. There's no external bulge or extra apparatuses required to add 3G/4G to the iPad, as Apple tucks a Verizon Wireless or AT&T module right within the friendly confines you're already used to seeing. "3G/4G" enables these iPads to flip over to a cellular data network when you stray from a Wi-Fi network, giving you a powerful secondary way to remain online in a pinch. Neither Verizon nor AT&T's 3G networks are as speedy as the average home broadband connection (though LTE can be, if the towers around you aren't overloaded), but for true road warriors, just being able to stay connected in the (relative) middle of nowhere could be a godsend.

NOTE   The term "3G," as well as "4G," gets thrown around like a ragdoll these days. Apple only sells Wi-Fi + 3G/4G iPads with support for AT&T and Verizon Wireless, but it matters not if you have cell phone service with either. It's important to note, however, that the 3G/4G module embedded in the iPad is there forever. You can't remove the cellular data from the iPad, but at least Verizon and AT&T allow you to transfer service to new iPads if you decide to upgrade. Furthermore, the new 4G LTE-equipped iPad is the first that allows for mobile hotspot functionality, and at no extra charge. Verizon's new iPad supports it with iOS 5.1, while AT&T is expecting to offer it soon. This allows the iPad to "share" it's wireless data with other nearby Wi-Fi devices.

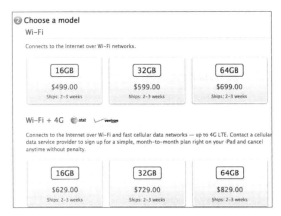

FIGURE 1-2: Decisions, decisions. But not too many decisions.

But here's the real kicker: the $130 price premium for a Wi-Fi + 3G/4G model is only the beginning. On the upside, the purchase of a 3G/4G-enabled iPad doesn't require a contractual agreement. That can't be said for most other 3G/4G slates. In fact, the vast majority of 3G/4G-enabled tablets are sold at a slight discount up-front, but the carriers force buyers to pay a recurring data fee for two whole years—similar to how your smartphone contract is presently arranged. One of the perks of paying more for the iPad up-front is the ability to pay month-to-month for data, or sell your device at any point sans any nasty strings attached.

Choosing between Verizon Wireless and AT&T

Apple offers two carrier options in the United States for those eyeing a 3G- or 4G LTE-enabled iPad: Verizon Wireless and AT&T, the nation's largest CDMA and GSM operators, respectively. There's no difference in the up front cost basd on carrier choice alone, but the monthly data rates do indeed differ somewhat. It's important to note that both carriers allow you to purchase data on a month-to-month basis; in other words, you can opt out of having data for a month that you know you'll be traveling overseas.

Although cost is naturally important (and, in regard to data plans, constantly changing), there's something else I should probably discuss while we're on this subject: coverage. You'd have to be technologically tuned-out in order to have missed the near-continual stream of griping from those in the AT&T camp, mostly from annoyed iPhone users in major metropolitan areas. Meanwhile, Verizon has managed to keep kvetching to a minimum, and, in fact, its 3G and 4G LTE networks are far more widespread than that of AT&T. Moreover, AT&T has gained more customers than it was prepared for in major cities, largely due to being the sole iPhone provider for nearly four years. If your local friends bang on AT&T, steer clear of that AT&T iPad, as seen in Figure 1.3.

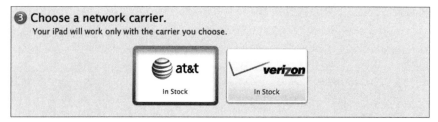

FIGURE 1-3: Choose wisely. There's no changing your mind or flipping the switch on this one!

BREAKING DOWN IPAD 3G/4G PRICE PLANS FOR AT&T AND VERIZON WIRELESS

AT&T

▶ Cheapest plan: 250MB for $15/month

▶ Midrange plan: 3GB for $30/month

▶ Largest plan: 5GB for $50/month

Verizon Wireless

▶ Cheapest plan: 1GB for $20/month

▶ Midrange plan: 2GB for $30/month

▶ Larger plan: 5GB for $50/month

▶ Largest plan: 10GB for $80/month

It's pretty clear that AT&T and Verizon Wireless have taken significantly differ-ent approaches to pricing data. The former offers the overall cheapest monthly option, but it only gives you 250MB to work with. Light users who focus mainly on e-mail and communication may be best served by this plan, but if you plan to frequently use Skype or any other video chatting application you will absolutely benefit from having a larger allotment. If you plan to stream multimedia—be it music, photos, or videos—the 250MB plan just won't be enough. Trust me on this one: The 250MB plan may be tempting on price alone, but it won't be enough if you semi-routinely use your iPad away from a Wi-Fi network for video calling or media streaming.

Why does this matter? Your iPad's speed and reliability on a 3G/4G network is only as good as the provider it's linked to, and there's absolutely no way to turn an AT&T iPad into a Verizon iPad, or vice-versa. Even if you currently reside in an area with historically solid AT&T voice and data coverage, I'd recommend picking up the Verizon iPad. I've traversed all fifty U.S. states, and I can say with authority that AT&T's 3G/4G reach is markedly less than that of Verizon.

> **NOTE** A major annoyance in the cellular industry is the inability to share a data pool over multiple devices. AT&T Mobility's CEO has affirmed that the carrier is considering it, but so far, no dice. In other words, those with a grandfathered unlimited data plan (or even a new tiered one, for that matter) on their AT&T smartphone can't simply affix an AT&T 3G/4G iPad to that plan, even if you'd be willing to have your smartphone's data disabled while you're online on the iPad. Although such a scenario makes perfect sense to the layperson, carriers have found a wildly lucrative revenue stream in forcing people to buy new pools of data for every connected device they own.

One vital thing to keep in mind here is this: It matters not who your current cellular provider is. You won't get some sort of "bundle discount" if you're using AT&T to provide service to your smartphone *and* your iPad. Just the same, there's no "penalty" for using AT&T as your cellular provider, while Verizon provides the service on your iPad. These devices are purposefully kept separate, so don't let your existing situation have any effect on choosing a carrier to service your iPad Wi-Fi + 3G/4G.

The iPad is all about enabling mobility—taking computers and their functionality to places you never before could. That functionality is severely hampered when the connection to the Internet is severed, and AT&T's 3G/4G data network are simply not as robust and wide-reaching as Verizon's. I won't ask you to think about the places you'll use your iPad most. The reality is this: You'll probably end up taking your iPad to places to which you would've never imagined taking a computer of any type, and it's those oddball, off-the-beaten-path locales where Verizon's entirely more apt to have 3G/4G coverage than AT&T. AT&T may claim to cover 97% of America, but it doesn't cover anywhere near that with 3G/4G.

▶ Both AT&T and Verizon offer bundle deals for folks using them for pay-TV, home phone, Internet, and mobile service, but there's no way to bundle the iPad into that.

▶ AT&T claims to blanket 97% of America's population with basic voice services, as well as EDGE—a terribly slow data protocol that does more to frustrate you than anything else. Don't confuse EDGE for 3G/4G.

UNDERSTANDING THE NON-EXPANDABLE STORAGE SITUATION

What's in a megabyte? Oh, 1024KB, which is comprised of... never mind. I could dig deep into the technobabble surrounding storage and be here for hours, so I'm just cutting to the chase: Apple provides but three options for storing files locally on the iPad. You can buy a 16GB model, a 32GB model, or a 64GB model. That's it. Despite the pleading of pundits, there's still no SD (Secure Digital) card slot on the slate itself, which means that you can never expand the quantity of storage via any means whatsoever.

Aside from deciding between Wi-Fi + 3G/4G or just the stock Wi-Fi model, choosing an iPad with adequate storage for your needs is of utmost importance. What you probably don't realize now is that you need far more storage than you suspect. Much like we do in our homes, we tend to fill our iPads with as much "stuff" as it gives us room for. What, exactly, takes up space on an iPad?

- ► E-mails
- ► Music
- ► Photos
- ► Videos
- ► Apps

Those are the heavy hitters (see Figure 1-4). Things such as Contacts, Calendar entries, and miscellaneous To-Do lists also take up space, but they're so insignificant that it's not worth harping on. The long and short of it is this: If you plan on using your iPad as a serious content consumption machine—loading it down with iTunes, TV rentals, and every album you've had since the second grade—buy the one with as much storage as you can afford. If you're willing to "clean house" every so often in order to only have the latest and most germane content onboard, the cheaper 16GB edition will do.

FIGURE 1-4: This capacity gauge within iTunes lets you know what's taking up space on your iPad.

The good news is that Apple's taking the focus off of internal storage in many ways with the introduction of iCloud, enabling users to simply stream in content that's hosted *elsewhere*, as opposed to on the device itself. Granted, this magic only seems magical if you've a solid connection to the Internet, but it's certainly worth considering. Thanks to iCloud—a feature that I devote more time to in the pages to come—there's at least a secondary option for storing TV shows, music, and movies, but you still need to keep local versions of your most favorite material right on your iPad. Wireless Internet isn't quite ubiquitous, in a literal sense.

SETTING UP 3G/4G (IF APPLICABLE)

Perhaps you decided early on that you just didn't need an iPad with 3G or 4G built in. If that's you, don't just glaze over this section—I have a snippet of advice for you, too. The bulk of this portion describes the art of linking your iPad with the wild, wonderful world of cellular data, but first I discuss an alternative for bringing 3G—or even 4G—connectivity to your iPad.

Opting for a Mobile Hotspot

What many consumers forget is that Verizon Wireless and Sprint both offered up this workaround not too long ago, but the advent of the 3G-*embedded* Verizon iPad quelled those offers. In effect, carriers were bundling Wi-Fi iPads with mobile hotspots, which are small, palm-sized modems that connect wirelessly to a carrier's data network and then share the connection over Wi-Fi (see Figure 1-5). They're known as various things: a MiFi, Overdrive, Hotspot, and so on. But they all serve the same purpose. They're battery-powered nuggets that broadcast a carrier's wireless data signal to between five and eight (usually) Wi-Fi devices.

If you're curious as to why these things are important to consider, allow me to explain. Let's say you've a laptop or two in the family, as well as an iPad, all of which need to be online from obscure places—or, perhaps, places that simply lack Wi-Fi. Instead of buying a monthly data connection for each device, it might make more sense to invest in a single MiFi that could share a WWAN signal among the group.

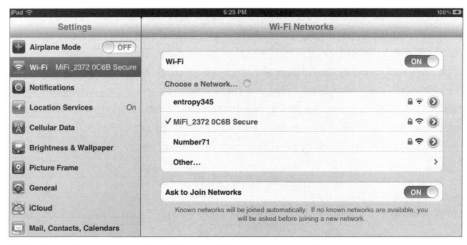

FIGURE 1-5: Here, an Australian MiFi is providing Internet to my iPad. It's cheaper to rent a local MiFi than to roam on AT&T.

Another upside here is 4G. *Real* 4G, not HSPA+ coated with clever marketing. Clearwire, Sprint, AT&T, and Verizon Wireless all sell their own WiMAX or LTE mobile hotspot devices, with plans all over the proverbial map. Clearwire is your best source for cheaper, month-to-month plans if you're a light user, whereas Verizon Wireless' on-contract LTE hotspots are a superior option if you know you'll be using it monthly (and heavily) for the foreseeable future.

> ▶ Humbly, I'd recommend choosing Verizon's LTE service over WiMAX. WiMAX is a wireless technology with waning support.

> **TIP** Samsung's SCH-LC11 Mobile Hotspot is a great LTE option on Verizon. It's one of the few that enables users to charge via USB while plugged into a computer—which is a common scenario, as it turns out. Some users have discovered power cycling issues, but I've found that a quick battery removal and replacement clears that up.

Selecting a 3G/4G Plan

Congratulations. You just purchased—presumably, anyway—an iPad with cellular data within. Celebrations are in order. *Wireless* ones, no less. But as alluded to earlier, picking up an iPad with a cellular data module within is only the beginning of the perpetually connected journey. You'll easily spot the Cellular Data option, shown in Figure 1-6, if your iPad is 3G/4G-enabled. In this selection, I explain a bit about how cellular data consumption works, why tiers matter, and what kind of data package makes the most sense depending on your usage model.

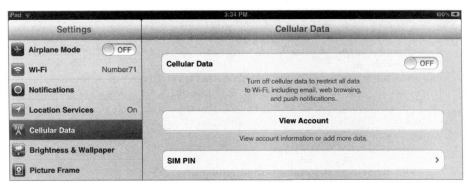

FIGURE 1-6: Cellular Data setup screen within Settings. Let the off-grid connectivity begin!

Defining 3G/4G could take up a book's worth of pages, so I'll try to keep it brief. If you own a smartphone, you're all too familiar with mobile data. It's a constant wireless data connection that enables you to sync with the Internet, pull down e-mails, send Tweets, and remain constantly dialed into your digital life. These days, it's hardly a foreign concept. 3G/4G on the iPad works in a similar fashion, but there are no voice capabilities to complement it. Imagine a smartphone that wasn't able to ring a typical nine-digit phone number, and you've got it.

You're probably wondering how exactly a 3G/4G-connected iPad sucks down data, and how much data is consumed by doing various tasks. Just two years ago, this wasn't even an issue. All four of the major U.S. carriers were offering unlimited data plans with their smartphones, so pondering the strain placed on the network by any given task wasn't something consumers were apt to do. Today, it's all different. The networks are being burdened by gaining new users faster than carriers can build new towers, so what we're left with is a world of tiered data plans.

As mentioned earlier, you have a handful of tier choices for iPad data. But it's nearly impossible to make an informed decision on which tier suits you best without knowing how much data is consumed by [*insert task here*]. Below is a rough and dirty guide to give you some basic perspective.

Got all that? Good. You can see from the figures in the sidebar just how useless AT&T's entry-level 250MB per month plan becomes if you decide to stream even a *single* half-hour TV episode. Granted, this doesn't affect your 3G/4G data pool if you stream said show while connected to Wi-Fi, but who says you won't crave a 1982 drama during a break in the park?

▶ It's possible to communicate over voice using the iPad, but only through VoIP (Internet-based) protocols. In other words, you need data access to yap, which you don't need on a typical cell phone.

WHAT'S IN A DOWNLOAD?

You can use the following approximate file sizes to have some idea of what kind of data plan you need based on what you'll be doing with your iPad:

▶ Sending an e-mail: 0.1MB, without attachments

▶ Loading a typical website: 0.2MB to 1MB

▶ Downloading a single song from iTunes: 3MB to 6MB

▶ Downloading the Engadget Distro app: 2MB

▶ Video chatting over Skype: 3MB per minute

▶ Streaming an SD TV show: 400MB for a 30-minute program

▶ Streaming an HD TV show: 1500MB for a 30-minute program

▶ Loading an Adobe Flash-based website (on iPad): 0MB

The facts are pretty clear: sending e-mails back and forth sans attachments doesn't require too much data, and loading the occasional website doesn't either. For users who plan to do little more than that, AT&T's 250MB plan may suffice. But I still maintain that Verizon's 3G iPad (and its LTE-equipped iPad) is both more practical from a coverage standpoint, and more sensible from a plan standpoint. Verizon's entry-level plan is $5 (per month) more expensive than AT&T's, but it gets you four times the data allotment: 1GB compared to 250MB.

If you plan to tap into the endless fount of multimedia streaming while on a cellular connection you'll certainly want to splurge for one of the pricier plans. It ain't cheap keeping that Netflix rotation moving while away from Wi-Fi.

Managing a Month-to-Month Plan

▶ Looking for ways to burn data? Download Hulu Plus, Netflix, SlingPlayer, Vevo HD, ABC Player, Plex, and EyeTV— just search for each in the Apple App Store.

The idea of having a "month-to-month" data connection is a new one. The only folks who'll be even remotely familiar with this are those who've been on the prepaid side of the cellular rollout. Most smartphone owners are forced to pay a monthly data and voice fee due to the multi-year contract they signed for subsidization on their handset, but because Apple doesn't discount the iPad's price in exchange for a service agreement, you're given the freedom to buy data only on months that you need it.

Apple (and the carriers, for that matter) has made it shockingly painless to get your cellular data connection up-and-running. You need to be in an area with decent 3G/4G data coverage when trying to activate for the first time, though, and you obviously need a credit card handy. As you can see in Figure 1-7, getting started is as easy as popping in a credit card number and your billing address and then selecting which plan you'd like to activate.

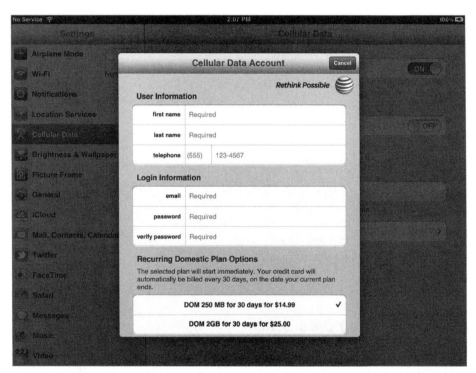

FIGURE 1-7: Pop in your credit card details, choose your plan, and you're connected. It's scarily easy to hand over cash for data.

In the AT&T example shown in Figure 1-7, you see the two tier options mentioned earlier. "DOM" stands for domestic. Whatever you do, *do not* allow data roaming (see Figure 1-8) when traveling overseas with your iPad. Well, you can, but you better have an exceptionally good reason. International roaming rates on data typically hover between $5 and $15 per megabyte, which means your average inbox refresh from a night of missed messages could leave a $20 to $40 impression on your next bill.

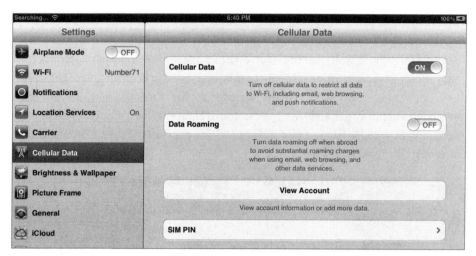

FIGURE 1-8: There should really be a giant, red "X" next to that Data Roaming option. "Last resort" is being generous.

> **TIP** Both AT&T and Verizon Wireless automatically renew your data every 30 days and charge you accordingly after you've initiated things. But remember: You're totally month-to-month. You need only to log in to your account and tell it to *not* auto-renew in order to have service halted when your current 30 days are up. If you know you need to pull the plug on data services for a given month, make yourself a reminder...on your iPad, of course!

Keeping Tabs on Data Usage

▶ Apple's built-in tool only applies to cellular data. There's no built-in way to see how much Wi-Fi data you've used, which is a real shame given that some home ISPs, such as Comcast, are capping monthly usage.

So, loading a few web pages should have only taken a few megabytes of your monthly allotment, but wouldn't it be grand if you could see—specifically—how much data you've used at any given time? It would. And it's possible. Apple doesn't go out of its way to make it clear, but there's a slightly hidden data meter that's always running in the background, calculating how much data you've sent and received right down to the *byte*. It operates in real-time, and it doesn't miss anything.

In fact, it's a fantastic tool for sniffing out "data leaks." If you're using the 3G/4G connection, and you have got too many push notifications enabled, you may be consuming data that you never intended to. I'd strongly recommend disabling push e-mail, Twitter, Facebook, and other social networking apps while using 3G/4G, particularly if you're dangerously close to exceeding your monthly allotment.

NOTE On Wi-Fi, having push notifications enabled is excellent for automating the flow of new information. On a cellular connection, it zaps data at an alarming rate. Sadly, there's no way to create two profiles on your iPad for push settings while on Wi-Fi or 3G/4G, so you're stuck disabling and re-enabling. Yet another reason to spring for a larger data plan.

TIP Apple might not support multiple profiles, but if you're brazen enough to jailbreak your device (which voids the warranty, hence I can't publicly recommend it), the iUsers app in the Cydia app store does just that. My guess is that this kind of functionality will be bundled into the next major iOS release.

To access the meter, visit Settings → General → Usage → Cellular Usage, as shown in Figure 1-9. Unsurprisingly, you'll only see this on a cellular data-enabled iPad. You should also set up a recurring reminder on your iPad that encourages you to reset that meter every 30 days. If you don't, it's practically impossible to keep tabs on how much data has been consumed on a new month's worth of data.

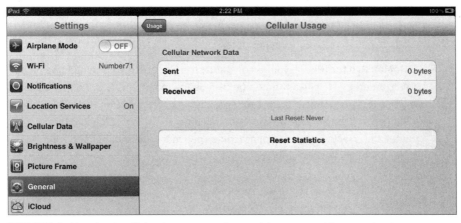

FIGURE 1-9: Ah, a fresh cellular data counter. Be careful not to run this up too fast!

SQUEEZING THE MOST OUT OF EVERY MEGABYTE

Pinching pennies is never a bad idea. Turns out, pinching bytes isn't a half-bad concept, either. Although the World Wide Web is largely developed with unlimited home broadband connections in mind, a few companies are mindful of the natural limits applied to wireless broadband. Here I've compiled a few of my favorite data-saving apps, which are all available after a quick title search in the App Store:

▶ **Opera Mini**: It's a free, fast, and compact web browser for iPhone. When you request a page, the request is sent to the Opera Mini server, which downloads the page from the Internet. The server then packages your page in a compressed format—dubbed OBML—that requires less data to download.

▶ **Skyfire and VideoQ**: If you're a YouTube addict, get the Skyfire browser and accompanying VideoQ app ($3.99), which has a multimedia compression feature that lets users spend less time loading videos and less data accessing them.

▶ **Onavo**: This is a free app that acts as a proxy server for your iPad. After it's installed, the app streams data sent to you from Safari, Mail, Facebook, Google Maps, Twitter, and other apps through Onavo's servers and then compresses it before sending it to your tablet. Users also receive access to compression reports and metrics on data savings. The app doesn't shrink or compress information that you send, though, so your image and video uploads still look as good as possible.

▶ **DataMan Pro for iPad**: If you're constantly fretting about your usage and can't remember to check Apple's built-in usage meter, this $3.99 app provides elaborate notification and monitoring services, enabling you to stay informed and curb usage as your monthly limit approaches. You get unmistakable alerts as you're approaching your monthly limit, helping you to dodge those pesky overage fees.

SETTING UP (AND UNDERSTANDING) FIND MY IPAD

Find my iPad is a brilliant service that ships with every iOS 5-equipped iPad (see Figure 1-10). If you update your existing iPad to Apple's latest mobile OS, you too will have it. Swell, eh? Put simply, it's a software and hardware solution that allows your Apple ID to keep tabs on the movement of your iPad, enabling you to rather easily track the iPad down if it's ever lost or stolen. Think of it as OnStar tracking for your tablet.

FIGURE 1-10: Make sure you tick Use Find My iPad here. Failing to do so will result in endless tears from yours truly.

Setting up this service didn't used to be so simple. In a prior life, this service required a MobileMe account, a paid service that only the hardest of hardcore Apple loyalists were apt to spring for. Sensibly, Apple figured it prudent to bring this highly valuable service to *all* iPad owners, completely free of charge.

▶ MobileMe was (mercilessly, albeit understandably) killed when iCloud was introduced. Existing users have a window of time to retrieve their data from the service, after which it'll be shuttered for good in mid-2012.

Enabling the service is as simple as accepting the opt-in notification for Location-Based Services upon iOS 5's install, choosing to turn Find My iPad on, and creating an iCloud account. If you skipped this while rushing through the startup screens in iOS 5, simply visit Settings ➜ iCloud ➜ Find my iPad, and flip the toggle to "On." I can't emphasize this enough: Please, take five seconds and enable this feature, as shown in Figure 1-11. It's never been easier to proactively protect your investment in anything.

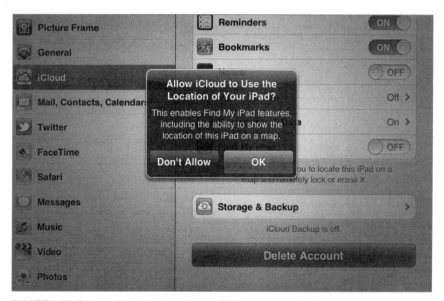

FIGURE 1-11: This confirmation should read, "Allow a potentially investment- and time-saving feature to run?"

Once active, it's downright staggering what you can do should your iPad become lost or stolen. For starters, you can sign into www.icloud.com on any Web browser in order to see precisely where it's at based on its GPS coordinates. If you're near a pal with an iOS device of his own, there's a Find my iPhone app that enables you to use *his* device to locate and interact with *your* lost device, as seen here in Figure 1-12.

And when I say "interact," I mean *interact*. You can force a pop-up message onto the screen of your misplaced device, encouraging anyone that finds it to drop it off at a given location or phone you at whatever number you please. The message you write is completely customizable. Moreover, you can force the alert to make an audible sound... even if you had the Mute function on when you lost the iPad!

FIGURE 1-12: Using one iOS device to hunt down another.

If you're concerned about ill-willed thieves prying into your personal information, you can remotely set a lock-screen password requirement, and if you know that your iPad has somehow fallen into the wrong hands, you can remotely delete *all* of its contents (see Figure 1-13). Oh, and if (and when) you do retrieve your tablet, a simple restore from iCloud brings it back to the state you left it in. Did I mention all of this was free?

FIGURE 1-13: Wipe away. With iCloud, you can restore your data in a few clicks.

WORKING WITH NETWORKS

Despite being a highly useful offline product, the iPad is truly at its best when connected to a live wire. And by that, I mean no wire at all. Ensuring that your iPad is connected to the Internet—be it over Wi-Fi or 3G/4G—also ensures the best possible experience and enables you to take full advantage of iCloud, Game Center, e-mail, and a litany of other incredible things that simply aren't available offline.

Right from the get-go, iOS 5's startup process asks you to connect to a Wi-Fi network in order to fully set up your device. *That's* how integral the Internet is to the overall experience. So, it goes without saying that you should be near the Web before you get too far into iPad setup. I'd recommend venturing to Settings ➜ Wi-Fi each time you situate yourself in a new place. As soon as you're in, the iPad begins an automatic perusal of the surroundings in search of nearby Wi-Fi networks. Connecting to one is as simple as tapping the one you're after and entering the security password (if applicable). (See Figure 1-14.)

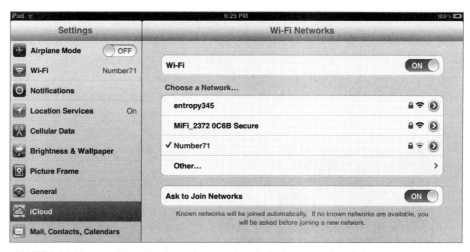

FIGURE 1-14: Hmm. . . Which to choose? Now, where's that password again?

If no suitable Wi-Fi networks are nearby, and you have a Wi-Fi + 3G/4G iPad, you can surf over to Settings ➜ Cellular Data in order to flip the toggle there and have it connect to your carrier's network. Just as a reminder: Keep that Cellular Data toggle set to Off until you know that there's no Wi-Fi nearby. No need in exhausting your monthly megabyte supply unless you have to.

I caution iPad users to not jump to any conclusions if they spot poor Wi-Fi reception right out-of-the-box. iPads have relatively poor antenna systems, at least compared to Apple's highly regarded MacBook Pro antennas. I've seen, on many occasions, my MacBook Pro receiving five strong bars of Wi-Fi signal, while my iPad beside it sees only one bar, or none at all. The reality of the matter is that tablets in general, as with smartphones, cannot match the reception capabilities of a full-on computer.

If your home router is located a great distance away from where you typically use your iPad, and you're pulling your hair out from dropped connections, it's probably worth investing in a Wi-Fi repeater or extender. My personal favorite is the AirPort Express. For one, it's an Apple product, which practically guarantees smooth sailing within the ecosystem. Two, it's widely available for less than $100—far less if you buy it from Apple's refurbished store. Third, it's wildly compact, and a new AirPort Utility app (shown in Figure 1-15 and free in the App Store) enables you to have complete control of the AirPort Express' settings and security right from your iPad—no Mac or PC required.

> Apple's original iPad was notorious for randomly dropping Wi-Fi connections, and even today it can occasionally get hung up and refuse to reconnect upon waking from sleep. Your best bet in that situation is to fully reboot the iPad while taking long, deep breaths.

FIGURE 1-15: AirPort Utility makes AirPort Express configuration way easier than surviving airport security.

TIP The AirPort Express is also an exceptional travel partner, just like your iPad. With the built-in Ethernet jack, it allows hotel wireline connections to instantly be shared with all of your devices on your own, homegrown Wi-Fi network. It quite literally converts a wired Internet connection into a wireless one, and you have absolute control over the SSID and password. Particularly in those hotels that charge you *per connection*, paying for just one while sharing the love between your iPad, phone, and laptop would make any frugal traveler smile.

UPDATING AND READYING ITUNES

Make no mistake: iTunes is still a very real, and very necessary part of the iPad experience. Apple has gone to great lengths in order to convince the world otherwise, but unless you've grown up entirely enveloped in Apple's ecosystem, you'll still find the occasional talk with iTunes a necessity. To Apple's credit, iOS 5, iTunes Match, and iCloud have made iTunes interactions far less necessary than in years past, but keeping the primary middleman between your stored files and your iPad in tip-top shape should be considered a mandate.

The truth of the matter is that iTunes is updated on a far more regular basis than iOS. Apple tends to only make major, deliberate changes to the latter, while the former seems to be in a perpetual state of improvement. Or perhaps "repair" is a better term, depending on your perspective. At any rate, it's extremely wise to ensure you have the very latest copy of iTunes installed on your PC or Mac before attempting to set up your iPad for the first time, or upgrade your existing tablet for its initial encounter with iOS 5.

CROSSREF   If you're immediately concerned with the process of reverting, I instruct you in Chapter 4 on where to find older builds of iTunes online. Newer isn't always better, though oftentimes it's required.

You have two options when it comes time to update. Either Check for Updates within iTunes itself, or cruise over to www.itunes.com and download the new installer from Apple itself. When the latest iTunes is fired up, and your iPad is plugged into your computer via USB, tap the Check for Update button to get things underway on your device. Have a look at Figure 1-16 for a clearer understanding.

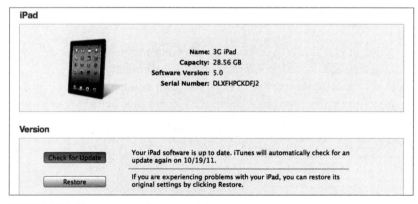

FIGURE 1-16: Fingers crossed for an update!

ORGANIZING YOUR ILIFE FIRST

You might be thinking, "Sheesh, *another* step in the process before I even dive into my iPad?" It's a fair question. But yes, that's exactly the case. I've set up a number of iPads in my time, and I've consistently found that those who put in the proper effort ahead of time are more greatly rewarded afterward. The entire iPad experience is enriched by one's organization, and a few key portions of Apple's iLife suite tie directly into the fabric of iPad.

How iPhoto Ties into iPad, and Vice-versa

The first component of iLife worth mentioning is iPhoto. Granted, this won't apply to those who aren't using a Mac (or, OS X, given that Apple's desktop OS can technically be hacked onto machines designed for Windows), but it's a surprisingly robust piece of software that's worth dabbling in if you're a self-proclaimed shutterbug. One of the real joys of using iPad comes in the form of sharing photos. For example, the built-in slideshow feature enables owners to quickly and beautifully share vacation and family pictures without having to lug a full laptop and external hard drive to a relative's abode (see Figure 1-17). But unless you organize your images ahead of time, they show up as a scattered mess on your iPad. "Garbage in, garbage out" has never been so accurate.

FIGURE 1-17: Yes, you can even slideshow your screen captures.

I dive deeper into Photo Stream in Chapter 14—one focusing solely on the merits of iCloud—but suffice it to say that this is yet another method for pulling down captured shots and displaying what's been happening most recently in your life according to the cameras on your various iOS devices.

How Movies and Content Share Homes

Let's go ahead and get this idea engrained in your head: Don't let content live solely on your iPad. Thinking of it in the following terms is guaranteed to save you grief should something ever go wrong on your device: Your movies, photos (shown in Figure 1-18), music, and other miscellaneous content should live either on your computer or in the cloud, and in an ideal world, in both.

It's absolutely worth creating a robust, well-cataloged file folder system for your local videos. And then, I'd sort them in iTunes. Anything that's prearranged in iTunes tends to sync beautifully with iPad. If you choose to sync it from some random file system on your computer, your mileage will obviously vary.

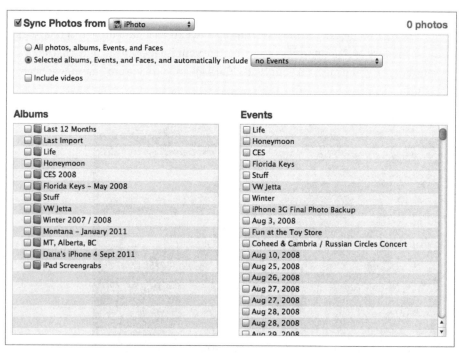

FIGURE 1-18: iPhoto integration is tight enough to let you cherry-pick select folders within the program for syncing.

As I discuss in the chapters to come, syncing is a *huge* part of iPad life. I've an inkling that Apple's doing all that it can to change that—it would love nothing more if everything you could ever want was available on demand from the cloud, but we aren't there yet. As it stands, you'll be reaching back to your computer for a great many files, and things aren't going to become magically organized on your iPad if they're strewn about on your home computer. The introduction of iCloud adds another option to that mix, which I'll describe in detail in Chapter 14.

Realizing that content will be living in (at least) two places is a bit tough for some to wrap their heads around. But I'm an ardent supporter of backing up everything on your computer, and it's something that's worth managing. If you acquire something fresh on your computer, make sure it's placed in the same file system or program that you initially sync your iPad to. That way, updates are shared with no fuss to speak of. If you happen to download a new app or iTunes song on your iPad, I discuss how to transfer those to your PC in the pages to come. The key is making sure the data continues to flow both ways, even after the initial setup. Computing families that talk together, stay together.

SUMMARY

Setting up one's iPad, particularly with iOS 5, can be done in the blink of an eye. But that's not the path you should take. Putting a proper amount of effort into cataloging and organizing your content before setting your iPad up initially ensures that subsequent syncs are smooth and predictable, and that no data is haphazardly left out or lost.

It's also important to carefully consider which iPad is right for you, and if the Wi-Fi + 3G/4G model is worth both the up-front premium and the additional monthly surcharge for access to cellular data. For those who already own (or want to own) a mobile hotspot, the Wi-Fi iPad is the perfect device to take advantage of a cellular data connection that you already own.

The proactive iPad owner is the happiest, and I've provided a number of apps and methods for keeping an eye on your 3G/4G data usage, as well as managing your network situation. An AirPort Express is not only a highly recommended iPad accessory, it's a travel companion that I never leave home without. Just like my iPad.

Arranging Icons and Folders for Efficiency

I've preached it throughout the first chapter, and I'm continuing to preach it here: Thinking about the setup involved in tailoring your iPad specifically for you is worth the effort. After you have things just so from an initialization standpoint, it's time to ponder the overall look and feel of iOS 5. After whisking through the first handful of setup panes, you are abruptly dropped onto the Home screen. Where do you go from there? Here.

In this chapter, I explain how to best tweak the iOS Home screen for maximum productivity. I share how to best arrange your dock and how to position icons that I'm sure you'll end up using the most. Fact is, it doesn't take a great deal of time to get your icons and apps ideally situated, and it saves you precious time and frustration in the future. When you first get an iPad, there's not a whole lot on it. But soon, if you lack a proper attack plan, you might be overwhelmed with the sheer quantity of apps and information onboard. Thankfully, there's a method to controlling the madness, and in this chapter I discuss shortcuts and suggestions for creating a sorting system that works best for you.

OPTIMIZING PLACEMENT FOR PRODUCTIVITY

Ever wondered why people tend to place things in "easy to reach spots" whenever possible? Because it makes perfect sense. If you let it, the iPad's Home screen eventually becomes an out-of-control slew of panes on which icons are arranged in the order that you downloaded the apps, as shown in Figure 2-1. Not surprisingly, that's no good for anyone.

FIGURE 2-1: A Home screen like this is visually confusing to make sense of.

The iPad is really an entirely new product category (or, a new breed of a category that never flourished in the early 2000s), and its usage model allows for a staggering amount of customization. I suggest that you take advantage of that. You probably wouldn't buy a new Mac or PC and then proceed to tweak absolutely nothing about the boot-up screen. I doubt you'd buy a new smartphone and never touch the layout

that's presented to you upon first boot. Taking a pinch of transitive property knowledge and a good guess from experience, I'd say that you're probably interested in
rearranging the iPad's furniture a bit, too.

> **NOTE** In a strange move that proves Apple's both listening to end user com-
> plaints but still forging ahead with certain initiatives regardless, the pesky
> Stocks app was completely yanked from iOS 5. However, Newsstand has been
> introduced, and Apple has made it impossible to file it away inside a custom
> E-reader folder. I guess Apple's not too comfortable with Newsstand and
> Amazon's Kindle app being buddy-buddy in a folder.

Arranging Frequently Used Icons

It may sound obvious, but it's worth clarifying. The iPad, due to its shape, tends
to place your thumbs in the lower right and left corners. Predictably, those are the
two hottest spots on the entire screen, and they're absolutely the easiest and most
convenient to access. The Dock has room for a grand total of six icons (it's full in
Figure 2-2), but don't be fooled—you can actually stuff many dozens of apps into
that lower bar without ever reaching for a jailbreak.

> ▶ If you're coming
> from the world of
> OS X, the term
> Dock is a familiar
> one. If you're not
> familiar with the
> Mac universe,
> it's the semi-
> translucent row of
> icons that's glued
> to the bottom of
> the iPad's display,
> regardless of what
> pane you swipe to.

FIGURE 2-2: There's nothing quite like a fully loaded Dock!

iOS 5 includes a feature called Folders, which is Apple's simplistic, albeit entirely satisfactory solution to now having more than 100,000 iPad-specific apps in the App Store. I dive deeper into folders in a bit, but suffice it to say, I'm a big fan of using 'em for the sake of organization.

> **WARNING** It's vital to think about where an app should be slotted as you're downloading it. Moving it to a sensible folder right away prevents your mind from expecting it to be somewhere that it's not, and it also prevents you from relaxing your efforts to maintain a clean and well-sorted grid of applications. There's no digital rug to sweep things under on iOS; it's either categorized nicely, or it sticks out on its own like a sore thumb.

The Dock as a whole is without question the most important locale for apps. It's the only row of apps that retains its position regardless of what pane you're on. Taking it one step further, the apps on the far left and far right of the Dock should be the ones you use the most. Remember that whole "close to your thumbs" thing? Yeah. If you're looking for a little advice on which apps you're *likely* to use the most, consider these:

- Mail
- Safari
- Messages
- App Store
- Music
- Photos
- Settings
- Newsstand
- Facebook
- Game Center
- Twitter

Yes, I can count. Yes, I know that's more than six. But I promise—everything's going to be all right. My personal recommendation is to make Mail and Safari the bookends, unless you have a stellar reason to do otherwise. From there, create a folder (see Figure 2-3) to house relatively similar apps that would normally be "overflow"—apps that would've been numbers 7, 8, 9, and 10 if the Dock were longer.

FIGURE 2-3: Folders . . . they do an iPad good.

An ideal Dock, in my mind, consists of four of your most commonly used applications (Mail, Safari, Settings, and Music for me) and two folders of overflow. You can cram up to 20 apps in each folder (an improvement of 8 over the iPhone's limit), but 9 per folder is optimal. Why? Because you see miniaturized icons of the first 9 apps in any folder, which—surprisingly enough—are large enough for you to make out what they are when you have a brain fart while trying to remember what apps are in what folder.

> **TIP** iOS 5 doesn't allow for multiple user profiles, unlike OS X. This means that owners who need a certain grid of apps at their fingertips for work and another set handy for play simply don't have the option of switching on the fly. If that's you, here's my solution: Use one of those overflow folders in your Dock to house your favorite additional "at home" apps, and use the other overflow folder for the apps you most frequently need for work. It's not quite a two-profile compromise, but it's far better than just shoving all of your office apps on the last (and hardest to reach) Home screen.

Pegging the Edges

The corners are undoubtedly the place to nail your favorite apps. The bottom corners are the easiest to reach, but the top two aren't lacking on the tantalization scale, either. But sadly, some estranged law in some scientific field I'm not qualified to opine on has asserted that only four corners be applied to each rectangle, and I know good and well you'll need hasty access to more than four apps or folders.

Just as surrounding yourself with good company is a wise move in life, it's also wise to surround your moderately used applications with your favorites. That's right—it's time to head to the edges. The outskirts of the app grid are naturally easiest to access (see Figure 2-4) without having to relocate your hands or fingers, and conversely, the central region of each Home screen is where I leave my most infrequently used programs.

FIGURE 2-4: Sorry, Newsstand—it's tough to get a seat on the edge!

TIP Unfortunately, Apple doesn't include any sort of launch counter to clock how many times you open any given app, so it's a bit tedious to actually keep track of what programs are being used the most. It's delightfully easy to re-locate an app, however, but more painful to relocate nine. Thus, I'd strongly recommend using folders whenever possible. If you realize you need to move your Travel or Foreign Language folders to a hotter spot on the grid due to an upcoming trip, you're now moving two icons instead of dozens.

Picking a uniform *modus operandi* and sticking with it is crucial in allowing the iPad to become an extension of your brain. If you know precisely where the apps that you need most given your current situation will be, it makes it far easier to locate them. Even if the apps or folders themselves change with the season, the placement is of the utmost importance. I'm guessing your favorite sneakers have a special place in the closet, and I'm also guessing the favorites of today aren't the same as they were a decade ago. Hopefully, that odd analogy helps drive home the importance of creating (and sticking with) a neat map of apps.

Masterfully Organizing Your Folders

Folders are perhaps the most wonderful introduction to iOS from an organizational standpoint, though they're oft overlooked when you get in a frenzy of slapping as many mouth-watering applications as possible onto the iPad when you first unwrap it. I'm not blaming the masses—grabbing hold of an iPad for the first time is indeed a thrilling experience. If you're calm, cool, and collected enough to be perusing these pages, however, you're probably thoughtful enough to add a bit of order to your iPad.

NOTE One of Apple's unofficial official trademarks is the art of letting people discover its products on their own terms. Particularly with the iPad, there's a certain level of intrigue surrounding the glaring lack of instructions. The iPad really isn't meant to be "used," in the common sense. It's meant to be what-ever you want it to be. Apple smartly realized that placing artificial boundaries around the possibilities here would have been a poor decision. Instead, it creat-ed an accessible App Store that has—in effect—allowed *users*, not Apple itself, to dictate what the iPad is truly capable of.

As mentioned earlier, you can shove up to 20 apps into a single folder, and you can name each one anything you desire. I recommend stopping at 9 apps per folder (or 4, as shown in Figure 2-5) in order to see each and every app thumbnail within each folder, but those with highly trained memories can feel free to go overboard.

FIGURE 2-5: Folders, folders, folders!

NOTE Oddly enough, it's not immediately apparent how one goes about creating a folder's worth of apps. Mercifully, it's more of a lesson in simplicity than anything else. All you need to do is press and hold one app's icon and then move it until it hovers above another icon. A moment later, a folder is born, and the iPad does its darndest to suggest a satisfactory folder label based on the categories of the apps you're bringing together. In my opinion, these suggestions are generally too vague. *Productivity* doesn't mean much; you're better off with separate folders named Photography, Word Processing, and Financial apps.

Outside of a few choice apps that you simply use over and over and over again, the only true way to keep your iPad organized for the long term is to rely on an elaborate system of folders. It's daunting at first, but far less harrowing than seeing 80+ apps untidily strewn across countless Home screens. What's difficult, however, is a wholesale change of how you arrange apps within a folder system. Here I share three proven—if a touch unorthodox—methods of attacking the issue of folders.

HOW TO ORGANIZE BY GENRE

This is absolutely my preferred way of organizing folders. But I'm a person who thinks in terms of subjects and topics, so it jibes with my natural mental flow. Before I get too physiological up in here, let me reiterate that Apple's suggested folder names are simply too vague for me. They work fine if you're only interested in lumping things broadly together, but you have 11 Home screens to work with. If you end up with 40 or so folders, so be it. I'll take highly specific folders—ones that are named so I can recall their contents at a mere glance—over folders that could contain just about anything.

Looking for suggestions on app folder names? Try these:

- ▶ Apple Apps
- ▶ Cloud Storage
- ▶ Navigation
- ▶ Travel
- ▶ Online Radio
- ▶ Web Browsers
- ▶ Social Networking
- ▶ VoIP
- ▶ To-Do

HOW TO ORGANIZE BY COLOR

Color, you ask? Why, yes! Not everyone's inclined to think about apps in terms of natural categorization, and in fact, some respond better to visual stimulants than descriptive phrases. I can't take complete credit for this one—a dear friend of mine at The Verge, Ross Miller, first brought this to my attention—but it is actually far more useful in practice than it sounds in theory. The majority of applications I've seen in the app store are launched with a logo that rarely, if ever, changes. And even if the design is mildly overhauled, few apps ever change their logos entirely.

Here's an example of how this would work: Create a folder called Red. Now, pop i.TV, Netflix, Photo Booth, and iTunes Movie Trailers in the folder. Black & Red? The AP's mobile news app and Opera Mini come to mind. Blue? There's Engadget, Skype, Twitter, Facebook, Dropbox, Distro, Echofon, FlightTrack Pro, PS Express, and Safari.

Because some apps simply don't use an icon that relies heavily on one single hue, this method works best if you reserve color-themed folders for your most frequently used apps, and then categorize the rest using the genre method discussed earlier. It's a hybrid system, but it might be just what your cranium ordered.

HOW TO ORGANIZE ALPHABETICALLY

I'm surmising that you can guess what I'm going to say next. This is the most elementary method of all, but setting it up isn't quite as straightforward as you might imagine. A simpleton may create a different folder for every letter of the alphabet, and although that's a fine approach, I'd bet that you'd see quite the imbalance very soon.

Folders N and S are apt to be overflowing, but less commonly used letters remain barren. Thankfully, it's fairly easy to create S2 if S1 fills up, but you may be better served by Sa-Sm and Sn-Sz. Depends on how heavy an app user you are, really.

If you go this route, I'd still look to place the letter folders you frequent most around the edges of your first Home screen; just because your apps are in alphabetical folders, that doesn't mean your folders have to be arranged in alphabetical order themselves.

GIVING EACH HOME SCREEN A PURPOSE

The first Home screen—the one that loads after you unlock the iPad—is clearly the most significant. Communication, productivity and your favorite content and game applications should reside here. But what about the other ten panes? The iPad and iOS 5 provide 11 total panes to work with, and if you're genuinely able to fill them all up, you've most certainly accomplished something. Newsstand is an oddball; although it shows as a single app, many magazines are now distributed here. Rather than having multiple apps for multiple magazines, this is Apple's inbuilt solution for housing them. In Figure 2-6, you'll see it moving about after a long-press on the icon opened up the ability to rearrange things.

The wild thing, is, however, you might come close. If you're the type who tends to leave no stone unturned—and thus, no pane left blank—the aforementioned categorization methods may need a bit of tweaking. Start off by keeping your first Home screen reserved for your most commonly used apps and folders. The first screen should always be home to the popular crowd. The good news is that science has yet to prove that apps have feelings, so those relegated to subsequent panes aren't apt to delete themselves in an act of rebellion.

FIGURE 2-6: Rearranging the furniture.

Apple doesn't allow each page to be labeled. You can call your folders anything you want, but you can't name panes. What I suggest is that you give each overflow pane a theme. It's certainly not as obvious as a label, but until Apple enables you to name panes, this is about as close as you can get.

Looking for an example? Let's say you're a huge news junkie, and you've downloaded just about every possible news application hosted on the App Store. Creating News 1, News 2, and News 3 folders is clearly not specific enough, so let's just theme an entire pane for news apps. You can create folders for Sports, Politics, Technology, Science, Travel and whatever other niche you're into, and for apps that encompass all aspects of news, you can pop those into a General folder. Just like that, you've assigned an entire pane to host news apps—no confusion about what lives where.

▶ You can't create a folder as a placeholder. In fact, you need two apps before you can create a folder. In other words, download a fair number of programs before diving headfirst into creating folders.

> **TIP** When organizing panes by theme, I generally leave my absolute favorite, most-used app from each theme as a standalone icon in the top-left corner. Not only does it prevent me from having to dig into a folder to access a favorite app, but it provides an at-a-glance way to see what theme is represented. For instance, the ESPN ScoreCenter app is in the top-left of my Sports pane, left out of a folder for better visibility and "marking" purposes.

Here are some examples of themes that tend to flesh out well:

- News
- Sports
- Audio Streaming
- Video Streaming
- Communications
- Productivity
- Business
- For the Kids
- Games
- Sharing / Storage

It'd be swell if Apple included a way to lock all panes except for that one dedicated to kids, but at least you can go ahead and arrange one specifically for their eyes. It's on you to keep 'em from swiping around and discovering that stash of tabloid apps, though.

GENERATING A WORKFLOW

At long last, it's the culmination of all the work you've put into the art of organizing. After you've populated your Dock just so, arranged your most commonly used apps along the edges of the first Home screen, and organized panes 2 through 11 by easy-to-recognize themes, it's time to focus on a workflow.

The most challenging thing about using an iPad after you pick it up is finding what you're after, particularly if you're keen on keeping dozens upon dozens of applications on your device. I'll be taking a closer look at push notifications in Chapter 12, but for the sake of organization you should know that they are completely valuable tools when properly set up and minded.

A great number of applications have been updated to support the more useful, less invasive push system unveiled with iOS 5. In prior versions of the operating system, push notifications simply popped up in the center of the iPad's display, regardless of what app you were currently engrossed in. Taking a note from Google's Android, Apple decided it prudent to shift notifications to their own pull-down bar at the top of the display (see Figure 2-7), where they collect and sit until you manually sift through.

FIGURE 2-7: A look at iOS 5's drop-down notification window.

I suggest enabling push notifications for any app that you truly find daily value in. Things like Facebook, breaking news apps, e-mail, and perhaps your favorite podcast can send you push notifications whenever a new message, alert, or issue awaits. With a reliable push system, you're presented with only the important changes upon reentering the iPad universe, giving you a head start on which apps to check first. Those that haven't sent you a notification are probably less urgent to reload.

TIP It's easy to become overwhelmed by push notifications. Being alerted of every MLB score update is probably overboard. Being alerted of a new iMessage from your significant other is probably useful—well, provided your relationship is in good standing. At any rate, be careful to not enable push alerts willy-nilly.

Another trick for accessing programs you use frequently is double-tapping the Home button from any pane on iOS. That brings up a lower bar with the apps you've used most recently shown first. A swipe to the right takes you even deeper into your recently used app stash (see Figure 2-8), whereas a swipe left enables you to change the orientation lock switch (or mute/unmute, depending on your settings), adjust screen brightness, control music playback, and adjust overall volume (from left to right).

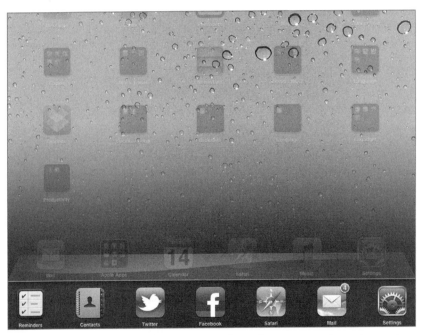

FIGURE 2-8: A double-tap of the Home button shows the most recently used apps along the bottom.

One inclusion that Apple *has* made, however, is the Universal Search screen (see Figure 2-9). For times when sifting through pages or folders just seems too burdensome, there's always a way out. At the initial Home screen—the one that automatically presents itself just after the lock screen—just swipe to the left one time, and a simple search bar pops up.

FIGURE 2-9: Universal Search—just type, and it starts finding.

That search bar is remarkably powerful, and it fields results incredibly quickly. What's most useful about the Universal Search function is that it actually digs *into* apps when it searches. In other words, searching for *Facebook* not only pulls up a shortcut to the Facebook app, but also returns any e-mail messages within the Mail app that relate to Facebook (see Figure 2-10). It's also capable of searching within Contacts, Music, third-party apps, and Calendar.

FIGURE 2-10: It's not just for finding apps. . .

No need to type out a full term. Universal Search updates and rearranges results with each additional letter you press.

Best of all, there are two shortcuts that appear for every search: Search Web and Search Wikipedia. Even if you can't find what you're looking for, one of those can probably help. I actually recommend using the Universal Search bar as a shortcut to Google search something. No need to actually launch Safari and search; just whisk over to the Universal Bar, peck your query in, and select the Search Web option.

SUMMARY

Just as important as setting your iPad up right is the art of organizing the applications that make it what it is. It's vital to think about the kind of layout you'd prefer, choosing a methodology for arranging folders and giving themes to each Home screen. I'd suggest keeping your most-used apps in the Dock, even if that means tossing a folder or two down there. Yeah, folders can fit into the Dock, too!

The iPad's edges are easiest to reach, so keeping your most commonly used programs around the perimeter is advisable. You're also more apt to maintain your sanity if you take full advantage of folders, but placing only nine apps in each ensures that you have a view to all of the app thumbnails within. In general, Apple's folder name suggestions are just too vague for serious cataloging; they are, however, useful for thinking of themes for home panes.

The easiest way to go digging through information that builds upon the iPad is the Universal Search function, which not only pulls up app names, but also finds information tucked within Mail, Contacts, and more.

CHAPTER 3

E-Mailing Like a Champion

It may be a bit presumptuous of me, but I'm guessing that you're going to be doing an awful lot of e-mailing on your iPad. And if you aren't exactly planning to do a lot of e-mailing, per se, you'll probably find that changes in due time. Fact is, the iPad is an absolutely stellar communication tool, and although it's long been possible to compose, reply to, and forward e-mails using a standard smartphone or BlackBerry, doing so on the iPad is a far richer, far more enjoyable, and far more productive experience. Having a full 10.1-inch keyboard to peck out e-mails is entirely more natural than attempting to wrestle a QWERTY keyboard with just the tips of your thumbs, and with the introduction of the split keyboard options within iOS 5, composing messages is even more natural. But, in typical Apple fashion, there are a few niggles with the overall e-mail experience.

Although it's far too easy to fall into the trap of believing that the iPad should act just as a laptop would, there are some intrinsic limitations that I've found particularly troubling when attempting to use the iPad as a productivity workhorse. In this chapter, I do a bit of composing of my own, digging through the App Store's vibrant third-party library in order to overcome some of the limits and stumbling blocks related to e-mail. I also show you a few alternatives to the factory Mail app, and if you're entrenched in Outlook or another enterprise service, I explain how to best make the iPad play ball there, too. Finally, I discuss e-mail syncing and the smattering of options available to keep your iPad, smartphone, and desktop web browser on the same page.

MASTERING GMAIL'S WEB APPLICATION

If you aren't an avid Gmailer, perhaps this section won't be near and dear to your heart. But if you are, it's probably worth a look-see. Most iPad owners dig right into the conventional Mail app settings—the e-mail app that Apple loads into each and every iPad Dock it sells—and proceeds with the built-in Gmail registration and setup tool. And that works. It's quick and painless, and for most, that's that.

> **NOTE**   E-mail is far from being the only productive thing the iPad can do, but it's really integral to the overall experience. One of the more interesting paradigms is the interplay between Google and Apple, particularly as it relates to e-mail. Google's Gmail service is widely used, and there's little disputing the fact that Android's native Gmail app is about as good as it gets for avid Gmailers. Knowing that Apple isn't going to let Google submit a native Gmail app into the App Store, Google approached a far more open workaround in the form of an iPad-specific HTML5 web app. Yes, a web app that's accessed via Apple's Safari browser. Clever!

But there's actually an alternative—an alternative that I'm convinced is far better in almost every way. There's no native Gmail app for iOS, and with Google and Apple becoming stronger rivals each and every day, I highly doubt that'll change in the near future. In an effort to encourage Gmail adoption and use on the world's most popular tablet operating system, the engineers at Google whipped up an HTML5 "web app" (see Figure 3-1) that brings a shockingly robust experience to the iPad via a back door that Apple can never really shut: the Internet.

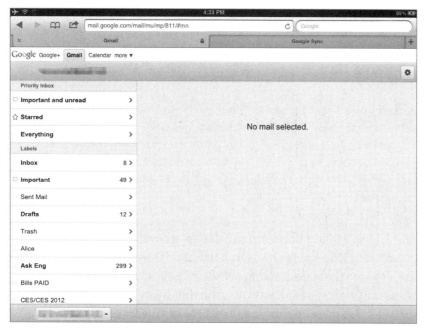

FIGURE 3-1: Looks crisp, no? It's not an app; it's the Gmail.com web app.

Comparing Gmail's Web App with Mail

Simply visiting gmail.com within Safari on your iPad redirects to the company's highly polished iOS Gmail interface; a split-pane view of your inbox that looks worlds better than Apple's Mail application. Moreover, the aesthetic improvements are just the beginning. For starters, this approach enables you to have Gmail open in one tab and related web pages open alongside of it. In other words, you don't have to jump completely out of your e-mail app in order to reference some other web page before continuing your message. It may sound minor, but those who need to flip back and forth between a reference page and e-mail can save a meaningful amount of time because of this. The less jumping between apps you need to do, the more productive (and sane) you'll be.

> **WARNING** Apple claims that iOS 5 allows for "multi-tasking," but the reality is quite different than the multi-tasking you're accustomed to within Windows or OS X. Think of it more like "background support." You can let Safari or Mail load messages in the background while you compose a graph in Apple's Numbers app, but you cannot load a split-app view that shows two or more applications on-screen simultaneously.

Gmail's web app also enables users to take advantage of their Google Contacts list. Yes, users can most certainly import their Google Contacts into the iPad's own Contacts app via an iTunes sync, but by using the web app, you never have to wonder if your contact list is up-to-date. If it's current within Google's database, it's current here.

> **TIP** Recently, Gmail began supporting multiple logins. In other words, those with more than one Gmail account can flip from one to the other in a matter of clicks. I have a personal account as well as a hosted **darren@engadget.com** account, and Google's Gmail web app even supports this flip-flopping feature. Just a tap along the bottom bar enables users to sign into another account or sign out of all accounts.

Perhaps most importantly, Google's Gmail web app knows how to handle e-mail threads and archives. iOS 5 has improved its handling of threads, but I've still seen many occasions where the built-in Mail app rendered a 20+ message thread incorrectly, whereas the Gmail web app always displays things just as I've come to expect from within Gmail. Archives are also a major part of daily life for Gmailers, and if assigning a label to a message before archiving it is vital to keeping your inbox organized, you'll be happy to know that this portal nails it every single time. Colored stars, too, can only be fully executed within Gmail's web app.

For as outstanding as the Gmail web app is, there are two major features that simply cannot be offered due to it residing within Safari. For one, you cannot receive push notifications of a message in the way you can if you're using Gmail through the iPad's built-in Mail app. Secondly, the iPad's Universal Search bar only sifts through messages in the device's Mail app; it doesn't reach out to an open Gmail tab within Safari.

Of course, you can manually refresh your mail list with a simple downward finger swipe, and the browser-based search function works swimmingly, but it's just not as seamlessly integrated. My advice here is to have your Gmail account also linked in the Mail app. That way, you'll receive a push notification of a new message via Mail, but you can open and respond to it via the web app. Furthermore, Universal Search digs through your Gmail messages within Mail, and if it finds a hit, you can simply dig through the web app.

> **WARNING** For as great as the HTML5 version of Gmail is, there's one major limitation for now: language. It launched with support for U.S. English only, though other tongues will be supported in the near future. If you can understand the words in this book, however, you probably won't be negatively affected by this limitation.

Understanding Horizontal versus Vertical Views

The Gmail web app maintains a two-pane view regardless of which orientation you're using. Your list of messages is situated on the left, and the e-mail of the moment is fully displayed on the right. Both orientations display the same surrounding icons and buttons, with the obvious difference being what you see more of. With the iPad flipped horizontally (see Figure 3-2), the individually selected e-mail gets more real estate; if flipped vertically, you've a better view to what e-mails have come in recently.

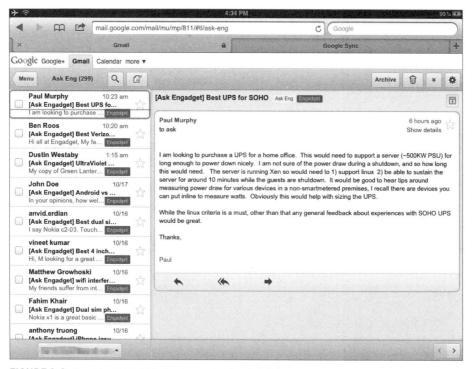

FIGURE 3-2: Gmail's HTML5 iPad web app, horizontal view.

In iOS 5, Apple made it easier to e-mail folks back with the introduction of the split keyboard. I'd recommend using the split keyboard at all times while you're in vertical mode (see Figure 3-3)—it's simply easier to compose messages when the keys are within reach of your thumbs. When you go horizontal, though, the full-size keyboard tends to produce fewer errors in my experience.

FIGURE 3-3: That split keyboard sure is handy while in vertical mode.

CROSSREF Expecting to type a lot on your iPad? A case that doubles as a kick-stand is a must-buy accessory. I cover the best of the best in Chapter 15.

Looking for a refresher? Use the vertical view with a split keyboard if you've nowhere to set your iPad (for example, when you're stuffed between two blokes in the rear of a taxi). If you have a table of some sort, and particularly if you have a Smart Case or some other kickstand apparatus around back, turn 'er sideways, plop it down and pretend that you're typing on a bona fide keyboard. Ahh... feels refreshing just thinking about it.

SWITCHING TO GMAIL'S TABLET INTERFACE

If you fall madly in love with Gmail's tablet interface and would actually prefer to use it on your regular computer, I've great news for you: It's possible. You need to do the following using Mozilla's Firefox browser:

1. Install the User Agent Switcher add-in (`https://addons.mozilla.org/en-US/firefox/addon/59?src=api`).

2. Go to Tools ➜ Default User Agent ➜ Edit User Agents.

3. Select New ➜ User Agent and paste the following code into the User Agent field:

```
Mozilla/5.0(iPad; U; CPU iPhone OS 3_2 like Mac OS X; en-us)
AppleWebKit/531.21.10 (KHTML, like Gecko) Version/4.0.4
Mobile/7B314 Safari/531.21.10
```

4. In the App Code Name field, enter **iPad**.

5. Now that it's installed, go to Tools ➜ Default User Agent ➜ iPad.

6. Surf over to **gmail.com**, and the iPad interface should load.

NOTE I've harped a lot on Gmail here, mostly because it's the only major mail client that also has a competing tablet operating system, but Yahoo! recently rolled out an iPad-specific web app, too. Similarly, Microsoft revamped Hotmail with plenty of HTML5 to go around, so it's fairly clear that companies are paying attention to what their users are increasingly using to check messages on: the tablet that Steve built.

PERFECTING THE MAIL APP

Even if you're dead-set on using a web app to check your e-mail, there's plenty of reason to *also* establish your addresses within Apple's Mail app. I generally discourage duplicity with things like this (okay, fine, I abhor it—pretty sure you can handle the truth by this point), but as I alluded to earlier, there *are* certain benefits in having an e-mail account registered with an app that's so finely woven into the core of iOS. Universal Searches won't ever pull up findings within your e-mail accounts unless they're established in Apple's own Mail app (see Figure 3-4), and push notifications cannot be sent down through Safari. You can set up any POP or IMAP in Mail, but these are preprogrammed to fetch all the required back-end data with a simple username and password.

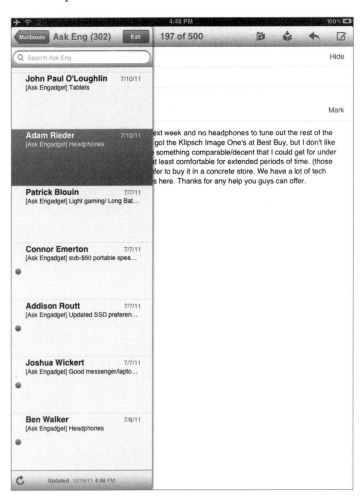

FIGURE 3-4: Simple and clean is Apple's iPad Mail app.

Beyond all that, though, Mail is a fantastic app on its own, but there are an abundance of settings and options to tweak—things that most folks don't ever take the time to investigate. Good thing you aren't lumped into *that* crowd. Apple makes it stunningly easy to get an e-mail account registered in Mail... provided you're using a Google, Yahoo!, Microsoft Exchange, iCloud, AOL, or Hotmail account (see Figure 3.5).

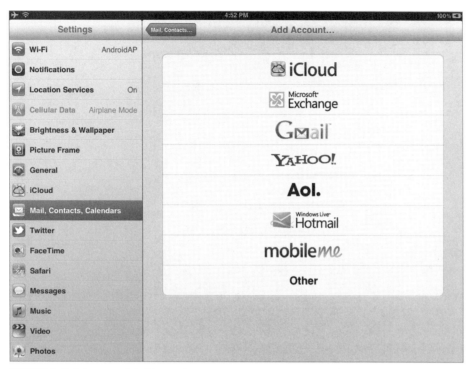

FIGURE 3-5: Take your pick. Plenty of automated e-mail setup awaits.

Discovering Setup Tricks (and Other Hidden Gems)

Here's a stunner: Mail setup leads you to all sorts of other non-mail related things. Take a moment to let that sink in. Apple has intelligently realized that you may not want to suck down associated contacts, notes, and calendars for every single e-mail account you load into Mail. To that end, each new account you create gives you the option to toggle the aforementioned extras off or on. If you're looking to add your work e-mail address to Mail just for the sake of having it there in case of emergency, but you've no desire whatsoever to see any weekly conference calls on your personal calendar, just venture to Settings ➜ Mail, Contacts, Calendars and select each account individually. See for yourself in Figure 3-6.

FIGURE 3-6: Syncing everything? Nothing? You have options.

NOTE As an example, I added my Engadget work e-mail into the Mail app for one reason, and one reason alone: To pull in associated calendar entries. Remember: There's no way to just add a calendar from an account without adding the account in Mail first. After you've done that, you can toggle what you want the iPad to pay attention to, and what to ignore.

You've probably heard a thing or two about "push" and "pull" systems related to e-mail. The iPad handles both. Push accounts—such as a Gmail account—automatically alerts your iPad that a new message has arrived, even if it's asleep or idling. It requires no action whatsoever on your end. Naturally, this "always alert" state has a slightly negative effect on battery life (think of it as your iPad sleeping with one eye cracked open), but more detrimental is the data required. If you're using a cellular connection, or you're counting kilobytes with more intensity than calories, you may want to disable push altogether.

To do this, surf over to Settings ➜ Mail, Contacts, Calendars ➜ Fetch New Data. Right (see Figure 3-7) up top is a toggle to disable or enable push wholesale. "Fetch" is another term for "pull," where you give the iPad a time interval in which to reach out to your connected accounts and pull in anything new since the last polling time. My suggestion is 15 minutes for those addicted to their digital lives, and Hourly for everyone else. Manually is fine, but why force yourself to remember what to refresh when the iPad does it for you?

▶ Push is a godsend for keeping you informed, but it can quickly become overwhelming. I've known people to disable push at 6PM each day in order to remove distractions and focus on family. It's worth considering.

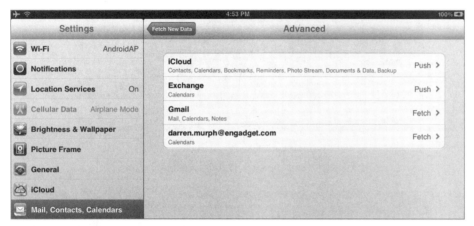

FIGURE 3-7: Pushing or fetching options can be applied separately to various accounts.

Another tip is to dig one level deeper. If, while in that same window, you tap Advanced, you are able to tell each and every mail or calendar account how you want it to push or pull. Perhaps pushing your personal account while only pulling your work account hourly is an ideal situation, as it saves precious battery life and data where you can most afford to. *Just don't tell your boss.*

There's another hidden gem here that more advanced users may very well appreciate. While in Settings ➜ Mail, Contacts, Calendar ➜ Add Account, there's a nondescript Other option beneath all the branded, pre-configured solutions (see Figure 3-8). *Mysterious!* I'll dig into the specifics of popping an unorthodox e-mail account in here shortly, but for now I'd like to draw attention to a foursome of obscure (to the simpleton, anyway) options below Contacts and Calendars. If you were hoping to connect an LDAP or CardDAV account for pulling in contacts, or a CalDAV/Subscribed Calendar for calendars, here's your opportunity. Make sure you bring your server address, username, password, and a crafty description, though.

FIGURE 3-8: Got your own mail settings? Punch 'em in here!

SETTINGS FOR MAIL, CONTACTS, CALENDARS

In the effort of saving you time, I'd recommend the following settings under the Mail options in Mail, Contacts, Calendars:

▶ **Show → 500 recent messages:** It doesn't demand that much extra space, and it's awesome to have a huge history when sifting for something offline.

▶ **Preview → 5 lines:** The more information you can see at a glance, the less time you waste diving deeper into something that's ignorable.

▶ **Minimum Font Size → Medium:** This setting is sufficient unless your eyes are troubling you.

▶ **Show To/Cc Label → On:** In most cases, the more information you have to glance at when communicating, the better off you are.

▶ **Ask Before Deleting → Off:** You can always resurrect things from the Trash if you need to.

▶ **Load Remote Images → Off:** Selecting On is a great way to accidentally buy into a phishing scam.

▶ **Organize By Thread → On:** Attempting to read e-mails sans threads could cause your iPad to burst into tears.

If you're one of those folks (like me—no shame in confessing it) who have a multi-tude of shared Google Calendars, getting them to populate in the iPad's iCal app is far more difficult than it should be. Although you may assume that simply flipping the Calendar toggle to On in your added Gmail account would be enough, that *only* adds the sole Google Calendar that directly links to said account. If you've access to shared Gcals from your significant other, colleagues, bosses, sports teams, and so on, those calendars won't just "show up." Defies logic, but it's true. Have a look at Figure 3-9 to see what it takes to remedy this.

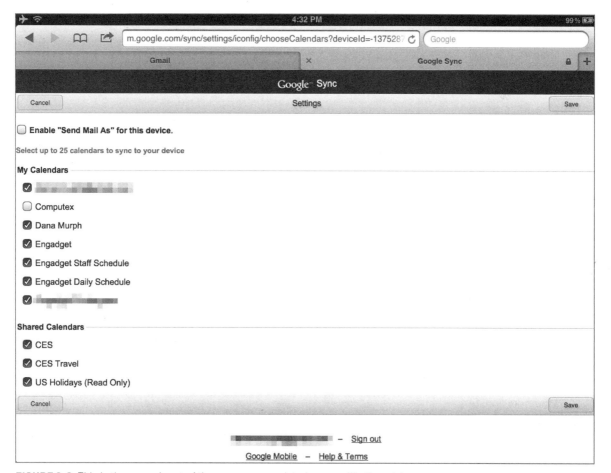

FIGURE 3-9: This is the second part of the process, completed on your iPad's web browser.

SYNCING GOOGLE APPS WITH IOS

Thankfully, Google has a workaround, but it certainly takes a little elbow grease. Here's how it's done:

1. Choose Settings ➔ Mail, Contacts, Calendars ➔ Add Account.

2. Select Microsoft Exchange and then enter your full Gmail address in the Email and Username fields.

3. Leave Domain blank and insert your Gmail password in the Password field.

4. Tap the Next button in the top-right, and when the Server field emerges, type **m.google.com**.

5. On the following screen, ensure that all options are toggled to Off except Calendar.

6. Open Safari and go to **m.google.com/sync**; find your iPad in the list after logging in and select it.

7. Tap to add any or all of your shared calendars. After you save your changes, your iCal updates in a matter of minutes if you're on a solid Wi-Fi connection.

Making Tweaks for Productivity

Although the iPad's Mail app is fully capable of handling as many e-mail accounts as you can throw it (within reason, naturally), there can only be one default. This is actually more important in relation to third-party apps that allow shortcuts to "mail" things from within. For example, if you select to e-mail an article from a news magazine, it'll send from whatever your default account is. If your work is fairly strict about what passes through its mail servers, make sure your personal account is the default at Settings ➔ Mail, Contacts, Calendars ➔ Default Account.

Also, leaving "Sent from my iPad" as your signature may seem a bit pretentious and played out—and let's be honest, it sort of is—but it definitely gives recipients a heads-up to expect curt replies, stranger than usual formatting, and a glut of typos. Better safe than sorry, right? Have a look at what the default signature *really* reads as in Figure 3-10.

▶ For what it's worth, I changed mine to something less colorful: "Sent from my mobile device; apologies for brevity and typos."

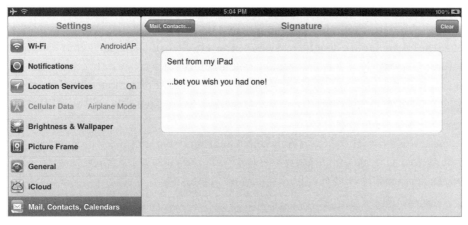

FIGURE 3-10: Now that's a way to make an impact.

If you're planning on traveling with your iPad (you should!), pay close attention to how your calendars are displayed. In the familiar Settings ➜ Mail, Contacts, Calendars ➜ Calendars section, make sure you deliberately choose to turn Time Zone Support on or off. The Off setting pleases those who want to see what times their events are with respect to whatever time zone they're currently in. The On setting pleases those who may change position in the world, but never mentally leave the time zone where their work takes place. In my world, Engadget revolves around Eastern Time, so Time Zone Support on my iPad is flipped to On. Even if it's 3 a.m. on a Thursday in Sydney, I want to be reminded that it's noon on Wednesday so far as my work is concerned (see Figure 3-11). There's hardly a productivity (and reputation) killer more ruthless than a confused time zone.

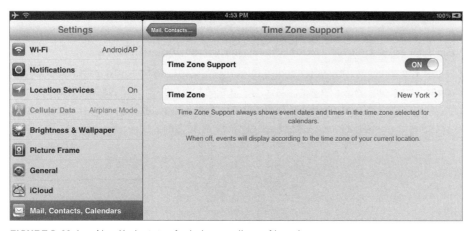

FIGURE 3-11: In a New York state of mind, regardless of location.

As mentioned earlier, I recommend reading your e-mails vertically if you don't have a table to rest your iPad on, and horizontally if you do. At first glance, it appears that the former is darn near impossible, as the left rail (which displays your list of messages) partially covers the selected e-mail. But a quick swipe from right to left across the panel removes that, and a swipe in the opposite direction brings it back when you're ready to move onto another message. In horizontal mode, the split-pane view remains there regardless.

Avid archivists should also know about another swipe trick: Sweeping left or right across a message *in the list of messages* will bring up a red "Archive" button, which does exactly what you think it does upon pressing.

Mark as Unread is another beast entirely. It feels like Apple changes the location of this feature on every iOS release, and it's located in a somewhat hidden spot in iOS 5. I use this function all the time for e-mails I want to quickly peek at but don't have time to fully reply to at the moment.

Within an open message, you need to take the following steps:

1. Tap Details in the upper-right corner.

2. Tap Mark.

3. Tap Mark as Unread.

I mentioned earlier that multi-tasking is more like backgrounding on the iPad. That doesn't mean that you should avoid keeping mental tabs on what's lurking behind your Mail pane. When composing an e-mail that requires you to reference something stored on Dropbox, in Numbers, on a web page, as an address in Maps, or data in practically any other application, a simple double-tap of the Home button (or a four-finger swipe from bottom to top) pulls up apps that are currently running in the background (see Figure 3-12). It only shows the six most recently used apps at first, but a swipe from left to right reveals more (and more... and more).

Just tap whatever app you need to reference in order to hop into it and then do the same bottom-bar emergence trick as before in order to find Mail sitting there in the lower-left corner. Your message remains just as you left it, ready to accept a new thought or even a paste of text that you copied from a different app.

▶ That little "drawer" icon in the top bar between the file folder and left-pointing arrow is another shortcut for Archive.

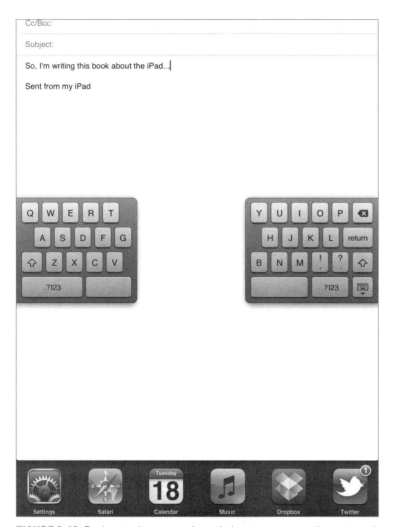

FIGURE 3-12: Background apps are shown below as a message is composed.

Managing Passwords and Multiple Accounts

Look, you're a popular person. There's no need to feel ashamed about having eight e-mail accounts. (At least, you can keep telling yourself that.) All jesting aside, there are a few snippets you should know about having a cadre of accounts within Mail. For one, the notification bubble on the Mail icon—which represents a view of how many unread messages you have—shows the *sum* of all unread e-mails across accounts. There's unfortunately no way to force the icon to only show unread message counts for a specific list of accounts, which may or may not bother those who go to great lengths to maintain a "zero inbox" in their most-used account.

I've already touched on the importance of carefully selecting which account is your default account, but changing from one to the next is fairly simple. While in the Mail app, just tap Inbox ➜ Mailboxes in order to pull up a list of your accounts. I recommend naming them with care. If you have more than a couple, using just your name, "personal," or "work" may not be descriptive enough.

For now, Apple has no feature that enables you to lock specific apps or e-mail accounts. When you're through the optional lock screen password—you can establish the passcode in Settings ➜ General ➜ Passcode Lock ➜—you've access to everything. This is particularly troubling when you need to hand your iPad off for a work presentation but would rather your nosey colleagues not "accidentally" read your e-mail or spot any personal push notifications. To date, there's no app in the App Store to remedy this, but jailbreakers have an option—a few options, actually. You can find FolderLock, Lockdown Pro, and Locktopus in Cydia or BigBoss repositories, and all are priced at less than $5. These enable you to set up very specific locks for apps and content. My suspicion is that Apple will see the light here and integrate similar functionality into a future iOS build.

S/MIME (Secure/Multipurpose Internet Mail Extensions) is one of the more advanced security features that most common folk just gloss right over, but for those obsessed with keeping track of signed messages (or those that have this requirement due to the sensitive nature of their work), it's a great feature to tap into. Apple has enabled support of this by default within iOS, and you need to dig into Settings ➜ Account ➜ Advanced for each e-mail account in order to enable it. From here, you can opt to receive signed messages and sign them yourself, but you first need to procure a certificate elsewhere. (VeriSign's a good place to head for one.) When you're in possession of the certificate, just e-mail it to yourself and have iOS install it.

TACKLING OUTLOOK, FIREWALLS, AND VPNS

Then there's Microsoft Outlook. Outlook is to enterprise mail clients what Word is to word processors. In other words, if you're working at a major corporation, chances are high that you've been ushered into an Outlook world. Although Apple makes it

▶ One idea is to switch less important accounts to manually fetch, so you aren't distracted by push notifications (and a surging unread count) for accounts that aren't urgent to keep tabs on.

▶ Jailbreaking isn't for the weak spirited or the cowardly, but you can use Google to find plenty of information if you want to dive in. It voids your warranty, though, so you're operating at your own risk!

simple to set up an Exchange account on your iPad, getting along with Outlook isn't something iOS prefers to do natively. Thankfully, as I've found so frequently, "there's an app for this, too."

OutlookReflex, a gem of an app by Karya Technologies, makes your desktop Outlook reachable via your iPad. You can search, view, reply to, and forward your mails from your device, as well as access Outlook contacts, view address locations on Maps, and so on. OutlookReflex is available in the Apple App Store and is compatible with Outlook 2003, 2007, and 2010. If you're hesitant to buy it without trying it, you can enjoy a free trial for 30 days. After that, you need to pony up for the $9.99 per year subscription cost. The app even supports multiple e-mail accounts and inboxes within your Outlook account, and the newest build enables users to flag e-mails, create and move folders, search, and mark messages as read or unread.

Things get tricky when firewalls are involved. If you're using your iPad in both a blockaded work environment and a free-as-a-bird home environment, you may want to consider how you set up your Microsoft Exchange or Lotus Notes e-mail accounts. Although both can technically be established via the iPad's Add Account function, the servers you instruct it to connect to while on a firewalled Internet are not accessible after you leave your workplace. My suggestion is to take advantage of the web-based interfaces available for both platforms. You can find Outlook's web app at www.microsoft.com/exchange/en-us/outlook-web-app.aspx, and you can find Lotus Notes at www-01.ibm.com/software/lotus/products/inotes/.

▶ The user interface on OutlookReflex isn't what I'd call "beautiful," but it serves the purpose, and the dev team has been steadily improving it.

NOTE Apple has realized that the iPad is forcing its way into business. Hundreds of Fortune 500 companies already use the product in one way or another. Although Apple has struggled to embed certain products in the enterprise (remember Xserve?), it's grabbing this opportunity by the horns.

Because business setups are infinitely more complicated than most personal scenarios—or, at least they can be—Apple has created a shockingly detailed guide that explains what ports need to be left open, what settings need to be enabled for VPN access and what security protocols are supported on the device. The topic of enterprise setup could fill a book of its own, and that's practically what Apple has done. If you're looking to become versed in corporate iPad integration, point your browser to http://images.apple.com/ipad/business/pdf/iPad_Deployment_Scenarios.pdf.

Another good resource for this information is *iPad in the Enterprise: Developing and Deploying Business Applications* written by Nathan Clevenger and also published by Wiley. The ISBN for this book is 978-1-118-02235-1.

WRAPPING YOUR HEAD AROUND ATTACHMENTS

One of the most troubling aspects of using Apple's Mail app on iPad is the inability to truly add a limitless number of attachments. Adding photos from your Camera Roll is a cinch (see Figure 3-13), but everything else requires a bit of backhand jiggering. In my mind, I'm assuming that Apple's done this due to the omission of a properly accessible file system in iOS. On a full operating system, there's a Desktop and My Documents folder to browse to in order to attach files. That doesn't *exactly* exist in the iOS universe.

FIGURE 3-13: If only adding things other than photos were this easy. . .

It's still possible to save PDFs, create documents, and house files on the iPad. So, how do you go about attaching those to e-mail messages? If you're a jailbreaker, AnyAttach ($1.99 in the Cydia app store) adds a stereotypical paperclip to every Mail message compose screen, and tapping it enables you to sift through iOS's file system in order to easily attach pretty much anything.

If you're looking to remain on the straight-and-narrow, I have a few suggestions, all available through a simple title search in Apple's App Store.

- ▶ **Quickoffice Connect (free for limited version; $14.99 for full):** Access, view, and share or e-mail files from multiple cloud storage services, including Dropbox, Google Docs, and Box.net.

- ▶ **Dropbox (free):** E-mail links to files you've stored within Dropbox, as well as view them offline on your device.

- ▶ **FileApp Pro ($4.99):** Send a wide variety of document types.

- ▶ **GoodReader for iPad ($4.99):** Manage and share files via iPad; widely regarded as the best, most updated app for this purpose.

- ▶ **iFiles ($3.99):** Manage files with this stellar app that doubles as an e-mail liaison.

Unfortunately, even the best sharing solutions still require you to start your attachment journey in a third-party app and then hop into Mail (AnyAttach notwithstanding). It's a bit baffling to think that the iPad isn't capable of natively attaching any file you want, but at least Apple's developer community is as robust as they come. For as long as Apple leaves this vital feature out, you can rest assured that there will be third-party alternatives for bridging the gap.

SUMMARY

For as enjoyable as the iPad is as an entertainment and content consumption product, it's a respectable communication tool, too. Due to the lack of a physical keyboard and the omission of a full-fledged file system, it's not quite as functional as an actual laptop, but working on it is far more viable than working on your average smartphone. The increased screen space and the introduction of a split keyboard make it a breeze to type on, and with support for myriad e-mail accounts, it's quite possible to juggle both work and play.

Knowing that it isn't apt to win over the tablet market share crown anytime soon, Google has invested quite a bit of effort into its HTML5-based Gmail web application, and in turn, both Hotmail and Yahoo! have followed suit. Managing multiple accounts—and perhaps even multiple tools for sending messages—is tricky, but worth the effort. Enterprise users also have a few extra hurdles to jump, but thankfully Apple has made great strides in bridging the gap and providing support for firewalls,VPNs, and stricter security protocols.

Those entrenched in Outlook and desperate to send attachments via their iPads have plenty to learn and plenty of developers to thank. The App Store is home to a litany of inexpensive programs that greatly enhance Apple's relatively straightforward mail experience, and for less than $20 you can transform your iPad from a basic message sender to a sophisticated e-mailing wizard. And who doesn't love wizards?

CHAPTER 4

Wrangling iTunes (While Maintaining Your Sanity)

Apple has gone to great lengths to remove the PC (or Mac, for that matter) from the list of necessary items when one first sets up an iPad. With the introduction of iOS 5, Apple introduced the idea of "PC-free" and forced the concept to the forefront of the entire user experience. Think of it less as an option and more like the new regime. Not that I'm complaining—making the iPad more of a standalone device can only mean good things for mobile professionals, not to mention those who just aren't interested in learning the intricacies of a computer operating system in order to properly set up an iOS-based device.

Despite Apple's remarkable efforts, however, an iPad's potential is still only fully realized with the help of a partner. As with most right-hand men, iTunes is both a blessing and a curse. This chapter helps you tame a necessary evil and hopefully, shows you how to make iTunes work with you (as opposed to the obvious alternative).

MASTERING THE INITIAL ITUNES SETUP

When Apple initially launched iTunes on Windows, it aptly proclaimed that "Hell Had Frozen Over." By bringing the liaison used with every modern iPod and iPad to the archrival operating system, the company took a huge step in opening itself up and finally playing toward the demands of the masses. Not surprisingly, it has been consumer electronics—not Macintosh computers—that have forced the company's shares northward and placed them on a nearly unbelievable path of record-breaking quarters. But the irony in Apple's clearly tongue-in-cheek statement is that there's more "hell" in iTunes than any other piece of software ever designed in Cupertino.

Year after year, and release after release, iTunes remains the most griped about piece of Apple software. Granted, it's about the only piece that works on more than 95% of personal computers, but there is much to learn about an application that's both a requisite to maximum iPad enjoyment and an absolute thorn in the side of computer users the world over. As with most frustrating things, iTunes doesn't have to be the boss of you, but you need a bit of underground knowledge in order to gain the upper hand.

Creating Your Initial iPad Profile

One thing that Apple doesn't make nearly clear enough is just how important the initial iTunes/iPad marriage is. As with bona fide matrimony, getting these two off on the wrong foot unquestionably leads to heartache, if not outright disaster. Being that prenuptial agreements are null and void in the computing space, you don't want to resort to a night of reformatting every other week. The trick? Think about how you want your media arranged *before* you smash every "Okay, Move Along!" confirmation button you see.

It's helpful to know what iTunes is going to ask of you before actually approaching the point of no return. While owners of the original iPad might be able to sync most of their applications, music, and preferences to an iOS 5-equipped iPad 2 (as an example) sans a PC, iPad owners who are new to the entire ecosystem inevitably end up touching iTunes sooner rather than later. Get started by plugging your iPad into your Mac or PC and ensuring that both the latest release of iTunes is installed and the very latest version of iOS is running on your tablet.

One of the more vexing things about Apple is its insistence that you keep your software and hardware up-to-date. I generally recommend holding off on updates for at least a week or two after their release in order to see what issues crop up (surprise incompatibilities with automotive infotainment systems, for instance), but it's smart to have everything up-to-date at the point of first contact. Like I said, getting off on the right foot gives you more control over where to take the relationship.

NOTE Long before the iPad was even on the public radar, Apple decided it prudent to make iTunes a multi-platform affair. If you're worried about not owning a Mac (or moreover, have no interest in ever joining that club) you can still own an iPad. Perhaps miraculously, Apple has designed the iPad to be fully functional with or without a Mac nearby, with the common link being the iTunes software. iTunes is free to download for Windows XP/Vista/7 and OS X at **www.apple.com/itunes/**, and historically updates to both platforms have been pushed out simultaneously. Phew!

Updating both is as simple as opening iTunes and then choosing iTunes ➔ Check for Updates (see Figure 4-1). If you're connected to the Internet, iTunes should proactively search for any available iOS updates when you plug your device in initially.

Post-updates, you should register the device when iTunes prompts you. The Find My iPad feature is covered in Chapter 1, but suffice it to say that setting up the Find My iPad service is the first step to ensuring that you can track your lost or stolen tablet down should the bad side of fate decide to remove it from your possession. Trust

FIGURE 4-1: Have you checked for an iTunes update lately?

me, it's easy to just tick Never Register (see Figure 4-2) and feel accomplished, but it's absolutely worthwhile to go ahead and hand over some information.

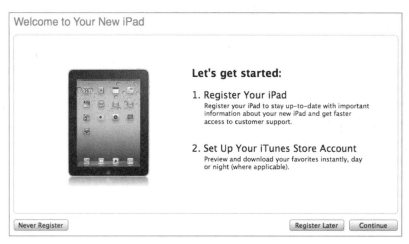

FIGURE 4-2: The Never Register option looks tempting, but go on and click Continue.

The next step is undoubtedly important: You're aiming to either restore your iPad from a backup (applicable to perfectly happy owners of older iPads) or create a new profile. For the sake of iOS newcomers (and those who just need a fresh start), the following sections assume that you're creating a profile.

> NOTE For owners of older iPads using an outdated version of iOS, it's vitally important to make sure you can find a copy of your existing iOS build *before* updating, as well as the outdated iTunes version that you originally used to install it with. Why? Because not all updates are better. Many iPod-compatible car systems won't communicate with the latest iOS builds, and the latest iTunes builds won't let you "downgrade" to older iOS builds, even if you have the restore file handy. Don't be anxious to update if you don't have to; if what you have works well, stick with it until some new feature pulls you ahead. (You know, like iMessage and iCloud in iOS 5.) Be sure to visit `oldapps.com` for archived iTunes releases and `iclarified.com` for archived iOS releases.

The Whys, Whats, and Wheres of iTunes

Before going any further, you'll be best served by having a few other ducks in a row:

- ▶ Are you using Google Calendar, an Exchange calendar, iCal, or something else for your date-tracking needs?
- ▶ Have you migrated all of your contacts into Gmail or Mac Address Book?
- ▶ Are all the photos you want on your iPad already sitting in organized folders within iPhoto?
- ▶ Have you already compiled an assortment of music for your iPad and thrown it all into a dedicated playlist within iTunes?
- ▶ Have you already converted your favorite video clips into formats optimized for iPad?

CHOOSING TO SYNC YOUR CALENDAR

▶ On a PC? Don't bother trying to find iCal—that's for Mac owners only.

Believe it or not, Apple's iPad actually syncs amazingly well with Google services. Rivals they may be, but they both understand that they need one another. I'm an avid Gmail and Google Suite user, and if you're like me, your entire world would crumble around you if Google Calendar failed to send reminders for a 24-hour period. The trick when setting up your calendar is to know ahead of time whether or not you'll be using Apple's built-in iCal app.

If you use Google's Calendar, make absolutely sure that you tell iTunes *not* to sync your calendar. It's a complete nightmare to have two conflicting (or worse, overlapping) calendars running on your iPad. It goes without saying that the same is true for any other calendar service other than iCal; if you use Exchange or any other cloud-based calendar service, don't let the initial iCal sync happen. (If you happen to dabble in both iCal and something else, feel free to have two calendars installed—just make sure you don't end up with duplicate entries.)

CHOOSING TO SYNC YOUR CONTACTS

Overseas travelers stuck in a hotel room with no cell service will certainly appreciate having a few pals from back home on speed dial, even if that means dialing a user-name instead of nine consecutive numbers. The rules described for calendars also apply here; iTunes gives you the option to sync Contacts from the OS X Address Book application should you choose; pick wisely, as duplicate (or triplicate!) contacts are both confusing to wade through and frustrating to cancel out.

Contacts? On a device other than a phone? A decade ago, your skepticism would be warranted, but times have changed. Regardless of whether you opted for a Wi-Fi only or a 3G/4G + Wi-Fi iPad, your slate is actually a powerful tool for communicating. The same address book you use in your phone is useful to have on your iPad, particularly if you're an iPhone, Skype, or Google Voice user. Although no iPad is capable of making voice calls over traditional cellular networks, all are able to make VoIP calls.

> VoIP, or Voice Over Internet Protocol, allows the Internet to supplant traditional cell towers in order to facilitate vocal communications.

ORGANIZING YOUR PHOTOS

I'm not the hugest fan of taking photos with a tablet; you not only look exceedingly strange walking around with a 10-inch camera, but the results are generally poor. That's your prerogative, however, but the iPad's photo abilities are thankfully more advanced—particularly when using the rear-facing 5MP iSight camera in the new iPad. The iPad is an ideal tool for displaying photo slideshows to colleagues or coeds, and the built-in Photos application nicely sorts images into folders. Here's the catch—you need to sort your photos on your computer ahead of time. On the Mac, the easiest way to do this is to toss the images you want to put on your iPad into iPhoto and then spend however long it takes placing them in galleries. iTunes is smart enough to automatically resize gargantuan 4MB JPEGs into more sensibly sized files for use on the iPad, but it's not smart enough to guess which image should go in which gallery. If you've never, ever sorted your heaps of vacation photos (*raise your hands—I won't judge*), this task is downright daunt-ing, but organizing things in iPhoto prior to that initial iTunes sync is time well spent.

> There's no iPhoto on the Windows side of things, but PC users can do similar organization using Adobe's Photoshop Album or Photoshop Elements.

If, for some reason, you'd rather avoid those programs altogether, you can choose the Sync Photos From option in the Photos pane of iTunes (see Figure 4-3) and then select the file folder that has your photos in it. This method is a bit messier, but it doesn't require as much legwork on the organization front.

FIGURE 4-3: Use Choose Folder if you'd rather avoid using a dedicated photo-management program.

> **TIP** iPhoto is also capable of displaying photos on a map based on location, which helps you easily visualize where you and your iPad have been based on photos captured.

READYING YOUR MUSIC FOR THE IPAD

When it comes to music, I'm happy to report that you don't need a third-party program. iTunes, the same program you use for syncing, is also the program I recommend for managing your music. It's not the most streamlined tool for playback, and older machines tend to have a tough time dealing with how many resources it ties up, but it's far and away the most sensible for use with iOS products. Syncing music to the iPad using any program other than iTunes is a hassle that's simply not worth dealing with, and if you happen to get an iTunes Gift Card, you'll find that it's even more logical to keep grandfathered and digitally purchased music in one central location. You need to think about storage before syncing music over. I have well more than 80GB of music, and, if you're in a similar boat, you're in the unfortunate position of not being able to sync 100 percent of your tunes to your new tablet. Time to pick and choose! The easiest way to do this is to create a new playlist within iTunes (see Figure 4-4).

FIGURE 4-4: Creating a New Playlist is as simple as a single click. . . or pressing Command + N (Control + N for PC users).

Decide now how much room you're willing to sacrifice for music. Roughly 50% of your storage is a safe bet, leaving the rest for e-mails, Dropbox attachments, apps, and photos, but feel free to adjust based on your particular needs.

> NOTE Thinking about storage? *Boring.* But trust me—it's vitally important! Running out of room when you least expect it is a real bummer, and nothing seems to swell uncontrollably like music. Leaving 50 percent of your available storage open for productivity tasks, unsuspected photo dump sessions, and all-night app download-a-thons is a wise move. Just force yourself to be smart about what's in your music playlist; if iTunes tells you that you haven't "Starred" or listened to a particular song in six or more months, you'll probably be okay without it on your iPad.

From there, create a playlist that's easy to recognize ("iPad Music" works magically) and then sift through your gigantic library to drag and drop your absolute favorites into the list. If you're willing to put in the extra time and effort you could actually create a number of playlists and simply add up how much storage they each require. iTunes handily tells you exactly how much space a playlist takes up on a small line at the bottom of the software—keep an eye on that (see Figure 4-5) to make sure you aren't overloading things.

When you're satisfied with your selections, it's important to tell iTunes very specifically what music you want synced. By default, it attempts to sync your entire library until it runs out of room (gape in horror at Figure 4-6), but that leaves no extra space for apps, photos, and other things. You need to tick the Selected Playlists, Artists, Albums, and Genres selection and then check off your individual playlist choices. Now, iTunes only copies the tunes in those lists, not your entire library.

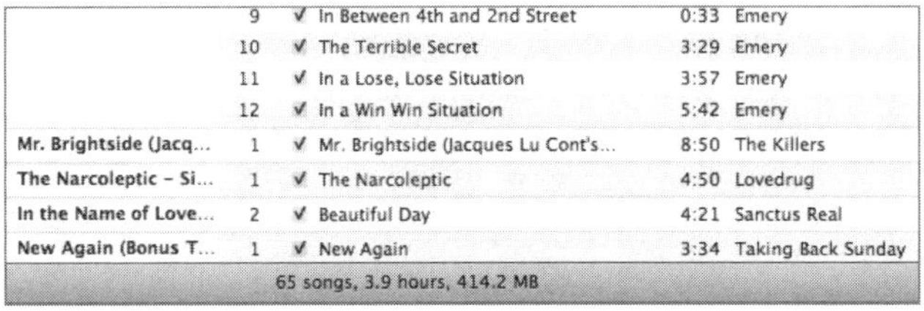

	9	✔ In Between 4th and 2nd Street	0:33	Emery
	10	✔ The Terrible Secret	3:29	Emery
	11	✔ In a Lose, Lose Situation	3:57	Emery
	12	✔ In a Win Win Situation	5:42	Emery
Mr. Brightside (Jacq...	1	✔ Mr. Brightside (Jacques Lu Cont's...	8:50	The Killers
The Narcoleptic – Si...	1	✔ The Narcoleptic	4:50	Lovedrug
In the Name of Love...	2	✔ Beautiful Day	4:21	Sanctus Real
New Again (Bonus T...	1	✔ New Again	3:34	Taking Back Sunday
		65 songs, 3.9 hours, 414.2 MB		

FIGURE 4-5: Total songs, total playtime, and total storage requirements. Pay close attention to that last one.

FIGURE 4-6: Syncing your entire music library to an iPad probably isn't wise. Unless you only own four albums, that is.

TIP It's important to remember, however, that you need to manually add any new music that you add to your master library to your iPad-specific playlist; otherwise, those new tunes won't ever migrate over in future syncs.

PREPARING YOUR VIDEO CONTENT FOR THE IPAD

When it comes to putting films, TV shows, or home movies on your iPad, you have two main options. The first is the one that Apple hopes you choose frequently. There's a movie and TV rental store right within iTunes. As you might expect, anything you purchase or rent from there lands preformatted to fit on your slate. That's notable for two reasons: First, it's optimized for size, so it doesn't take up unnecessary space. Second, it's optimized to fit the screen resolution of the iPad, so it's guaranteed to look crisp and not distorted. In other words, renting or buying content from the iTunes Store removes gobs of hassle, and anything you download from there immediately files itself nicely into an iTunes subsection on the left rail.

What if you're dealing with footage you've already captured? Home videos or Digital Copy films acquired as part of a DVD or Blu-ray combo pack may not always be optimized for viewing on the iPad, and unlike with photos, iTunes isn't built to do the converting without your intervention. The good news is that iTunes is *capable* of doing it, but you need to put in a little elbow grease. Just choose the Advanced → Create iPad or AppleTV Version option. If you'd like more control over how videos are re-encoded, you can also use iMovie HD or Final Cut Pro, or any other video conversion software that can downsize to 1024×768 for the iPad and iPad 2 or 2048×1536 for the latest iPad.

UPDATING YOUR APPS

If you're brand new to the iOS/iTunes ecosystem, you won't have any apps to worry about updating, but if you already have a few kicking around, it's worth updating them all before throwing them on the iPad. Within the Apps section of iTunes, you can click Check for Updates to get the process started (as seen in Figure 4-7 below). As with most everything else related to iTunes, you need a live Internet connection to accomplish anything.

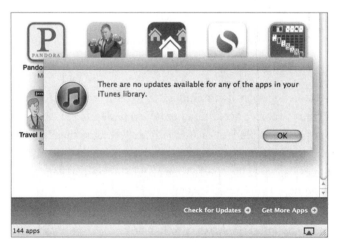

FIGURE 4-7: One of the best sights an iTunes user can see—everything's up-to-date!

▶ Remember: If an app doesn't say "iPad" in description, it only displays on a small part of the iPad's panel.

It's important to realize that not all apps are created equal. Although there are well more than 100,000 applications in the App Store that are built for the iPad's screen, far more are built only for the iPhone's smaller panel. When searching for new apps, Apple does a commendable job separating apps that are only for iPod touch and iPhone and apps that are suitable to display on all three platforms.

You also cannot assume that your iPhone apps will simply upgrade themselves to look nice and shiny on the iPad. You might need to download an entirely separate application as the iPad version of a given program, though many developers are now crafting single app downloads that display correctly on iPod touch, iPhone, and iPad. Figuring out what device an app is for couldn't be easier: In the Apps subsection along the left rail in iTunes, any app in the iPhone and iPod touch Apps section (as opposed to the iPhone, iPod touch, and iPad Apps section) doesn't display full-screen on your tablet (see Figure 4-8).

FIGURE 4-8: Any apps that file themselves under this category fit optimally on your iPad display.

Here's one final point on managing apps within iTunes: If you're an organization junkie, which you likely are if you're poring over these words, you'll want to put extra effort into arranging your apps in a sensible fashion *within iTunes*. I discuss specific patterns and recommendations in the pages to come, but it's worth knowing up-front that you don't want to sync your apps haphazardly, only to then manually arrange them on the device. If you do the arranging within iTunes, that layout "sticks" to your profile.

Consequently, if you just let the apps fall where they may on the initial sync you'll have *that* pattern overwrite any organization work you then do on-device. It's a frustrating cycle that's only ever put to rest by arranging your apps within iTunes.

TIP If there's one thread that repeats itself here, it's this: Take the time to organize iTunes prior to your initial sync. It's worth it.

UNDERSTANDING ACCOUNT LIMITS

You might assume that content purchased in the iTunes Store can only ever be played back on the machine that you originally used to complete the transaction. Or, if you're in the other school of thought, you might assume that a single purchase in one place should be readily available anywhere else. With the introduction of iTunes Match and iTunes in the Cloud, Apple has vastly extended the usability of iTunes purchases. However, when it comes to actually playing things back and syncing via hardwire, there are still a few limits (and, of course, ways to deal with them) that you need to know about.

In the iTunes world, your system is either authorized or deauthorized, and there's no in between. In order to access purchased content, play it back and—perhaps most importantly—sync it to your iPad, you need to have access to a live Internet connection as well as your iTunes credentials. In essence, iTunes requires you to log in before doing any of these tasks as a means to double-check your purchase history before enabling you to copy that content onto other devices (such as your iPad).

The good news is that you can have five computers simultaneously authorized. For the vast majority of consumers, that's plenty—a home desktop, a laptop, a work machine, and a netbook shared by the family. But if you're one of *those people* (much like myself, I might shamelessly add) who have more than five machines within reach, you need to figure out which of the five you want to have authorized.

This proves particularly tricky when you're visiting a friend and want to play back content that you purchased on a foreign machine. If you're already at your five-machine limit, your friend's copy of iTunes informs you that you can't authorize a sixth. Stuck? Not quite. There's a fairly simple workaround, but Apple curiously buries the option in a place most folks don't think to look.

You need to first log in to your iTunes account on the guest machine and then click your username in the top-right corner. When you enter your password, a full profile page is shown. The typical fields are there (name, address, billing information), but if you scroll all the way to the bottom, you get a glance at how many computers you currently have authorized. From there, click Deauthorize All (see Figure 4-9) in order to

> ▶ If you attempt to play a song purchased on iTunes during the DRM era, you need a username and password. If you type that in, you've just authorized a machine.

> ▶ Regardless of anything else, Apple's hard limit is five authorized machines.

remotely deauthorize all five machines and start over with only the guest computer you're using. Yes, this means you need to quickly reauthorize the systems that you just canned at a later date, but that's as simple as signing in again.

Apple ID Summary

Apple ID:		Edit >
Payment Information:		Edit >
Country/Region:		Change Country or Region >
Computer Authorizations:	5 computers are authorized to play content purchased with this Apple ID.	Deauthorize All

FIGURE 4-9: Click the Deauthorize All button to start fresh.

▶ Always remember to sign out and deauthorize any guest computers when you're done using them.

WHAT CAN BE SYNCED, AND WHERE?

Syncing files between a computer and an iPad can be a magical, if not mysterious, experience for the uninitiated. With a few choice clicks, content housed on a PC becomes content housed on a tablet—all neatly organized and ready for mobile consumption. Apple purposefully leaves many of the particulars vague for the sake of simplicity, which is a company value that oftentimes annoys power users who'd rather have access to the minutia going on behind the scenes.

Where Files Go in a Sync

Unlike Android 2.x, which enables users to simply mount their devices and drag content over as they would on an external hard drive, iOS takes a vastly different approach. For instance, the MP3 files stored on your computer are renamed and reorganized when synced onto an iPad; they're shuffled into an esoteric file pattern that only iOS can accurately digest. Why mention this? Because getting files off your iPad isn't nearly as easy as getting them on.

▶ These bodies, among other things, largely control what content is released, and how it's released, and what you can or can't do with it after you've purchased it.

Let's say your hard drive fails, and the only place your music remains is on your iPad. You might assume that a simple "reverse sync" to the new PC would be all that's required to shift those files back from the iPad and onto a new system. Sadly, it's not that easy. The reason likely has nothing to do with Apple, but with the RIAA and MPAA—America's two largest content overlords. They look out for the rights of content creators, which means that end users are frustrated.

If iOS had the capability to reverse sync content unchecked, you could theoretically purchase thousands of songs and movies and then place that purchased content onto an unlimited number of guest computers, thereby distributing "stolen" content at will. In reality, the restriction makes it impossible to use your iPad to restore any lost files. *Bummer.*

If you plug in your iPad to a new machine, you *can* right click on the mounted device and choose to Transfer Purchases back to the connected machine. (See Figure 4-10.) It works like a charm for content that you've procured via the iTunes Store, but that's the extent of the functionality. Any content you purchased elsewhere—be it a physical record store or Amazon's rival MP3 service—is not eligible for a reverse sync.

FIGURE 4-10: While in the Apps or Music section in iTunes, right-clicking your device's name brings up a Transfer Purchases option box.

Apple's nice, but it's not *that* nice. While redownloading things you've already purchased within the iTunes Store is kosher, it's not Apple's responsibility to do so for content you procured elsewhere. Because this function only checks your prior receipts within the iTunes Store, any content not matched up there is not available for download. In other words, make *sure* you have a great backup solution for your other content, be it an in-home NAS or Time Machine, or an off-site solution such as Mozy (mozy.com).

> **NOTE** For honest restoration situations, there is a way to reach into your iPad and pull your stored music back into your computer. For Mac users, there's a free program called Phone to Mac, and it's useful for rescuing songs from your iOS device and placing them back on a new or different computer in an organized fashion. For Windows users, SharePod accomplishes the same thing. I obviously recommend against piracy of any sort, but it's great to have these programs in your back pocket just in case disaster strikes.

How to Revert Your iPad to a Prior State

If you manage to create problems for yourself while using your iPad—by downloading a problematic app or something else—Apple makes it fairly painless to restore your device to a prior state. If you allow it, Apple backs up every single morsel of your iPad before every new sync, so if something goes wonky you can plug it back in and select the Restore option (see Figure 4-11) and revert the entire system to a place of peace—before trouble struck.

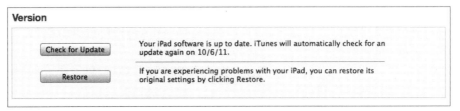

FIGURE 4-11: Don't worry if you tap Restore by accident—Apple gives you one final chance to confirm.

OPTING OUT OF A BACKUP

As mentioned earlier, there's tremendous value in allowing iTunes to back up your device while it's still in a recent, useful state. Should anything go wrong, it's extraordinarily comforting to know that a backup is available to get your iPad back on its feet. But the harsh reality is that we're all busy, and sometimes, that means we're too busy to sit around and wait for a system backup to complete.

For example, imagine that you purchase a new album from iTunes, drag those new tunes into your iPad Music playlist, and plug in your iPad to have those songs added. This process sounds like it ought to take two or three minutes, but if it's been a month or so since your last sync, the initial backup process could take in excess of 20 minutes. In other words, you have got more than 20+ minutes of waiting ahead of you before the new tracks even think about migrating over.

When you're rushing out of the door, the example scenario is a buzz kill of epic proportions. Thankfully, Apple makes it possible to opt out of backups, but, unsurprisingly, it doesn't go out of its way to advertise that. Apple's obsessed with user experience, and by not-too-subtly coercing iPad users to back up their devices with every sync, there's a far smaller chance that you'll be flustered by not having a recent backup to revert to.

Here's how to opt out of the backup process: After you've initiated a sync to add new files to your device, a tiny X displays to the right of the Backing Up message. (See Figure 4-12.) Just click that X one time, and iTunes immediately jumps to the transfer process, leaving you ready to eject your iPad and be on your merry way in mere minutes. Realize, however, that any restoration you do in the future will not contain any files that were added on sessions that you opted out of the backup. Opt at your own risk, so to speak.

FIGURE 4-12: No time for backups? Just click that tiny X on the right.

HOW TO MANAGE MULTIPLE COMPUTERS

It won't take you long to realize that Apple intends for you to use one computer to manage your iPad. Do you have a couple of machines at home, plus one at work? Brace for frustration. The good news is that you can calm most of the multi-machine mayhem with a few sly workarounds, which is what this section covers.

Secrets on Partial Syncs

Believe it or not, you don't have to sync everything from one machine to your iPad, but it's not as easy as being able to completely pick and choose what comes from where. You can sync music and contacts from one host machine, and use another only to sync photos and apps.

The trick is to be exceedingly careful about what you check to sync. If you carelessly leave the Sync Music box ticked on a machine with no music on it, your iPad will soon be devoid of Devo (and whatever else you had on there). From there, the only way to get the tunes back is to resync with the machine from which the music originally came—there's no "undo button" to syncs.

> **TIP** A partial sync makes sense when your music library is on a home desktop but everything else is stored on your laptop.

Cautions on Using Secondary Machines to Add Content

One common misconception is that you can use Machine A to sync your music and then use Machine B to simply add a newly downloaded album while keeping your existing playlist in place. Unfortunately, this is absolutely not the case. The reasoning, as best I can tell, relates to the same piracy concerns as explained earlier. In an ideal, honest world, Machine B would be able to suck down your existing music structure, back it all up, and then add the newly downloaded tunes atop that. The concern here is that you would've just given Machine B a wealth of content that perhaps the owner didn't actually purchase. So, Apple makes it impossible, *except* for music purchased in the iTunes Store. In theory, if you acquired every single song on your iPad via the iTunes Store, this scenario would be possible. It's food for thought, anyway.

The secret here is that the same is true for apps. The difference, notably, is that most consumers will have acquired every single app on the iPad via the App Store. Usually only developers who might have sideloaded test programs run into issues with an app not being eligible for transfer in a reverse sync. So, a reverse sync works with apps, but there's a catch: A new iTunes master doesn't recall the exact app structure that you painstakingly organized on Machine A, so if you pull over your apps, add a few newcomers, and then resync with Machine B, all your created folders are eliminated, and you're left to manually reorganize the location of every single app.

SUMMARY

iTunes is a powerful tool, and it's one that will almost certainly become a necessity in your continued iPad use. It's of paramount importance to organize your photos, music, movies, and apps before ever making the initial iPad sync, and it's vital that you deselect contact and calendar syncing if you're planning to pull those tidbits from the cloud on another service (Google, Microsoft Exchange, and so on).

Planning ahead and staying organized within iTunes is the best way to guarantee a seamless and satisfactory experience when syncing with iPad, and it's important to always let the program back up your tablet whenever you have ample time. If you're in a pinch, opting out of a backup is as simple as clicking a single X, but remember to plug things back in when time is more plentiful so that you keep your restore file current in case of disaster.

Finally, I recommend against having multiple iTunes masters on a single iPad. Although it's possible to pick and choose which machine syncs which sections, this method makes it impossible to ever have a completely whole restoration file, leaving your iPad susceptible to vast downtime if you ever have problems.

Part II

ACING THE ADVANCED FEATURES

CHAPTER 5

Making the Most of Multitasking

IN THIS CHAPTER

► Learning the shortcuts
► Discovering what's hidden
► Managing your background apps
► Universally searching
► Gesturing your way around iOS

I've alluded to this before, but Apple's definition of multitasking on the iPad doesn't jibe with the definition that was (and still is) used within the desktop operating system realm. iOS 5 can most certainly have multiple applications running at once, but you're forced to look at 'em one at a time. In my estimation, that's more like "backgrounding," but I won't spend any more time arguing semantics.

Instead, in this chapter I explain how to make the very most out of what Apple has to offer in terms of multitasking (or whatever you prefer to christen it) and how to think about your workflow in a way that follows logic in the iOS world. You find out about shortcuts, dig deep to figure out what's hidden, and see how to manage the apps that are running in the background. You discover how to reduce resource load by killing apps that you aren't actively using, and I show you why Apple's Spotlight is the unsung hero of iPad productivity. Finally, I touch (ahem) on the expanding world of multitouch gestures, which Apple has placed at the forefront of iOS discovery. Your iPad is nothing without your touch, and having the full gamut of gestures in the forefront of your mind will undoubtedly improve your overall experience.

SHORTCUTS GALORE

Half of the fun in owning an iPad is "discovering" new ways to use it. At first, it's little more than a mystery. Pop a couple of productivity apps on it, and soon it's an essential part of your workday artillery. Load up a few language-training tools, and it morphs into your favorite teacher this side of Mrs. Phelps. But there's another part of the equation, and that part is usability.

> **NOTE** With every new iteration of both OS X and iOS, Apple has grown ever more attached to multitouch gestures. In a way, the company pioneered this paradigm as the primary control mechanism on slate-style smartphones, and although multitouch control has become widespread across all types of devices, the touch response on iOS products remains world-class. What started out as a fascination with two-finger gestures (such as pinch-to-zoom) has blossomed into four-finger gestures that can accomplish a variety of tasks. Apple even ushered the Magic Trackpad into existence in order to bring the gestures that people were learning on iOS products onto its laptops and desktops. If you've yet to explore what using all of your digits can do on the iPad, you're only feeling a part of the experience.

The iPad is immediately and infinitely usable, even to those who don't understand the concept of multitouch. I've seen children who can't even spell their own names grab an iPad and figure out how to swipe through a photo gallery. There's just something intrinsically natural about control via touch, and few companies have implemented it as well as Apple has on the iPad. But smooth scrolling on web pages and seamless shuffling of photos is just the tip of the proverbial iceberg.

Mashing Buttons

Go on, admit it: You always were one of those kids who couldn't resist pressing the big, red button, despite obvious warnings to avoid doing so. Apple's minimalistic approach means that there aren't too many buttons and switches on the iPad, but that *also* means that each and every one of them is highly important to understand.

Starting at the top of the iPad, you find what rocket scientists affectionately call the Power button. Take a moment to ponder its possibilities. In all seriousness, the Power button itself does have a few undercover features, some of which are only revealed when you use them in conjunction with other buttons. Aside from turning an iPad on from a powered-off state, a single press also turns on or off the display. Moreover, holding it down for a few short seconds brings up an otherwise impossible-to-find option to turn the unit off entirely. If your iPad ever becomes completely unresponsive and unusable—yes, this can and has happened before!—holding down the Power button as well as the Home button for approximately ten seconds initiates a "hard reboot."

> A hard reboot on the iPad is the equivalent to holding down the Power button on a Mac or PC computer in order to force a shut down. It ain't pretty, but sometimes it's the only way out.

While I'm on the topic of using your Power and Home buttons in conjunction, there's one other function this tandem can pull off. Mashing the Home and Power buttons simultaneously causes a white flash and a camera shutter sound, which lets you know you just took a perfect capture of your iPad display and stored it for safe keeping in your Photos app. The Photos app is the same place that photos you take with the iPad camera are housed, and you can easily pull them over to your Mac by firing up iPhoto and initiating an import. Each captured image is saved natively as a .PNG file, with a resolution of 1024 × 768 on the iPad and iPad 2 and 2048 × 1536 on the latest iPad.

If you're curious as to why the screen capture function is important, just ask any author of a book about iPad secrets or any journalist at Engadget. In all seriousness, the two-button screen capture feature is a real godsend for those working in the media industry, but it's also equally beneficial for consumers. Troubleshooting remotely becomes a lot easier when you can capture on-screen errors in order to show others, and those who need to permanently capture something on-screen for offline viewing later will also be thrilled to have this in their back pocket.

In the effort of being thorough, I should also point out that holding down the top Power button for roughly four seconds brings up a Slide to Power Off option, which is useful when you know your iPad will go unused for a day or so (and you're looking to conserve battery). It's also not a bad idea to do this every week or so. Even the iPad can get caught up in its own mire sometimes, and giving it a fresh start every six or seven days helps to ensure that it doesn't become too bogged down. You probably wouldn't let your PC run a solid week without a single reboot, so why let your iPad carry on without the same?

Playing with the Volume Rocker and the Mute Switch

Sliding around the edge a bit, there's a subtle shortcut on the volume rocker. Although you can't crank things to 11 by holding the "up" portion for an extended period of time, you *can* mute things entirely by simply holding the "down" portion for just longer than a second. It might not seem entirely important in and of itself, but combine it with a tip on the diminutive button just above it, and you have a killer combo.

You see, the tiny toggle switch that sits just above the volume rocker is a dual-purpose switch, but there's a catch: Changing "purposes" requires a bit of monkeying around in the software. In fact, it's probably worth explaining a bit of the background here.

On the original iPad (and in an earlier version of iOS), this switch served a single purpose: It locked the orientation of the display. In other words, if you were holding the iPad horizontally, and you "locked" that switch, then even a gentle tilt vertically wouldn't flip your on-screen content. It was great for people on bumpy buses and subways, or those giving landscape presentations who couldn't afford any accidental rotations.

Eventually, though, Apple decided to switch things up on us—without any warning whatsoever. Starting with iOS 4.2, that switch turned into a mute button for the device. In order to revert the button to being an orientation lock switch, you have to change a setting in the iOS software. And that brings us up to current devices. I recommend changing the switch to being an orientation lock switch, and use a long press of the Down Volume button as a makeshift mute switch. Wondering how to do just that? I figured.

By default, the switch simply mutes or unmutes your iPad. To change it, simply go to Settings → General and look on the right pane for the Use Side Switch To field (see Figure 5-1). To revert the switch to use as a lock switch, make sure Lock Rotation has a check beside it. If, for whatever reason, you'd prefer to use the switch as a Mute switch, you need to dig even deeper to see the alternative way to lock orientation.

> NOTE In my experience, having the ability to lock the screen orientation with a simple hardware switch is far more useful than a secondary way to mute your iPad. Few things are as frustrating on this product than accidentally flipping your on-screen content vertically, then horizontally, without meaning to.

To find the more deeply hidden orientation lock option, you have to use *another* button-mashing shortcut. Pressing the Home button twice in quick succession brings up—for lack of better terminology—the multitasking menu. It's a secondary Dock bar that contains each and every app that is currently "running" in the background, even if the apps are idle. They are arranged from most recently used (left) to least recently used (right), but there's a hidden area here pertinent to this discussion. Have a gander yourself in Figure 5-2.

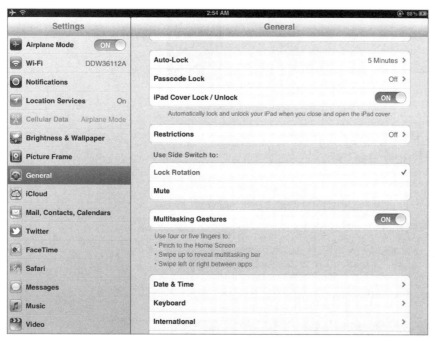

FIGURE 5-1: Take your pick. Either Lock Rotation or Mute will do. (But pick the top one!)

Swipe from left to right on that multitasking menu, and you find a new layout with a few vital buttons and sliders. What you're looking for is on the far left—the circular lock icon. (This assumes you have your side switch set to control mute/unmute; if it's assigned to lock orientation, you see a Volume icon, as shown in Figure 5-3.) Tap the lock icon once, and your orientation is locked. Tap it again, and it unlocks. (In case you're wondering, this icon reverts to being a mute/unmute software switch when your side switch is set to dictate screen orientation.)

I've made it extra clear that using your iPad as a camera is probably a horrendous idea (and a surefire way to embarrass yourself in public), but for those who aren't hearing any of that, here's a shortcut for you. When you're in the Camera app, you can press the Volume Up key to either capture a snapshot (if in Still mode) or begin and end a video (if in Record mode). It's a bit more natural than reaching all the way down to the lower portion of the iPad's display to mash the software equivalent. Of course, sharing this tip with others will out you as a tablet camera user, so consider yourself duly warned.

FIGURE 5-2: The Secondary Dock, sitting pretty beneath Engadget's Distro app.

FIGURE 5-3: Hidden menus! Hooray!

While the iPad's native lock screen still isn't as useful as some lock screens that are available to jailbroken devices, there is one highly appreciated extra tossed into iOS 5. If you double-tap the Home button while the screen's locked, you see a top bar that enables you to play or pause a track, move forward or back within the last accessed playlist, and even adjust the volume—all without ever sliding to unlock the device. (See Figure 5-4.)

FIGURE 5-4: Enjoy an album, right from the lock screen. Switchfoot is highly recommended, too.

Using the Secondary Menu Bar

Before moving to the keyboard, which is covered in the next section, take a moment to examine the other shortcuts located on the secondary menu bar. The left-most slider controls screen brightness, and the trio of buttons in the middle control music playback (skip backward, play/pause, skip forward). The right-most slider controls the volume level, and the right-most icon (Music) pops you directly into your music application. If you've used the Videos app more recently than Music, you see that shortcut in place of the Music icon. I've found that double-tapping the Home button and using that secondary bar to get into my Music app is far more convenient than exiting to the Home screen and then hunting for the icon. Furthermore, knowing that this shortcut is always available might encourage you to stash your Music app on a less important home pane, which saves more room for other apps on that all-important first pane.

MASTERING YOUR INNER KEYBOARDER

Not surprisingly, the iPad relies on touch for just about every single interaction. But there's one antediluvian aspect that's oft overlooked, though just as important: the keyboard. Although you can admittedly get quite a bit accomplished on the iPad sans any input on a QWERTY layout, its uses become significantly limited if you never use the keyboard. Apple has shown extra care of late when it comes to the device's on-screen virtual keyboard.

From day one, critics extolled Apple's slate for having a remarkable keyboard and input system, and despite having to type on a flat, hard screen, composing e-mails and the like on it is actually quite enjoyable. And quick, to boot. But one keyboard really doesn't fit all. I've known many people to jailbreak their iPhones *solely* for the opportunity to install a modified keyboard, but thankfully—with the advent of iOS 5—you don't need to void any warranties to find one of the best virtual keyboards on the market. Now, you just need to know how to best take advantage of it.

Splitting It Up

For starters, there are two different "styles" of keyboards in iOS 5, which I already mentioned in Chapter 3. As a brief refresher, Apple has introduced the notion of a "split" keyboard in its newest mobile OS refresh, which—predictably—cuts the virtual keyboard layout in half, compressing each side and leaving an ergonomic gap in the middle (see Figure 5-5). It makes thumb typing an absolute breeze while you're in vertical mode, and just makes keystrokes more natural and comfortable in horizontal mode. I'm an avid user of an *actual* split keyboard on my desktop, so if you're already acclimated you'll probably never revert back to the traditional full-screen keyboard layout.

Apple has (thankfully) made it exceptionally easy to switch back and forth between the normal and split keyboard right from the keyboard itself, so there's really no excuse to not have the split version active in case you want it. To make the switch, head to Settings → General → Keyboard → Split Keyboard and flip the slider to On (see Figure 5-6).

FIGURE 5-5: Look, ma! Split keys!

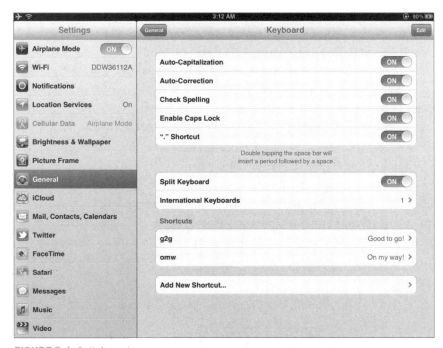

FIGURE 5-6: Split 'er up!

Now that you've turned on the split keyboard option, there are two ways to get your keyboard broken in two. When you're in an application where the keyboard is on the screen, tap and hold the icon in the bottom right until you see a pop-up choice to Split. The better, quicker and far more magical way to split the keyboard is to simply take two fingers, lay them on the keyboard and spread them apart—as if you're pinching to zoom on a photo. That's a tactic better known as a reverse pinch. Better yet, taking two fingers on a *split* keyboard and dragging them to the center reattaches the keyboard, making it whole again.

While we're on the topic of touching and keyboards, you should also know that you can move the keyboard up and down the screen as you see fit in both the split and non-split modes. However, doing so is tricky. You see, that bottom-right button (the same one that brings up a secondary menu if you long press it) is the button you need to tap to release the keyboard from its current position. Tap it too quickly, and your keyboard simply vanishes into the ether. Hold it too long, and you get that afore-mentioned pop-up menu. You need to tap and hold it for merely half a second, acting quickly to drag it north or south to your desired position. If you see the pop-up menu, you've held it too long. It might take you five or six tries to nail the execution, but don't be too down on yourself.

Kbrd Shrcts

▶ TextExpander (www.smilesoftware.com/TextExpander/) is a remarkable $35 program for Windows and Mac that lets you assign short abbreviations to frequently-used snippets of text.

Kids these days. Who has time to actually type out full sentences? All jesting aside, there's more to keyboard shortcuts within iOS 5 than LOL and JK, and Apple has intelligently pulled in functionality from things such as TextExpander in order to make the overall typing experience faster, without you having to revert to commonly known acronyms to do so.

There's no third-party app required here. Just surf over to Settings ➜ General ➜ Keyboard ➜ Shortcuts in order to get started. The idea here is pretty simple, as evidenced by Apple's one inclusion from the factory: omw. When you type omw on the iPad, it automatically expands to "On my way!" By pressing Add New Shortcut, you can add any number of similar shortcuts (see Figure 5-7). Perhaps g2g for "good to go," or iirc for "if I recall correctly." These shortcuts make it easier for legitimate typers to quickly type out *actual* words and phrases. On the other hand, quick messagers may actually *prefer* the shortened version out of respect for space. At least Apple's giving you the option.

While you're in the Settings pane, look at the five shortcut sliders that Apple has On by default. Auto-capitalization, auto-correction, check spelling, enable Caps Lock and "." These shortcuts are all useful to keep turned On in my estimation, but it's worth making special mention of two of 'em. Auto-correction can be a serious pain for those who use iMessage frequently. "Yo" is almost universally corrected to something other than "yo," and you need to get used to tapping the X in the bubble that pops up a suggested word if you'd prefer to skip it. The "." shortcut is actually one of the more useful shortcuts in the keyboard; just tap the space bar twice after you complete a standard sentence, and the iPad automatically adds a period, adds one space, and primes your next letter to be capitalized as you begin a new sentence. Handy!

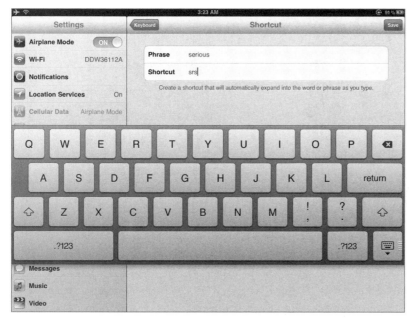

Apostrophes are important, but not when using a virtual iPad keyboard. If you simply type a normal contraction sans the apostrophe (for example, doesnt, cant, wont, dont, and so on), iOS 5 adds it automatically. Don't waste time doing it yourself.

FIGURE 5-7: The only limit to these shortcuts is your imagination.

Speaking specifically for the U.S. English keyboard—which is the only one my feeble brain can understand—there's a bit of extra value in trying out the oh-so-popular long press. Long pressing select keys brings up menus containing extra characters (see Figure 5-8), and if you tap the .?123 key in order to switch over to the numeric pad, the trick works on a few keys there, too. Finally, a double-tap of the Caps Lock key (it's the up arrow just below the A and Return keys) activates caps lock; another double-tap deactivates it. (A single tap capitalizes just the next letter.)

FIGURE 5-8: Pick an A. Any variation will do. . .

TIP In the same vein as TextExpander, Safari lets you create an app shortcut to just about anything. Many great websites already have iPad apps in the App Store, but not all of them. Although you can certainly create a bookmark within Safari for any site, you can also add some of your most-loved sites to a Home screen pane or in an app folder. Simply tap the menu icon to the left of the URL bar within Safari then select Add to Home Screen. Customize the title, click Add, and then adjust it to the position you want on the Home screen. Just like that, you have an app-sized web shortcut (see Figure 5-9).

▶ When you use the keyboard in Safari, there's a convenient .com key at the bottom. Long press that for a multitude of other domain name endings, such as .net, .org, and .edu.

Although the on-screen keyboard is certainly capable of handling its fair share of e-mails, if you're drop-dead serious about input into the iPad you might opt for a docking or Bluetooth keyboard. When using an external keyboard, the world of shortcuts opens up even further. Many shortcuts from OS X work on iPad as well.

FIGURE 5-9: Web shortcuts shaped like apps. What will they think of next?

Here's a list of surefire keyboard shortcuts that external typists should do their best to commit to memory:

- **CMD + C** (copy)
- **CMD + X** (cut)
- **CMD + V** (paste)
- **CMD + Z** (undo)
- **CMD + Shift + Z** (redo)
- **CMD + Delete** (deletes current line to the left of cursor)
- **CMD + Up** (top of document)
- **CMD + Down** (bottom of document)
- **CMD + Left** (start of line)
- **CMD + Right** (end of line)
- **Option + Delete** (nixes the word to the left of the cursor, and its preceding space)
- **F1** (dims the display)
- **F2** (brightens the display)
- **F7** (prior track)

- **F8** (plays or pauses music)

- **F9** (forward track)

- **F10** (mutes volume)

- **F11** (volume decrease)

- **F12** (volume increase)

- **Eject key** (displays or conceals on-screen keyboard)

► Speaking specifically for Pages, Apple's acclaimed iPad document processor, there's a laundry list of shortcuts to learn. Head to http://www.apple .com/support/pages/ shortcuts/ to learn more.

On the off chance that you're typing a word without actually knowing the defini-tion (or, perhaps more likely, you spot a curious word that your mate typed), you can simply long press the befuddling word in order to bring up a Define option. As a bonus, the pop-up definition box is just gorgeous (see just how gorgeous in Figure 5-10), proving once again that Apple overlooked few details.

FIGURE 5-10: Definitions never looked so beautiful.

MAKING THE MOST OF MAPS

As an avid traveler, having the world in my pocket has been one of the biggest boons to smartphone ownership. There's only one thing better than a smartphone with Google Maps onboard: an iPad with Google Maps onboard. Some might say a 3G/4G-equipped iPad is the best mobile navigation experience out there. The inbuilt Maps application can help you explore the big, bold world out there, but to best experience it, there are a few tips you should know.

For starters, you need to activate Location Services (see Figure 5-11), at least for Maps. Go to Settings ➜ Location Services and flip the top option to On. You *should* already have this active if you have Find My iPad active. If you've switched some apps off because you're uncomfortable with everything having access to your current coordinates, keep Location Services on for Maps. Without it, well. . .you won't do much navigating.

FIGURE 5-11: Location Services. Flip 'em on. . .with care, of course.

TIP Every so often, a new wave of fuss is made over location-based services on mobile devices. Mostly, there's fear that corporations could take advantage of knowing your location, using it for marketing or solicitation purposes without your consent. But if you're only using it for Maps, there's nothing to get worked up about. If you're tremendously paranoid about your location being shared, you can disable it altogether and not use one of the iPad's greatest features. But by the same token you should probably also put away every credit card you own, given that the powers that be can certainly trace your movements in other ways. Moral of the story? Location services aren't the devil—you just need to use them judiciously.

While you're on the Location Services pane, hop on down to System Services. The top six options, all of which should be On by default, are just fine to leave that way. I strongly recommend that you switch the Status Bar Icon option to On, too. Why? With the Status Bar Icon option active, you get a Location Services icon in the top menu bar (beside the battery life indicator) whenever an application is using your location. Think of it as a heads-up to when your coordinates are being shared. If you object to some unknown app using your location, you can quickly shut things down and uninstall the app, or you can adjust the preferences to disable location sharing on that particular piece of software. To date, there's no way to see *specifically* which app is triggering the location seek.

Now that your sharing preferences are squared away, it's time to focus on a few hidden features of Maps. You won't go far without getting your bearings, so tap that northeasterly arrow in the top bar. That's the shortcut for pinpointing your current location, and it's useful to tap it before you start seeking any guidance from Maps.

After you've searched for a locale you'd like to head to, tap the pin that drops on the destination to see directions that will get you there (see Figure 5-12). When the pop-up displays, you can *typically* get walking, driving, and public transportation directions to the destination.

▶ You need a Wi-Fi or 3G/4G connection to use Maps.

▶ You'll only see a public transportation option when you're in a city that has a public transit system.

FIGURE 5-12: Tap that pin and get going!

That's all pretty straightforward, but it may be easy to overlook that turned page corner in the lower right of the map. Pull that corner toward the center to uncover a few options—mostly visual tweaks—that you might be pleased with. Turning this page reveals four Map options (Standard, Satellite, Hybrid, and Terrain), and, if you're in a dense population center, the Traffic overlay gives you a real-time view to congestion on the roads surrounding you. Perhaps the most useful nugget is the Drop Pin function (see Figure 5-13), which enables you to place a visual marker on an area that you'd like to remember—such as your hotel in a foreign city—which can act as a central point of reference. I cover the Print function in a future chapter, but suffice it to say that those of you who are zany enough to actually think about printing a virtual map can do so (wirelessly, to boot) from this options pane.

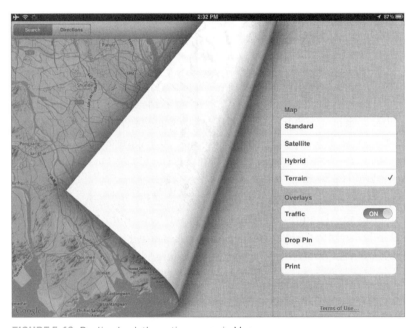

FIGURE 5-13: Peeling back the options pane in Maps.

MANAGING YOUR BACKGROUND APPS

Apple's iPad is chock full of surprises, including one that involves apps running in the background. The art of multitasking is truthfully still being mastered by iOS, but the devices are a lot closer to true multitasking today than they were a few generations prior. iOS doesn't allow you to have two separate apps open and on-screen at the same time—the closest you can come to that is the use of multiple tabs within Safari—but thanks to an expertly constructed backgrounding scenario, flipping back and forth among programs is just about effortless.

As with all computers, the iPad has its limits. There's only a specific amount of memory in the device, and although it'd take a hardcore power user to truly see a performance dip from using too many programs at once, those who fail to do a bit of housekeeping might unintentionally end up seeing some effect on performance.

> **NOTE**   Apple designed the iPad so that end users wouldn't have to actively think about what is or isn't running. By-and-large, you can just use the iPad at will without ever stopping to think how many programs you have open, and you never see a performance hit or a decrease in battery life. But why leave it to chance? Managing your background apps is categorically simple, and it's well worth the time investment.

The first step to managing background apps is figuring out what wheels are in motion. By initiating a four-finger gesture from south to north (within any app or on the Home screen), you get to the secondary dock pop-up at the bottom. It's a sight you should be familiar with by now, but here's something you might not already know. Each app in that tray is active, albeit idle, in the background. Each app is also claiming its own share of resources—however small—which may eventually affect performance and battery life if the build up becomes too great over time.

Seeing that the app you used longest ago is all the way at the end of line, I'd suggest swiping towards the right until you reach the app on the far right. Then long press on any infrequently used app that you aren't planning to use in the near term. A small minus sign displays in the corner of the app icon (see Figure 5-14); give that minus sign a tap, and the app closes, freeing up whatever resources were assigned to it.

FIGURE 5-14: Minus means gone!

MAKING YOUR IPAD A BACKGROUND DEVICE

Ever longed for a way to convert your iPad into a photo frame? In a way, it's the ultimate background application for a tablet in which you just can't let the screen go dim, and Apple's made it extra easy. Well, sort of easy. Actually, not entirely easy. But finding out how to do the not-so-easy things is why you're reading this book.

In order to flip the Picture Frame option on, go to Settings ➜ General ➜ Passcode Lock ➜ Picture Frame, and slide the toggle to On. No, I still haven't figured out why this is tucked in here instead of the Settings ➜ Picture Frame pane (shown in Figure 5-15), but I digress. When you've turned on that option, head into Picture Frame to customize a few options. Now, when you press the Power button or Home button and wake the iPad from sleep, you can tap the small Slideshow icon (the flower) to the right of the Slide to Unlock message in order to start a slideshow—without even having to unlock the device. Nifty!

FIGURE 5-15: Apple iPad: the world's most overpowered digital photo frame.

Predictably, the accessories market has caught on to people using the iPad as a frame. Wall and table mounts galore are available, the latter of which can double as a book stand when you're actually using your iPad. Read more about accessories in Chapter 15.

▶ Unlike Android devices, there's no built-in app manager to kill all programs. You have to do it manually if you don't reboot. An alternative way to get a fresh start is to simply hold down the Power button and reboot the iPad.

UNIVERSALLY SEARCHING WITH SPOTLIGHT

Without qualification, one of the most useful aspects to OS X is Spotlight. It's simple, well integrated, and eerily accurate. In short, Spotlight is a baked-in search apparatus that peeks into whatever folders and file systems you deem fit in order to find programs, documents, and even snippets of code hidden *within* documents. And while this functionality has been on the iPad in the past, in the iOS 5 version it is even better.

As described earlier, accessing Spotlight is as easy as swiping toward the left from the Home screen. From there, you can start typing, and the iPad begins to shoot out tailored results with each additional letter or character.

Here's a tip: Apple lets you customize (to some extent) what Spotlight indexes and searches. In order to see what's being included (or, perhaps more importantly, excluded), you need to go to Settings → Spotlight Search and have a gander at the options (see Figure 5-16).

▶ Unfortunately, you can't include web apps here, so avid users of the Gmail HTML5 app won't be able to use Spotlight to dig through archived messages.

FIGURE 5-16: Don't want your Contacts cluttering Spotlight results? Uncheck 'em!

> **TIP** I highly recommend that you use Spotlight to look for reminders or calendar events. No more sifting through days on end looking for that one birthday of that one colleague whose name you can't quite remember. Even if you know the first two letters (or just "birthday"), Spotlight should come through in the clutch.

While I'm on the topic of searching, I should also point out that Apple now gives you the ability to change which engine it uses for searches that you initiate in the top-right Search bar within the browser. Check out Settings ➜ Safari ➜ Search Engine and find a trifecta of choices: Google (default), Yahoo!, and Bing. My personal preference remains Google, but if you prefer either of the alternatives you can change it here. Have a peek in Figure 5-17.

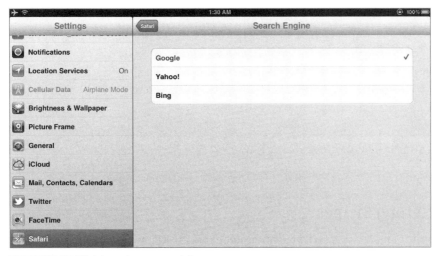

FIGURE 5-17: Which engine to search by. . .

GESTURES TO LIVE BY

Gestures have always been a crucial part of the iOS experience, but Apple has really gone overboard (in the best possible way, mind you) with the touch input experience in iOS 5. Everything from gesturing back to the Home panel to pinching in order to zoom within the Camera app is included. This section highlights the best of the best that Apple seems to have forgotten to tell you about. Oddly enough, the original iPad lacked support for Multitasking Gestures (even after the iPad 2 supported them at launch), but the iOS 5.0.1 update brought them over. There's no excuse to leave Multitasking Gestures (accessible through Settings ➜ General ➜ Multitasking Gestures) off. Hop in there and flip that switch to On, as shown in Figure 5-18.

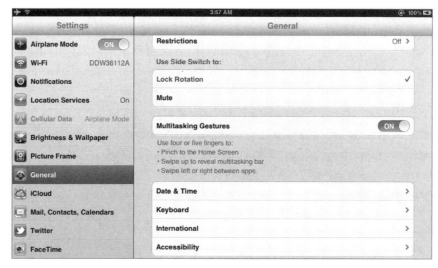

FIGURE 5-18: If Multitasking Gestures isn't On, you're doing it wrong.

Shutterbug Swipes

Within the Camera app itself, you might not expect too many extras with regard to touch. Turns out, that's absolutely not the case. For starters, you can pinch-to-zoom in order to get tighter or further away from a shot. Remember: You're dealing with *digital* zoom here, which introduces a plethora of noise in order to get closer to your subject. Optical zoom, which isn't available on the iPad, is the type of zoom that's preferred, as it doesn't inject pixilation into your resulting images after zooming.

A simple tap on the subject you're aiming to focus on makes the focus lock key in on whatever you've touched. After you've captured your masterpiece, you may think that the easiest way to access the Photo Roll is to tap that icon in the bottom corner. That's certainly one way to accomplish the task, but there's an easier way that relies on gestures. A three-finger swipe from left to right drags you to the photo you most recently took, and a tap along the top of the screen puts you just one more tap away from the entire roll.

Home Screen Dexterity

Apple created something special—if not outright addictive—with the advent of the Home button. It's been the constant throughout years upon years of iOS devices, and although I don't envision it vanishing anytime soon, the proliferation of gestures is making it all the more. . .well, useless.

How so? Users who are engrossed in any application can hop back to their first Home screen with one simple gesture. While in any app, grab the screen with your thumb and ring/middle/index fingers, and grasp toward the center. Think of it as pinching away the app you're in. Like magic (or just really, really well written code), your app vanishes and your Home screen appears.

When on the Home screen, a four-finger gesture from south to north pulls up the same secondary dock bar that used to require a double-tap of the Home button. That same four-finger swipe in the opposite direction conceals the bar.

If you're in an app—any app—the aforementioned four-finger swipe up and down also reveals the secondary dock bar, meaning that you don't even have to head back to the Home screen to see what's humming along in the background (or hop from one app into another).

Speaking of app hopping, there's an even *easier* way to do it. While you're in a program, just initiate a four-finger swipe in either the left or right direction; if you were successful, you are immediately taken to the app that you opened just prior to or after the one you're exiting. Keep the swipes coming in order to jump back and forth through a number of apps.

▶ If multi-finger gestures become second nature, and you're a Mac owner, have a look in your OS X settings for similar gesture support on your desktop or laptop.

Pinching and Zooming

Pinching and zooming are about as universal as it gets on the iPad. These simple techniques provide a smorgasbord of effects throughout iOS, and it's something that I recommend you learning, STAT.

In the Photos app, the simple act of taking two fingers on-screen and pulling them closer together allows you to zoom in on a shot; reversing the movement zooms out. In Safari, pinching in brings a full page in view, and reverse pinching enables you to focus on a specific area of images or text.

In Maps, as mentioned earlier, pinching and zooming helps you to get a broader or tighter view on the area that immediately concerns you. This technique is popularized in a litany of third-party apps, making it nigh impossible to list out what you can accomplish in every scenario. One thing's for sure, though: Pinching almost certainly does something in every app, so be sure to give it a go before fussing with a less intuitive way to navigate.

SUMMARY

I'll never discourage you from discovering the iPad in a way that suits you. Part of the magic of the iPad is the ability for this slate to become whatever it is you truly want it to be. However, most of us are in a hurry, and this chapter is designed to give you a look at shortcuts and navigation tips that make your time with the iPad both productive and efficient.

Shortcuts are as important as ever with iOS 5. From keyboard shortcuts to gesture-based navigational tricks, there's an easier way to get around your iPad. Long pressing buttons and apps both frequently enable users to get where they're going with fewer steps, and searching for content, apps, and text clippings via Spotlight is bound to keep your wild goose chases to a minimum.

Finally, it's important to fully realize the power of gestures. Don't stop with just single-finger swipes to the side. Multi-finger gestures are more powerful and prevalent than ever within iOS 5, and more often than not, their uses aren't entirely obvious. Simply initiating these swipes (along with the pinch-to-zoom technique) could help you to fall in love with any given program all over again.

CHAPTER 6

Making the Most of FaceTime. . .and Those Other Video Calling Solutions

IN THIS CHAPTER

▶ Getting comfortable with FaceTime

▶ Friending and finding

▶ Understanding connection requirements

▶ Integrating Skype

▶ Tying Google Voice into the equation

▶ Avoiding traditional communication charges

The iPad's rear-facing camera isn't anything to write home about, and taking pictures on a tablet—as a rule—isn't advised. (That said, the new iPad's 5 megapixel iSight camera is a respectable upgrade, and shines primarily when capturing 1080p video.) In my estimation, optical sensors and slates are being married for one simple, albeit powerful, reason: video calling. Chatting over webcam has been possible for years. The concept itself isn't hard to *grok*, but the primary issue that kept it from truly hitting critical mass was the difficulty in finding and organizing contacts.

The conventional phone number, for all of its faults, still excels in being easy to distribute, catalog, and reference. A username, however, is vastly more flexible. Internet-based chatting applications such as FaceTime, Skype, and Google Voice are infinitely more approachable, and any device with access to the World Wide Web can join in. In this chapter, I discuss the ins and outs of using the iPad as a video communication tool, and I point out the intricacies of getting (and staying) connected inexpensively via video while traversing the globe. Or just different rooms in your apartment.

MAKING FACETIME YOUR GO-TO VIDEO-CALLING APP

In a way, Apple took video calling to a mainstream audience in a way that no prior company could. Skype was well on its way, and its recent acquisition by Microsoft will no doubt hasten that, but FaceTime is what truly got people talking. Perhaps strangely, FaceTime was actually launched on the iPhone line, as the original iPad didn't even have a built-in camera. So, if you're reading this book with an original iPad in hand, you'll unfortunately find that most of this section isn't applicable to you. The inclusion of a front-facing camera in the iPad 2 (as well as the latest iPad) made it obvious that Apple was now serious about video chatting with tablets, and iOS 5 has made the feature even richer than it was before.

▶ Owners of Mac desktops can dive in to FaceTime as well thanks to Apple's 27-inch Thunderbolt Display with FaceTime HD camera ($999). You need a Mac with DisplayPort in order to use it.

To start, it's helpful to know what products can use FaceTime. So long as the FaceTime protocol is supported on a platform, a webcam is available, and a connection to the web is available, two users can link up for video calling. Right now, any iPhone with a front-facing camera, the iPad 2, the new iPad, the iPod touch (again, with a front-facing camera) and any modern-day Mac can enjoy the spoils of FaceTime. Smartly, Apple has made FaceTime a platform in which a phone number isn't required for the call to work. Although you can still request a FaceTime call with an iPhone user by pinging the number, the majority of devices are pinged by e-mail address. This is particularly handy if you own multiple FaceTime-equipped products; regardless of the device, people can initiate FaceTime calls with you using your same e-mail address.

How to Find Friends with FaceTime

One of the biggest strengths of FaceTime is that no accounts, in the most literal sense of the word, are required. You simply provide the e-mail address that's associated with your iCloud and iTunes accounts, and boom—it's connected. People search for you on FaceTime with just your e-mail address, so I'd highly recommend using an e-mail address that the bulk of your friends, peers, and colleagues are already familiar with. The setup pane is shown in Figure 6-1.

You may be wondering, "How on Earth do I know if any of my friends have FaceTime, and if they're connected over Wi-Fi?" The unfortunate truth is that making and receiving a FaceTime call is far more difficult than simply ringing a phone number, mostly because FaceTime calls require users to be on a Wi-Fi connection. To that end, some level of planning is typically required to have a FaceTime chat.

TIP FaceTime defaults to using the e-mail address tied to your iTunes and iCloud accounts, but you can easily add another e-mail in Settings → FaceTime → Add Another Email. Be aware, however, that you can only add addresses that have never been used with Apple's ecosystem before. Also, you need access to the addresses you add, as you have to verify each one before FaceTime enables that address to be linked to your profile. When that's done, however, folks can connect with you via FaceTime with more than just one e-mail address. It's a great trick for those who have certain sects of acquaintances familiar with various e-mail addresses.

FIGURE 6-1: Fill in your array of alternate personalities here.

NOTE The most magical aspect of video chatting is the cost savings. By replacing conventional landline and cellular networks with the Internet, consumers are able to significantly cut costs that are oftentimes associated with long distance or global calling. Part of the Internet's magic is being able to send bytes across fibers that end up looking like someone's face on the other end; the other tidbit is just how cheap it is to access this compared to options of just a score ago. That notion alone is causing a generation of landline droppers to also drop phone numbers that are directly linked to legacy carriers, a point which I explain in detail a bit later.

Thankfully, Apple *does* make it relatively easy to see if a contact is capable of receiving a FaceTime call. When scrolling through your contacts list within iOS, there's a FaceTime button (see Figure 6-2) beside Send Message, Share Contact, and Add to Favorites. It's a bit misleading, though, as every last contact has this button, even if a person owns an Android device, has no e-mail address, and won't even think of telling you her phone number. If you attempt to FaceTime with someone who meets one of these criteria, you receive a Failed message, as seen in Figure 6-2.

FIGURE 6-2: Give it a push. At worst, the person will reject your call.

> **NOTE** Interestingly, FaceTime is a protocol that could be adopted elsewhere. To date, no other companies have created applications based on the platform that Apple has built, leading to a serious amount of fragmentation. For example, you can't FaceTime someone simply by finding them in your Skype contact list. Too bad there's no easy way to merge all of the most popular video-calling apps into one!

If you're looking to start a chat within the Contacts list in the FaceTime app itself, you may end up a bit disoriented. There's no FaceTime logo as there is in Contacts. Instead, you need to tap on a mobile number (if the person is an iPhone user) or the e-mail address to attempt a conversation. Of note, you need to know ahead of time what e-mail address the person used to sign up for FaceTime. For example, if you have a colleague with a work e-mail address as well as a personal address in your Contacts list, you have no way of knowing which he used to register. This is where trial and error comes in (see Figure 6-3 for the "error" end of it). Try one, and if no one picks up, try the other. Of course, that's not anywhere near efficient, and I'm all about efficiency.

FIGURE 6-3: Ah, well. It was worth a shot.

NOTE   To date, Apple hasn't allowed any third-party applications into the App Store that solves the dilemma of not knowing when your friends are available to video chat. I'm keeping a close eye on Faceplant, though. This app is slated to give you a heads-up when your friends are available to video chat, and it even enables you to leave a video voicemail if they're offline when you try to contact them.

How to Make FaceTime Calls over a Cellular Connection

With the introduction of iOS 5, Apple also enabled FaceTime over 3G/4G for the first time. It's a feature that was already enabled on apps such as Skype and Fring, but until the newest build of iOS, FaceTime *required* Wi-Fi on both ends of the conversation. Here's the trouble, though: It's up to individual carriers to support it. Not surprisingly, no U.S. carrier currently supports FaceTime over 3G/4G. The reasoning is that the networks simply can't handle the excess load of a zillion high-bandwidth FaceTime calls going on, but some carriers—such as Rogers in Canada—have enabled it. My guess is that the major American carriers will never open this option up, but there *are* a couple of workarounds for those who simply cannot locate a solid Wi-Fi connection. It's also worth pointing out that iPad Wi-Fi users won't run into this issue—after all, they have no cellular module to enable—but those with Wi-Fi + 3G/4G models may wonder what they're missing out on.

The first option is only applicable to those who have jailbroken their device. I can't openly recommend that you void your warranty in order to enable something that carriers are obviously discouraging. Furthermore, video calling on the iPad eats up around 3MB of data *per minute*, so unless you have an unlimited data plan grandfathered in from yesteryear, you won't want to dip your toes into this pool, anyway. To add some perspective, a FaceTime call over 3G/4G would blow through AT&T's entry-level 250MB plan in 83 minutes. That's right—video chatting with your mum on Mother's Day for fewer than 1.5 hours would obliterate your data pool *for the month*. Yikes.

▶ Outside of data usage, FaceTime is completely free. No matter what FaceTime member you call, in what country, across what ocean, it's always free.

> **TIP** If you're familiar with Cydia—a repository for apps in the world of jailbroken devices—you need to search for My3G. That's your ticket to enabling FaceTime to work over a 3G connection, but don't expect it to work *well*. Even a solid 3G (or 4G) connection can't compete with most at-home Wi-Fi connections, so you can anticipate at least a sporadic cellular connection!

The other workaround doesn't require any tomfoolery—well, not any of the warranty-voiding kind, that is. As I mentioned earlier, opting for a Wi-Fi iPad and a separate 3G/4G mobile hotspot seems like a far more sensible and flexible solution to getting your tablet (and other Wi-Fi devices) online from just about anywhere. If you need more convincing, think about this: If you fire up a mobile hotspot (which should get you online via 3G or 4G networks, depending on what model, carrier, and plan you select), you can connect your Wi-Fi iPad to it.

Through a crazy combination of wireless tubes, you have your Wi-Fi iPad connected to the Internet via a cellular data connection—the very kind of connection that U.S. carriers don't want you to use FaceTime on. But, because your iPad sees that you are connected over Wi-Fi, it allows FaceTime to function normally. So, you can make and receive FaceTime calls just fine, though the quality depends on the strength of your mobile hotspot's connection (see Figure 6-4 for a typical shot of the video quality). And, of course, you'll be demolishing around 3MB of data per minute, so you need to be mindful of that. Most mobile hotspots these days let you use up to 5GB of data per month, so you'd have to video chat for many, many hours to use it all. But if you're already cutting it close for the month, initiating a heart-to-heart with your best bud over FaceTime probably isn't advisable.

FaceTime with Todd Davis...   End

FIGURE 6-4: What's this "FaceTime" thing all about, anyway?

> **NOTE** If you're planning to use the mobile hotspot trick to FaceTime over a cellular data network with any level of frequency, I'd strongly recommend selecting one of Verizon Wireless' LTE hotspots. Its 4G LTE network is the fastest and most widespread 4G network in the U.S., and it's expanding at a breakneck pace. There's plenty of bandwidth there to handle clear FaceTime calls, but remember—the faster your Internet works, the easier it is to blow through a 5GB monthly allotment.

Video Calling from 35,000 Feet

There's this crazy invention from the future, and it just so happens to be available today. It's called Gogo, and for all intents and purposes, it's Wi-Fi in the sky. Gogo has been around for a few years now, but they're still expanding to various new markets and airlines. In a nutshell, a Gogo-equipped plane enables you to connect to the Internet while sitting in an airplane at more than 10,000 feet. In the U.S., Delta, Virgin America, and JetBlue are your best bets for finding a Wi-Fi flight.

Frequent fliers would be well advised to spring for a monthly pass, but even those who only find themselves on an aircraft every so often can buy a single-flight pass for less than $13. You can identify Gogo on your flight by connecting to the gogoinflight network when you're higher than 10,000 feet. If you pass the point of "It's okay to use electronics" and you don't see this network, you're on a disconnected flight. To better your chances, take longer flights on non-regional jets, and be sure to consult the website of your airline ahead of time to see if your flight is listed on the Wi-Fi list. A more universal solution is found at http://haswifi.com, an online repository that crowdsources data for informing passengers about which flights do (and do not) have Gogo onboard.

Why spend so much time poring over in-flight Wi-Fi? Because it relates directly to FaceTime. If you manage to get on board an aircraft with Gogo, you can connect your iPad to the network so you can make and receive FaceTime calls. It's important to realize that Gogo is little more than a highly extended cellular network, so you shouldn't expect stellar performance. That said, I've seen it work in a number of instances, and it's certainly a fantastic way to pass the time and touch base with your loved ones. Just remember to use headphones with an inline microphone; your fellow passengers probably aren't interested in overhearing your conversation.

> **WARNING** Gogo has already blocked select VoIP ports on their service, locking Skype users out. I suspect it's only a matter of time before they do the same for Fring, FaceTime, and a slew of other Internet calling applications. It's probably less of a bandwidth thing, and more of a passenger distraction thing.

Showing Off Your Surroundings

Although the front-facing camera is obviously there to enable video chatting, the iPad also touts a rear-facing camera. You might as well take advantage of it! While you're in a FaceTime chat, simply tap the Camera Rotate icon (positioned beside the End key) in order to flip your camera to the rear-facing one. On the other end, your recipient sees whatever is facing the rear camera. This is an excellent trick for showing off the kids playing without having to physically turn the iPad around, and in the same vein, the person you're chatting with can tap the Camera Rotate button (see

Figure 6-5) on his end to give you a different perspective. In case you're wondering, the audio remains the same regardless of which camera angle you're using.

FIGURE 6-5: The caller's rear camera is active in the lower-right.

When you use FaceTime, be cautious of the lighting behind you. If you're in a sunny park, for instance, and the sun is unleashing its wrath on your neck, there's a better-than-average chance that the person you're chatting with will see nothing but a silhouette of your mug. It's a good idea to minimize the light flooding in behind you, particularly if you sit next to large windows. Those windows may make you the envy of the working world (congratulations!), but you have to reposition yourself before initiating a FaceTime call.

▶ You can relocate that mini window that shows off your own face (what the person on the other end sees) by tapping it, holding it, and dragging it to another corner.

NOTE iOS 5 is tailor-made for multitasking, and this applies to FaceTime, too. If you need to hop into another app while on a FaceTime call, simply tap the Home button to be taken to your Home screen. On the other end, your recipient sees a frozen image of you, but your audio still works. You can continue yapping while fiddling in another app, and when you return to the FaceTime call, the video feed picks up again.

Troubleshooting FaceTime

FaceTime was engineered to be simplistic, but it's worth covering a few troubleshooting angles in the event that you hit any snags during use.

- ▶ FaceTime doesn't like firewalls. Hotels are full of them. If you're trying to video chat with your family back home, you need port forwarding enabled on ports 53, 80, 443, 4080, 5223, and 16393-16472 (UDP). Rather than using hotel Wi-Fi, try using a mobile hotspot or heading to a nearby café.

- ▶ If you need to tweak the ports on your own router, open a browser page and cruise to 192.168.1.1 (or consult your router's tech support line).

- ▶ Apple's Smart Cover is great, but it'll block your rear-facing camera if flipped over. Try removing the cover if you're getting a black image when rotating your camera angle. (Read more about accessories in Chapter 15.)

- ▶ If you can't make any FaceTime calls at all, be sure you've enabled it through Settings → FaceTime.

- ▶ Remember to position your face just north of where you probably think it should be; otherwise, the person on the other end gets an eyeful of your nostrils.

- ▶ If you're having a conversation within iMessage, and the person hops on Wi-Fi, you can tap the Person icon in the top-right and select FaceTime to initiate a video chat from there.

EFFECTIVE USE OF SKYPE

It took Skype well more than a year to finally dole out a proper iPad app, despite being previously available for the iPhone. Now that the Skype iPad app is here, it's hard to ignore. Skype's main advantage is the traction behind it. By landing at the right time, offering the right features, and enabling people across the world to call and chat with each other for free, Skype has amassed millions upon millions of users. Chances are, if you know someone with a smartphone, they also have a Skype account.

The other *major* advantage to using Skype on the iPad (see Figure 6-6) is cross-compatibility. Skype is available on every major platform—both desktop and mobile—giving you a far larger pool of potential chatters. Because Skype supports Windows, Mac, Android, BlackBerry, iOS, and a myriad of other operating systems, you stand a far greater chance of finding all your friends on Skype than on FaceTime. As it stands, you need an OS X or iOS-enabled device to use FaceTime, so unless you hang with an Apple-only crowd, there's a good chance that some of your buds will feel alienated.

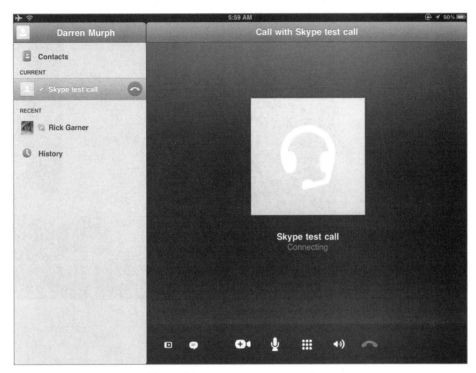

FIGURE 6-6: Skype's test call is a great way to ensure your settings are correct.

The good news is that you can have FaceTime and Skype running concurrently on the iPad, ready and able to accept calls from either platform at a moment's notice. Furthering the good news, Skype for iPad supports video chatting, and although it's not using the FaceTime protocol, it still works just fine with the built-in cameras (see Figure 6-7).

NOTE Skype for iPad is a free download in the App Store, and it accepts the same login credentials that you've probably already been using with a different form of Skype. If you're new to Skype, installing it on the iPad enables you to register with a new account and find friends via username or e-mail address.

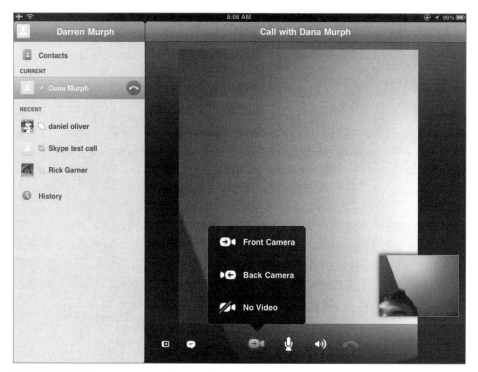

FIGURE 6-7: Pick a camera. . .any camera!

Replacing Your Landline with Skype

While you can't actually use the iPad as a gigantic cellphone (though, just the thought of it is enough to conjure up a chuckle), you *can* use the iPad to call conventional telephone numbers. Unlike FaceTime, which is a highly specialized application, Skype is a multifaceted communications tool. Just tap the dial pad icon in the top-right corner of the app, and a conventional dial pad appears (see Figure 6-8). You need to purchase Skype Credits (which you can do in your Skype account) in order to dial out to phone numbers across the globe, but if you're looking for a great reason to drop your landline, this just might be it.

Calling actual phone numbers from within Skype ranges from a few cents per minute on a pay-as-you-go plan, to $4.49 per month in an all-you-can-call plan that services the U.S. and Canada. You can find Skype's full list of calling plans at www.skype.com/intl/ en-us/prices/, and no matter how you slice it, it's a far saner deal than a traditional landline. Pair up a Bluetooth headset with an iPad and a Skype subscription, and you'll wonder why you didn't cut that cord long ago.

Skype for iPad beautifully melds with both conventional calling and VoIP/ video, so you can always hop from a familiar dial pad to a list of Skype usernames with no fuss to speak of. I always recommend dialing a Skype username (for voice or video) first. Skype-to-Skype calls are free within the app itself, but if you dial a phone number, it costs you. You can check your **Skype Credit** balance from within the app (see Figure 6-9).

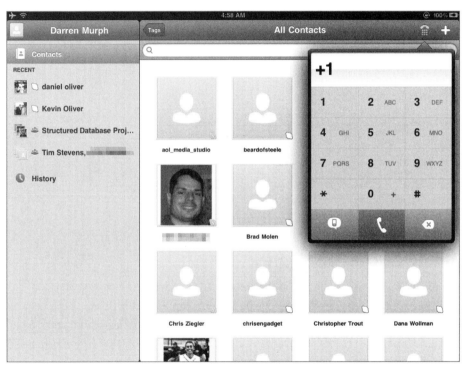

> Although Skype-to-Skype video (and voice) calls are gratis, it eats up around 3MB of data per minute. If you're using a rental SIM overseas, or you have a tiered data plan at home, make sure you factor this in!

> International travelers can't always initiate free Skype-to-Skype calls, but using Skype to dial back to wherever home may be is always cheaper than roaming on a foreign cellular network.

FIGURE 6-8: A telephone. . .on your iPad? It's true!

There are a couple of other advantages of Skype over a traditional landline. For one, you can view Skype calling logs and conversation histories from any Skype device, which cannot be said for a traditional landline. And because your iPad can go with you, so too can your phone number. I'm a firm believer that the phone number as we know it is a thing of the past, and it's only a matter of time before people begin porting those numbers to Internet-based hosting services such as Skype.

FIGURE 6-9: Skype Credit allows you to dial conventional phone numbers from within the app.

Receiving Calls on Skype

Of course, dialing out is only half of the equation. If you still want people to be able to ring you via Skype, you need a Skype Online Number. Basically, this is a brand new phone number—one that looks like any other number on the outside—but instead of ringing a landline, it rings whatever device you have Skype enabled on. By visiting Skype's website, you can apply for an Online Number. What's perhaps even more amazing is that U.S. users can procure a number from a country *outside* of America. That's right—you can claim ownership of a Hong Kong phone number without actually owning property there. Welcome to the future.

If you're a business owner that deals with foreign nations, stocking up on various "local" phone numbers in these countries could save you a bundle on roaming rates, and it certainly makes it easier for your clients (and perhaps more importantly, potential clients) to phone you.

> **WARNING** Although a Skype Online Number makes total sense for a lot of things, it cannot be used for emergency calling.

Exploring Skype

Skype for iPad is full of subtle additions that enrich the overall experience. I've included a list of my favorites here:

- ► You can send an instant message while a video call is ongoing, which is particularly useful for pinging just one person while a group call is being held.

- ► Skype can automatically forward your calls to a number that you dictate; just click into your profile and flip the Call Forwarding switch to On. (Requires Skype Credits.)

- ► Skype is capable of sending conventional text messages (SMS) via the dial pad. (Requires Skype Credits.)

- ► If you set up a secondary Skype account on your iPad and set it to auto-answer, you can mount it on a wall with the camera facing into your living room; dial that account from your mobile, and you now have a homegrown home security camera.

- ► QuickVoice (free), Audio Memos 2 ($0.99), and ScreenChomp (free)—all available in the App Store—can record calls and notes for future playback.

VIDEO-CALLING APPS YOU'VE NEVER HEARD OF (BUT SHOULD)

FaceTime and Skype for iPad are probably enough for most folks, but for hardcore iPad communicators, there are plenty more options out there. In fact, some of those options fill tiny holes that are glossed over by the two power players.

- ► Google's still working on an iPad version of Google Voice (free), but the iPod version works just fine for now, even on the iPad. Much like the Skype Online Number, getting a Google Voice number is infinitely powerful. It not only enables you to dial out and receive calls to a conventional-looking number (but through an Internet-based calling program), but it also enables you to receive e-mailed transcripts of voicemails.

- ► Fring (free) supports group video chatting with up to four participants, and unlike FaceTime, this app allows video calling over 3G or 4G regardless of carrier. It's also cross-platform, so you can use your iPad to video chat with pals using Android or Nokia devices.

▶ ooVoo (free) is a sassily designed messaging app that supports six-way group video chats. It also enables you to converse via audio and IM.

▶ WhatsApp Messenger ($0.99) doesn't support video calling, but it does support group chatting, multimedia messaging and a whole heap of platforms (Android, BlackBerry, Nokia, and so on).

▶ Tango (free) supports video calls over 3G/4G and Wi-Fi regardless of carrier, and it's one of the only cross-platform alternatives that has a future with Windows Phone 7.

▶ Nimbuzz (free) supports video calling. Additionally, it allows users to have a host of other communication protocols open. It also supports push notifications.

SUMMARY

FaceTime is easily one of the most substantial Apple product rollouts in recent memory. In effect, it allowed video chatting to turn from a niche to a mainstream event. But as a fledgling product, it's still only loosely tied into the fabric of iOS, and it's not nearly as seamless to use as iMessage or Music. With a bit of time to find and add your friends, however, you can slowly begin the process of ditching voice minutes and SMS for something far more personal.

FaceTime isn't the only option for communicating on the iPad, though. Tying Google Voice and Skype into the equation makes a lot of sense, and it gives you even more (free) ways to stay connected to your networks of peers—regardless of which platform they use. Of course, having a nearby Wi-Fi network is essential to staying connected, but if you've got a 3G/4G mobile hotspot nearby, you can use that loophole to complete chats.

If you fall head over heels for video calling, you've got plenty of alternatives to turn to, and if you rely on a Google Voice number, making and receiving calls on your iPad is as easy as doing likewise on your phone.

CHAPTER 7

AirPlay: Streaming Secrets of the Multimedia Variety

IN THIS CHAPTER

- ▶ Mastering the audio stream
- ▶ Playing nice with your Mac and PC
- ▶ Selecting your next (wireless) speaker system
- ▶ Adding video streams to the mix
- ▶ Tapping the power of Apple TV
- ▶ Mirroring secrets to make your HDTV smile

With the introduction of iCloud, Apple took a stand. A stand against wires. Cords have always been the necessary evil that has plagued consumer electronics, and although we've managed to consolidate them somewhat over the years (the multifaceted Dock Connector is proof of that), one cable is still one too many in my mind. I'm still waiting on wireless power to be a reality across the board, but until then, I have to be content with technologies such as iCloud and AirPlay.

The latter of the two is the focus of this chapter, in which I dive into the underpinnings of one of Apple's slickest tether-free implementations yet. AirPlay is an overarching term that describes a wireless protocol that's capable of distributing audiovisual content with no cables to speak of, and the real magic of it is the simplicity in setup. Still, a hassle-free setup doesn't mean that there aren't nooks and crannies to explore. If you're buying an iPad and aren't taking the time to explore its wireless streaming possibilities, you're selling your purchase short. Let's dive in and make sure you nip that in the bud.

WHAT IS AIRPLAY?

AirPlay is a relatively new term, even for Apple loyalists. The term was introduced at a September 2010 iPod launch event, but rather than being entirely new, it actually took the place of a term that had existed since 2004: AirTunes. Over the years, Apple realized that people were interested in streaming more than just audio. With video in the mix, converting AirTunes to AirPlay made more sense than using two separate protocols.

Even today, AirPlay is in its infancy. The true potential lies in the hands of Apple's blossoming developer army—an army that has already developed more than 100,000 iPad-specific apps. Optimists might say that Apple's headfirst approach into wireless video streaming is only being tested on the iPad and iPhone, with the real killer app to be the forthcoming Apple-branded HDTV. At this point, those are still rumors, but the smoke that leads to fire is certainly becoming tougher to ignore.

THE IN(PUT)S AND OUT(PUT)S OF AUDIO STREAMING

For years, most average consumers have assumed that setting up a wireless home audio system requires a professional installation, gobs of money, and tons of research. And in a lot of cases, those assumptions are both warranted and accurate. Whole home audio systems have traditionally required a high-end receiver, plenty of in-wall cabling, mounting brackets galore, and a networked remote to control it all. Those remotes alone could easily cost more than $500. These days, things are a bit simpler, particularly for owners of the iPad 2 and the latest model.

Beginning with iOS 4.2, Apple enabled the movement of video from the iPad onto other devices without the use of a cable. At first, only select applications could stream video, and a heap of limitations kept the functionality in check. But there's a lot more to talk about now that iOS 5 is out. AirPlay Mirroring has been unveiled.

All that said, audio is still at the core of AirPlay, and although the "Tunes" moniker has since been dropped, it's still very much a part of the overall experience. To better understand the intricacies of AirPlay, it's important to understand how AirPlay-compatible products are divided. AirPlay sender devices include the iPad, other iOS products, and computers running iTunes. All of these are capable of broadcasting audio or video wirelessly, for something else entirely to catch and comprehend. Those "catching" devices are called AirPlay receivers. As of now, there aren't too many receivers to keep track of. The AirPort Express—which I recommended earlier in the book as a fantastic iPad companion from a networking standpoint—is the primary

▶ AirPlay Mirroring is currently only available for the iPhone 4S, the iPad 2 and the newest iPad. Owners of older iPhone handsets, the iPod touch, and the original iPad aren't able to enjoy the spoils without a jailbreak.

AirPlay receiver from an aural perspective. Outside of that device, there's the Apple TV and a small but growing stable of AirPlay-compatible A/V receivers and speakers.

Configuring AirPlay on Your iPad

Unfortunately, select portions (mostly video streaming) of AirPlay's functionality are only available on the iPad 2 and the new iPad. However, the original iPad is more than capable of handling the audio streaming so long as you have installed iOS 5 on it. AirPlay setup may be a breeze compared to similar solutions, but there are still a few things you'll need to know ahead of time. Indeed, you cannot set it up at all without external equipment already in-hand. If you pore over the Settings menu within iOS 5, you won't see a single hint of AirPlay (see Figure 7-1). Evidently, that's intentional.

FIGURE 7-1: If you're seeing this on your iPad, you've done something right. Congrats!

> **TIP** One little-known fact about AirPlay? Any previously paired Bluetooth speakers (such as the fantastic Jambox from Jawbone) *also* show up in the list of AirPlay-enabled devices, enabling you to start streaming music even to Bluetooth devices from the same menu, using the same controls. Handy!

Considering that at least some external equipment is necessary to receive any wireless streams emitting from the iPad, Apple has hidden AirPlay's settings from view until your device *detects* one of those outside products. To find AirPlay, you need to ensure that your iPad and your AirPlay accessory are connected on the same Wi-Fi network. If they are, the "discovery" process happens automatically on the iPad, though you might have to reboot it if it doesn't recognize the device(s) right away. To find out, simply double-tap the Home button (or initiate a four-finger swipe from south-to-north) to bring up the secondary Dock bar at the bottom. Swipe from left-to-right to bring up the control bar, and look for a rectangular icon with an arrow on the bottom. That's AirPlay, which is shown in Figure 7-2.

FIGURE 7-2: "Hi. I'm AirPlay. Let's stream something."

▶ Unfortunately, there's no "alternate" place to find the AirPlay icon. Digging to find it is a bit of an ordeal, but using the new multi-finger gestures supported in iOS 5 is the simplest way to get there.

Tap the icon, and your discovered devices should be shown. You select whichever one you want to stream to, give it a moment to pair, and you're configured. If only washing dishes, mowing the lawn, and filing taxes were this easy. . .

TIP While you're in the setup mood, it's worth your while to download Apple's Remote app from the App Store. It's a free program that enables you to use your iPad to control your Mac's iTunes library wirelessly. It also gives you total control of AirPlay-connected devices (with a highly intuitive user interface), and you can search for things by typing on a pop-up QWERTY keyboard right on the display. It quite literally turns your iPad into an oversized touch panel remote. For free.

Another Reason to Consider AirPort Express

As if you didn't have reason enough to spring for Apple's $99 AirPort Express (remember how useful it is in spreading a single hotel Ethernet connection to all of your Wi-Fi travel companions?), it also acts as the cheapest, most seamless way to send a signal to an audio system you already own from the iPad. And yes, that includes wired audio systems. The AirPort Express has a 3.5mm minijack that supports both analog and optical audio cables (see Figure 7-3). Connect the minijack to an existing A/V receiver or speaker input, and it'll be the last cable you'll need to run. From there, your iPad can send audio from the Music app directly to the AirPort Express with no wire in between, enabling you to dictate the tracks and volume remotely to whatever speaker system is attached to the AirPort Express.

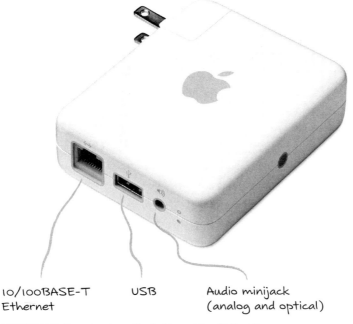

10/100BASE-T
Ethernet

USB

Audio minijack
(analog and optical)

FIGURE 7-3: Three ports on the bottom of the AirPort Express. So little, doing so much.

The AirPort Express is easily one of Apple's most awkwardly named and universally understated products. But then again, I'm not really sure there even exists a succinct way to name a product that does so much. Sure, it's a mobile broadband router that can be plugged into any home outlet. But the audio jack on the bottom is extremely powerful in conjunction with AirPlay. You can connect your AirPort Express to your home stereo or powered speakers using a digital fiber optic cable, analog mini-stereo-to-dual-RCA cable, or mini-stereo to mini-stereo cable (depending on what type of connectors your stereo uses) connected to the Line Out port. Better still, you can stream iTunes music to more than one AirPort Express at a time by choosing Multiple Speakers from the Speakers pop-up menu. In other words, you can place an AirPort Express in every room where you have a receiver or speaker setup, and then broadcast music to each of those rooms from a *single* iPad. House parties just became entirely more feasible.

> **WARNING** Although there's definitely a USB port on the bottom of the AirPort Express, it's not meant for speakers! USB speakers aren't compatible with this device. That USB port is meant only for printers that you'd like to make wireless; plug a USB printer in here, and it shows up on any Mac or iPad that's connected to the same Wi-Fi network.

Configuring Your AirPort Express

Setting the AirPort Express up is as simple as tapping into the AirPort Utility on your Mac or the like-named app on your iPad (it's available as a free download from the App Store). But there are many possible configurations, which are worth going over in detail here.

▶ You can use an AirPort Express exclusively as a wireless streaming liaison, without ever tapping into its other powers in the networking space. Simply connect your speakers to the 3.5mm jack, plug the device into a nearby AC outlet and select it as an AirPlay-compatible streaming device within iTunes or on the iPad's AirPlay menu.

▶ If an AirPort Express is your primary wireless router, you need to ensure that your speaker system and Internet modem are near enough to both reach the device. Then in AirPort Utility ensure that Enable AirPlay/AirTunes is checked in the Music tab when you create a new wireless network.

▶ If your AirPort Express is acting as both a music-streaming device and an extension of a network that's connected via Ethernet, you need to again ensure that both your speaker(s) and router are within reach. When the

Ethernet and 3.5mm cable are connected, you need to use AirPort Utility to configure the AirPort Express as part of a Roaming network, and ensure that Enable AirPlay/AirTunes is checked in the AirPort Utility Music tab.

▶ If you're connecting your AirPort Express to your wireless network in client mode—in other words, only for its wireless printing and audio streaming capabilities—you need to join the AirPort Express SSID from your list of available wireless networks. On a Mac, you can use the AirPort status menu in the menu bar; on a Windows-based computer, hold the pointer over the wireless connection icon until you see your AirPort network name.

▶ If you're setting your AirPort Express up as a wireless repeater or extender to your existing wireless network, you simply need to ensure that Enable AirPlay/AirTunes is checked in the AirPort Utility Music tab and connect to it as you would in the first example.

WARNING If you're planning to use the AirPort Express as a wireless repeater or extender to your existing wireless network, it's worth investigating the protocols supported on your other wireless router. If it's in 802.11b/g mode, switch your AirPort Express to the same. If one is using 802.11b/g/n, set your AirPort Express to follow suit. Don't mix and match network protocols across devices. I've seen lots of connection problems and interference when various routers on the same network are using different wireless technologies to broadcast.

UNDERSTANDING WHAT CAN BE STREAMED WHERE

With every new iteration of iOS, and even the new model in the Apple TV line, the visual map of what can be streamed where gets a little more complicated. In fact, it's so perplexing already that it's worth taking a look at the specifics. The two newest iPad models can accomplish a few AirPlay tricks that the original iPad cannot, and in similar fashion, the Apple TV 2 is required to accomplish a few feats that the original Apple TV cannot.

You might also be wondering if your NAS drive or Time Capsule can be used as an AirPlay source. Unfortunately, they cannot, *unless* a host computer is connected, is online, and is running iTunes. I'm hoping that Apple removes the middleman in a future update, but if you absolutely have to tap into a NAS library of music, Sonos's systems may be a better option.

Here's a list of places that content can be streamed from on the iPad.

▷ From the Videos, iPod, Photos, Music, and YouTube apps on iOS devices, you can stream videos, music, and photos to an Apple TV 2.

▷ From the Videos, iPod, Photos, Music, and YouTube apps on iOS devices, you can stream music to an AirPort Express or compatible third-party device (including AirPlay-certified speakers and A/V receivers).

▷ With iOS 4.3 and later, you can also stream video and audio from a website or a third-party app installed on your iOS device as long as the developer for the app or website has added AirPlay functionality.

Here's a list of places to which you can stream content from your iPad.

▷ **To Apple TV 2**: Play streamed videos, music, and photos from an AirPlay-enabled iOS device (including all the members of the iPad family); you can also play streamed videos or music from iTunes on your computer.

▷ **To Apple TV (original)**: Play streamed audio from iTunes on your computer, but no video content whatsoever.

▷ **To AirPort Express**: Play streamed audio from an AirPlay-enabled iOS device (including all members of the iPad family) or iTunes on your computer.

In any situation, it's important to remember that your iPad software and Apple TV software (and even your AirPort Express firmware) are up-to-date. Some of the more advanced streaming functions are only enabled when everything in the streaming family is running the latest software. If you're still facing troubles, you may want to temporarily disable firewalls (both network and local) as well as security software. Also, ensure that two or more devices aren't trying to connect or stream to a single AirPlay-enabled device. For example, if your nearby iPhone 4S has connected to your Apple TV 2 unknowingly, that would prevent your iPad from connecting to it. (Don't blame the iPhone—streaming's fun!) It's also worth disabling your Bluetooth radio (in Settings → General → Bluetooth) to prevent any unforeseen interference or connection confusion issues.

> ▷ Notice here that the first-generation Apple TV is left out from the AirPlay fun. Bummer. The hardware in the Apple TV 2 is clearly more sophisticated, and in turn, entirely more suited to handle the rigors of video streaming.

> ▷ As of now, iPad devices can only stream to a single AirPlay device. But iTunes libraries on Macs and PCs can stream to multiple AirPlay speakers and receivers.

WIDENING YOUR REACH WITH HOME SHARING

Here's a situation: What if you'd like to use your iPad to stream audio to a wireless speaker setup, but you have only 16GB of onboard storage? Perhaps even more importantly, what if the bulk of your favorite tunes are stored on your Mac or PC? You're left with two options: You could either use your Mac or PC (and the accompanying iTunes library), *or* you could take advantage of the Home Sharing library (see Figure 7-4).

FIGURE 7-4: Activating Home Sharing from within iTunes.

Home Sharing is a relatively new technology that's pretty involved to start, but using it is simple after you're established. You need a computer with the latest build of iTunes (one that's logged in using your Apple ID) as well as an iOS device (that's where your iPad comes in).

The key is to match the Apple ID on your iTunes and your iPad. To get this squared away, visit the Preferences section within iTunes → Sharing → Share My Library on Local Network. Then, on the iPad, go to Settings → Music and input the same Apple ID and password. From there, ensure that your iTunes computer and iPad are both online and then open the Music app. To switch to a shared library, tap More → Shared and locate the library that you just made available (see Figure 7-5). It's not exactly obvious, but it's there if you gave the right inputs. Apple has a fairly robust start-up guide and FAQ on Home Sharing at www.apple.com/support/homesharing/.

▶ You can also use another Mac or PC (or even an Apple TV 2) in place of the iOS device if you feel like streaming to something other than iPad.

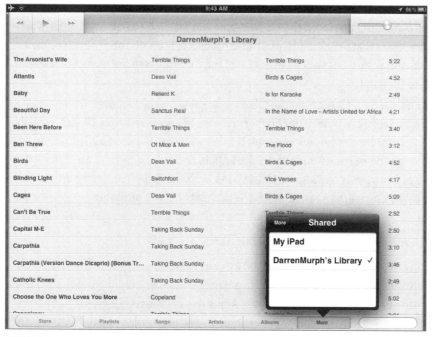

FIGURE 7-5: My shared library. No shame.

TIP Make sure the iTunes computer that's sharing its library doesn't fall asleep or go offline while you're streaming. None of that library is stored locally on your iPad; if the host drops out, all you get is silence.

HACKING EXTRA FUNCTIONALITY OUT OF AIRPLAY

Apple, like any for-profit company, cannot reasonably support an aging product forever, and at some point, the updates simply have to cease. The original Apple TV was always dubbed a "hobby" by the late Steve Jobs, and nowadays, there's really no major support to be found for it. For all intents and purposes, Apple has moved on to the Apple TV 2, with no real promise to add any more functionality to the first one. Thankfully, the hacker community has found a way to add AirPlay support to the original, and if you're mildly familiar with coding and have the ability to follow step-by-step directions, there's a solution waiting.

Perhaps unsurprisingly, AirPlay isn't exactly buddy-buddy with Windows, either. But even *more* unsurprisingly, there's a workaround for that, too. In this section I discuss a few hacks that are absolutely out-of-bounds for those who aren't into voiding extended warranties, but pack an awful lot of fun for those who are fond of throwing caution to the wind.

Thanks to a clever hack from the folks responsible for the Remote HD plug-in, AirPlay functionality can indeed be shoehorned onto the original Apple TV. Accomplishing this isn't for those who lack courage. It takes a fair bit of underhanded tinkering, and although the warranty on your original Apple TV has long since expired, meddling with the code inside of one's Apple TV has been known to leave the device unusable. If you're still interested, you can unearth the complete how-to guide at:

```
www.appletvhacks.net/2011/01/05/
airplay-streaming-hacked-into-the-old-apple-tv/
```

If you already have a Windows-based PC connected to your TV, or you'd simply rather broadcast video from your iPad to a Windows XP-, Vista-, or Windows 7-based rig instead of an Apple TV 2. . .good luck. Apple doesn't natively support it, but an older project dubbed AirMediaPlayer enables it. You don't have to jailbreak your iPad to pull this off, but you might have to do a bit of searching to locate download links for the software itself—it's not hosted on a centralized FTP due to its unapproved status. Check for a how-to install guide here:

```
http://compixels.com/8974/enable-airplay-on-windows-pc-to-wirelessly-
stream-audio-video-from-ios-devices
```

iTunes for Windows streams audio from your PC library to any AirPlay-compatible device, but if you want to stream music *to* a PC *from* your iPad, you need a handy piece of freeware called Shairport4w. Ensure you have the latest version of iTunes, download the software from http://sourceforge.net/projects/shairport4w/, and make sure that your PC is on the same Wi-Fi network as your iPad. If done properly, your PC shows on your iPad as an AirPlay-compatible device to stream to.

If you're also dabbling in the world of Android, you can install the doubleTwist AirSync add-in from the Android Market ($4.99) in order to stream audiovisual material from your Android device to an Apple TV 2. Twonky Mobile is a free alternative, but it lacks the tight iTunes integration that AirSync has.

AirPlay for Windows Media Center is a free piece of software that enables your iPad to beam content directly to your Media Center PC. It's perhaps the perfect mix of Apple and Windows, and you can find the install instructions at:

```
http://thomaspleasance.com/2011/05/23/
airplay-for-windows-media-center-beta-1/
```

If you're comfortable jailbreaking your iPad, and you need to pipe all manners of content *from* your tablet and *onto* your Mac, AirServer has you covered. It's a $7.99 app that you can download from `www.airserverapp.com/?page_id=182`.

SELECTING YOUR NEXT SPEAKER SYSTEM

As explained earlier in this chapter, the purchase of a $99 AirPort Express is all you need to convert *any* wired speaker system or A/V receiver into an AirPlay-compatible speaker. But in that scenario, you're still forced to move your AirPort Express and speaker system together if you want to reposition it. That's probably not a huge deal for surround systems that you've no intention of moving, but for smaller systems that are suitable for moving from room to room based on your current location, asking an AirPort Express to tag along isn't idyllic.

Slowly but surely, a host of AirPlay-certified speakers are rolling out that include the wireless AirPlay functionality from the factory. In other words, an AirPlay-certified speaker has Apple's wireless transceiver technology baked right into the device, so no extra accessories are required in order for the speaker to receive audio signals that are sent out from your iPad. Perhaps not surprisingly, most of these speaker systems are at least somewhat mobile—after all, a wireless speaker makes the most sense when you can easily move it from the outdoor patio to the kitchen, or toss it in the rear of the truck for a day at the beach.

In a nutshell, an AirPlay-enabled speaker system—if situated within range of your iPad—shows up as an AirPlay device in your secondary dock menu. When you select it, you can stream audio from your Music app to it while also dictating the volume remotely. Speaking of range, AirPlay's usage of Wi-Fi technologies enables it to be effective over a much greater distance than typical Bluetooth speakers, which are limited to about 30 feet. Wi-Fi signals can be sent up to several hundred feet away, so even if you have a miniature mansion you shouldn't have a problem using an iPad in the kitchen to send AirPlay commands to a speaker in the sauna. Granted, said speaker probably won't last too long in that kind of environment, but when you've got a sauna, what's another AirPlay speaker?

> **WARNING** Although Wi-Fi may be superior to Bluetooth for situations like this, it's still not perfect. AirPlay connections take around two seconds, as do subsequent actions, and full-on drop-outs aren't unheard of. Wireless might be convenient, but it's not flawless.

The following sections cover the pros and cons of a few recommended AirPlay speakers—everything from stay-at-home options to iPhone-friendly ones.

Stay-at-Home AirPlay Speaker Options

One of the major draws to AirPlay is the ability to kill those unsightly wires running through the home when hooking up a respectable speaker system. The following choices are my picks for a solid, all-in-one AirPlay speaker option for the home.

- **Bowers & Wilkins Zeppelin Air:** This is, perhaps, *the* stay-at-home AirPlay speaker. Why? For one, it's on the "somewhat enormous" side, and two, its shape makes it really impractical to carry around without fuss. The upside to this, of course, is that the sound quality is far more impressive than any of those pocket-sized alternatives. B&W is a name oft associated with high-quality aural experiences, and the Zeppelin Air is definitely a showcase piece for the home. There's also a unique docking arm that holds (and charges) your iPod or iPhone. It's a perfect ornament for game rooms, dens, or patios, but at $600, it's also one of the most expensive AirPlay speakers on the market. You get what you pay for, as the saying goes.

- **Libratone Lounge Speaker:** Say hello to the king. Or, at least the king in terms of price. This high-end AirPlay speaker checks in at a whopping $1,300, but it's the closest you can get to finding an AirPlay-enabled sound bar right now. It's big, classy, and understated, and it will undoubtedly bring the house down (while simultaneously breaking the bank). The Libratone app (available free from the App Store in iTunes) enables you to enhance and customize your FullRoom musical experience—you can input information about the placement of your Libratone Lounge and it then automatically adjusts the sound to fit your room.

- **Philips Fidelio SoundSphere AirPlay Speakers:** If you're looking for AirPlay speakers that involve more than a single, elongated bar, look no further. The Fidelio SoundSphere duo ($800) consists of two separate satellites. The design is certainly worth showcasing, and the 100-watts of built-in power should be plenty to fill the average room. Better still, there are no wires running between the left and right driver, making it entirely wire-free outside of the power cord. These are also compatible with Philips' free Fidelio app (available in the App Store), which enables you to remotely access more than 7,000 Internet radio stations, sound-setting controls, a clock and multiple alarms, and a sleep timer.

Highly Mobile Options

Have AirPlay, will travel. If you're looking to keep the music streaming even while away from home, these picks will do the trick. Sans wires, of course.

- ▶ **iHome iW1**: In my estimation, this $300 option strikes the perfect balance between a stay-at-home option and a mobile option. It's big enough to produce laudatory sound, but the built-in lithium-ion battery ensures that you can toss it in the car for a spontaneous getaway. (Boy, couldn't we all use one of those right about now?) There's also a convenient carry handle and a complementary iHome Connect app for easy network setup. You can find the latter in the App Store as a free download, while the former can't be purchased separately for any sum. Sorry!

- ▶ **Audyssey's Lower East Side Audio Dock Air**: The only major gripe I have here is the absence of a built-in battery pack, but the remarkably mobile design helps me to forgive that nitpick. The company crams an awful lot of drivers into a tight package, and although the $400 price tag isn't easy to swallow, you'd be hard-pressed to find the kind of audio fidelity here in an enclosure this portable.

- ▶ **JBL On Air Wireless Speaker System**: Besides having an omnidirectional speaker design that cleverly doubles as a carry handle, this is also one of the first AirPlay speakers to tout a built-in LCD. That screen is perfect for displaying album artwork or song information to those nearby, though you can control and shuffle things through your iPad from afar. It also offers an FM radio tuner and dual alarm clocks, as well as a perfect docking and charging port for an iPod or iPhone. At $350, it's also one of the cheaper options—yes, I said cheaper. None of these AirPlay speakers are "afford-able" by most definitions.

> **NOTE** Pioneer's X-SMC3-S Music Tap doesn't quite fit in either of the preceding two categories, but it just might be the best bang-for-your-buck AirPlay system, period. Aside from supporting Apple's wireless protocol, it also supports the more universally accepted DLNA wireless streaming technology. There's even a 2.5-inch LCD for showcasing album art, a built-in Ethernet port, iPod/iPhone charging dock, and a video output to boot. Quite versatile for $400.

AirPlay-Enabled A/V Receivers

▶ The $49
upgrade is merely
a firmware update.
Consult your
individual owner
manual for a how-to
on downloading and
applying the new
software.

The simplest route to adding AirPlay functionality to speakers you already own is the purchase of an AirPort Express, but serious home theater buffs may scoff at such a notion. For those considering something a bit more—shall we say—*robust,* there's the newfangled option of an AirPlay-certified A/V receiver. Apple's been working hard to add partners to its list, but so far there are only a handful of companies that are producing AirPlay receivers. In fact, a few older A/V receivers are being offered AirPlay upgrades, but the unfortunate part of that is the $49 upgrade fee. Apple's not exactly giving away this AirPlay stuff; any partner company that buys in has to pay a stiff licensing fee, and in the case of older units that are being blessed with an update, that fee is being handed down to the consumer. It's far from ideal, but, then again, it's better than having to buy an entirely new piece of kit.

While I'm on the topic, you're probably wondering what A/V receivers fall into that "upgrade-eligible" camp. Glad you asked!

- ▶ Denon AVR-4311CI
- ▶ Denon AVR-3311CI
- ▶ Denon AVR-991
- ▶ Denon AVR-A100
- ▶ Denon N7 Networked CD Receiver and 2.0 Channel Speaker System
- ▶ Marantz SR7005 A/V Receiver
- ▶ Marantz AV7005 A/V Preamplifier
- ▶ Marantz NA7004 Network Audio Player
- ▶ Marantz M-CR603 Networked CD Receiver

Denon and Marantz were two of the first companies to bite into the AirPlay agenda, so it's no surprise to see a litany of their devices on the upgrade block. That said, I can't wholeheartedly recommend that the average consumer go out and procure an A/V receiver from either of those firms. Despite producing outstanding equipment, anything with either of those labels is prohibitively expensive. At least it is for the average consumer.

▶ With more
than 250 member
companies, DLNA
is the de facto
streaming protocol
that almost everyone
uses. Except Apple.

Thankfully, there's an alternative. Pioneer has introduced a smattering of AirPlay-enabled receivers of its own, all of which are drastically cheaper than the options offered by Denon and Marantz. The $550 Pioneer VSX-1021 is the starlet of the bunch. It's only marginally more expensive than some of the mid-range AirPlay speakers, and it also streams content from DLNA devices when your iPad takes the occasional break. If that

7.1 piece is still too pricey, the VSX-521, VSX-821, and VSX-921 all feature AirPlay as well, and they're priced at $249, $349, and $449 respectively.

WHAT'S NEXT FOR AIRPLAY?

Put simply: *plenty*. AirPlay is still in its infancy, and Apple is still building out its partner list. Recently, Klipsch and Logitech decided to join in, and both companies have plenty of AirPlay-certified speaker systems en route. And that's just on the audio front. The next logical step would be for Apple to license AirPlay video streaming. You can already mirror your entire iPad experience onto your HDTV if you have an Apple TV 2 in between (video included), so it's clear that Apple's already in possession of the technology. Now, it's only a matter of logistics before that same video support trickles down to A/V receivers and perhaps even rival set-top boxes. Check out a visual example in Figure 7-6.

FIGURE 7-6: iPad + Apple TV + HDTV = streaming bliss.

And then, of course, there's the long-rumored Apple HDTV. It's unclear if the company is actually going to put its name (and more importantly, its software) directly into a television of any kind, but I have it on good authority that huge names in the industry are knocking at Apple's door in order to produce exactly that. Companies have struggled to produce cost-effective, lag-free wireless HD equipment, and tight integration with other products (namely, smartphones and tablets) is all but non-existent outside the Apple universe. The iPad is a fairly powerful controller today. If AirPlay is allowed to sink its tentacles into more than just a handful of speakers, receivers, and the Apple TV, it could become the world's most multifaceted and versatile universal remote.

KEYING IN ON VIDEO STREAMING

To date, AirPlay is predominantly about audio streaming. In fact, the only way to actually stream video content from the iPad and onto an AirPlay-certified device is to have an Apple TV 2 around. At least that's the case if you're doing things by the book. But with the introduction of iOS 5, Apple made clear that video is going to be the next big push with AirPlay, and I have a host of tips for making the most of that initiative. Using your iPad not only as a video controller, but as a video *source*, opens all new avenues of enjoyment, and it brings your tablet one step closer to truly being the center of attention in your multimedia universe.

Apple did something unique with the Apple TV 2. It opened up the world of iPad streaming in a way previously only thought possible in the world of jailbreaking. In fact, the capabilities that are given to one's iPad simply by having an Apple TV 2 connected to a television make it a must-buy accessory in my book. Like the similarly important AirPort Express, the Apple TV 2 is also $99. Not exactly "nothing," but hardly a bank breaker for those already investing $500+ in a tablet.

I've previously alluded to some of the video streaming capabilities, but here I focus on taking full advantage of a little thing that Apple calls "mirroring." AirPlay Mirroring is a completely new addition in iOS 5, and it's this addition that really makes the Apple TV 2 purchase worthwhile.

> **WARNING** AirPlay Mirroring is a fantastic technology, but it doesn't always work. . .fantastically. Too many walls, flaky routers and bad karma have all been blamed for sporadic dropouts, so if you're planning to watch a movie or play a game that requires multiple hours of beaming, I suggest picking up a Digital AV Adapter ($39) so that you can have a corded HDMI connection to connect your iPad and HDTV. Although it's hardly as convenient, the signal is a lot more stable.

Without any trickeration on your behalf, you can send anything and everything on an iPad (the two newest models) display to your HDTV, so long as there's an Apple TV in between. This has long since been possible with a dongle that protruded from the iPad 2's Dock Connector, and the original was able to output a very limited amount of content via the iPad Dock Connector to VGA Adapter, but cutting the cable entirely makes a world of difference.

▶ Sadly, the original iPad is left out of the mirroring fun. The only iOS devices that support it are the iPad 2, the new iPad, and iPhone 4S.

What does mirroring (see Figure 7-7) really mean for you? For one, it means that you can now use your iPad to showcase photo slideshows, streaming video, and even Keynote presentations on a big screen. This is also a cheap way to get out of buying a new game console for the 45-year-old kid in your life. How so? Even games are beamed wirelessly to whatever television your Apple TV 2 is connected to, so that $9.99 racing app can be more than just a personal piece. In fact, it's not inconceivable to think that single-player gamers wouldn't opt for this type of setup over a traditional console; after all, the average iPad game is four to five times cheaper than a home console title.

In order to activate mirroring on the iPad, simply ensure that your Apple TV 2 and iPad are connected to the same Wi-Fi network. Then, double-press the Home button and swipe from left-to-right as the secondary dock bar emerges at the bottom. The AirPlay icon should be in that central row of buttons; give it a tap, and select the Apple TV 2 from the list of options. Also, switching from landscape to portrait mode on the iPad even rotates the image on screen. If you're watching a movie and you'd prefer that things remain horizontal for a bit, be sure to activate the orientation lock when you're situated.

FIGURE 7-7: Pick a destination. Any destination!

TIP Although mirroring may focus on video, there's actually much more you can do with an Apple TV 2 connected to an entertainment center. AirPlay-enabled speakers and receivers work well, but if you already have your speaker systems linked to your television you can actually skip a step. If you're using your Apple TV 2 to be the wireless liaison between your speakers and iPad, you're able to DJ a party from your tablet without having to invest in new speakers or a new A/V receiver. Moreover, with everything tied together, it's one less fragmented portion of your home entertainment setup. Oh, and you can even have a fancy visualizer running on your television as the music pumps. (I won't be offended if you take the credit when your new pals drop by and ask about it.)

MAKING AIRPLAY (AND YOUR IPAD) EVEN BETTER

AirPlay, as with most Apple technologies, is pretty fantastical in its own right. But AirPlay, as with most Apple technologies, is purposefully limited on the original iPad. If you ask Apple engineers, they'd probably give you some line about the original's hardware not being potent enough to adequately handle the stresses of multi-touch gestures and AirPlay mirroring, but the reality is probably closer to "we want you to have sufficient reason to upgrade." Not that I'm complaining—Apple is a for-profit corporation, after all. The good news is that Apple's logic doesn't have to affect you.

Adding Multi-Gesture and Mirroring Support to the Original iPad

In most scenarios, adding special functionality to a product that Apple itself doesn't deem "doable" requires a tricky software hack dubbed a "jailbreak." It's a common term that describes the modification of certain files on the iPad in order to let unapproved applications and scripts run free. Naturally, it opens your device up to all sorts of *schadenfreude*, but if you're smart, you can open your device to all sorts of functionality that would otherwise be out of reach.

In a weird twist of fate, two of the most outstanding features on the iPad 2 and the newest model can actually be ported to the original iPad *without* jailbreaking. It's true! Thanks to the efforts of determined hackers ("d.B.," in this specific case), the famed redsn0w jailbreak is capable of being tweaked in order to unlock just two specific functions, without the entire jailbreak having to be applied. Technically, you're modifying so little that you don't actually have to run a full jailbreak, which ought to please you if you're worried about ruining a warranty. It's infinitely easier to do with a nearby Mac, but Windows owners can modify iPads as well with a few extra steps. You can find the full details at Gizmodo:

```
http://gizmodo.com/5851877/how-to-enable-multitasking-gestures-and-
display-mirroring-on-the-ipad-1-without-jailbreaking
```

Creating a Wi-Fi Network

Perhaps you're planning to take your iPad and Apple TV to a vacation home that has no Wi-Fi network to speak of. In order to prevent those "friends" you're allowing to tag along from laughing you out of your own rental, all you need is for someone to bring along an iPhone 4, or any smartphone capable of creating a wireless hotspot.

You see, an iPad and Apple TV have to be on the same Wi-Fi network in order to enable mirroring, but all you really need to do is bring the network with you. By creating a mobile network that both devices can connect to, streaming can commence.

Even if you don't have a mobile signal where you are, the network itself facilitates iPad-to-Apple TV signal transfers. However, there's a downside in that a live Internet connection is needed on the mobile device if you want to stream material with DRM, because that has to ping an outside server as a form of authentication before the stream is sent. The *other* suggestion is to bring along that AirPort Express that I've *surely* convinced you to purchase by now; even if an Ethernet plug isn't connected, you can still use it to create a local Wi-Fi network so your other devices can talk to one another.

Jailbreaking, and Why You'd Even Bother

I won't go into great detail on *how* to jailbreak your device for one simple reason: It voids your warranty. Apple has made no secret that it's strongly against the practice, but I'm including this section for a couple of reasons. For one, your iPad may be out of warranty already. Secondly, there's at least a sliver of chance that you couldn't give two hoots about what Apple is for or against. And finally, the reality of the situation is that jailbreaking is a heck of a lot of fun, and the apps found in those unapproved app stores can be way, way more titillating that the ones certified for distribution in the *actual* App Store.

iOS 5 has been one of the toughest builds yet to crack. That's not surprising given that Apple has been making it more and more difficult for coders to do so with every release. There are a handful of names that you need to know in order to stay up-to-date on the ebb and flow of the jailbreak. Comex, Grant Paul (chpwn), Jay Freeman (saurik), and MuscleNerd are the ringleaders, and all of these fine folks can be found on Twitter with a simple search.

Two websites (www.jailbreakme.com and blog.iphone-dev.org/) are go-to sources when it comes to jailbreaking, and you can rest assured that they'll have up-to-the-minute information about the latest cracks.

After you've applied a jailbreak, you need to surf over to the Cydia app store. There are a few other repositories, but that's the main one. It's effectively an app store that Apple doesn't approve of, and you should know that any app in here is "download at your own risk." Nothing here has been quality-checked by Apple, but if you're adventurous (and you feel like trodding through online forums regarding the latest and greatest unauthorized app), you can find all sorts of programs that enable you to customize notifications (SBSettings), tweak your lock screen (LockInfo), multitask differently (Activator), and even use your iPad's 3G/4G Internet connection (if applicable) as a mobile hotspot with MyWi.

Making Anything and Everything AirPlay-Compatible

If you're serious about hacking, and you're comfortable coding, there's a program you should know about: ShairPort. It's an unofficial dump of the ROM trapped within Apple's AirPort Express. Now that it's exposed, you can effectively add AirPlay audio streaming support to any piece of software in existence. So long as you can interweave the ShairPort code into an application, it'll register as an AirPlay device. In fact, if you're into DIY electronics, you could even embed this code into your own homegrown AirPlay hardware. Crack your knuckles and download it from here:

```
http://mafipulation.org/blagoblig/2011/04/08#shairport
```

Extending the Functionality of Your Apple TV 2

Surprise, surprise! You can jailbreak your Apple TV 2, too! Jailbreaking the Apple TV 2 isn't free like it is with iOS; it requires some dough, but you (and your iPad) will appreciate the added functionality.

Firecore's aTV Flash is available for both the original Apple TV and the new Apple TV 2, with pricing between $20 and $30 per device. By visiting the company's website (`http://firecore.com/atvflash-black`), you can purchase access to a point-and-click update procedure that requires minimal hacking knowledge and no physical alterations.

You can use the Remote HD app—mentioned earlier in this chapter—to give your iPad control over aTV Flash, which enables robust codec support, NAS streaming, web browsing, Last.fm access, and more. If you're using your iPad to interact with your Apple TV, and you're just searching for *more* than what Apple's willing to give you, this might be worth an install. It's easy to remove, too, should you decide that the new interface just isn't for you.

To close, there's a trick that doesn't require a jailbreak. If you're in possession of an iPad 2 or the new iPad and you have an Apple TV 2 hooked to a television, you can engage in big-screen video calling without investing in one of those HDTV cameras. Better still, you can use your VoIP app of choice. By firing up Skype, FaceTime, or any other chatting application and mirroring your screen onto an HDTV, you can now let the whole family watch as you (or they!) converse with that beautiful face on the other end.

SUMMARY

Tapping into the (mostly undercover) AirPlay functionality that's tucked within iOS 5 is a surefire way to justify your iPad purchase, but it's the iPad 2 or newer owners that are apt to see the most value. That said, a few relatively easy hacks and tweaks can bring a couple of highly useful features (multi-gesture support and mirroring) to the original iPad. All it takes is a bit of searching, clicking, and patience.

On the audio front, you're just a speaker system (or AirPort Express) away from being able to use your iPad to wirelessly DJ a party. And because AirPlay uses Wi-Fi instead of Bluetooth, the range is far greater. There aren't a plethora of AirPlay-certified speaker options out just yet, but the ones that have made it to market are really impressive. And expensive.

As for video? There are plenty of secrets to learn there, too. The mirroring functionality—unlocked in iOS 5—gives you the ability to send streaming video, photo slideshows, and even FaceTime calls to the big screen. But if you're down for digging deeper, there are plenty of jailbreaking options for extending the capabilities of both the Apple TV and the iPad itself. One thing's exceptionally clear: The iPad (and to an even greater extent, the iPad 2 and the latest iPad) is opened up to an entirely new world of control with the purchase of Apple's $99 Apple TV. It's worth budgeting for.

Taking Advantage of Wireless Functionality

If I didn't make it clear enough in Chapter 7, the iPad is at its best when no cables are involved. It just feels less like a tool, and more like a...magic wand. I'm sure Harry Potter would agree. In newer builds of iOS, and iOS 5 in particular, Apple has granted the iPad wireless abilities that some may argue it should've had from the start. Things such as wireless printing, syncing everything from contacts to music over Wi-Fi, and using the gorgeous 9.7-inch IPS panel that your iPad possesses as a secondary display for an honest-to-goodness computer.

This chapter covers the ins and outs of the remaining wireless features that are oft overlooked on the iPad, and I even dive into the art of wireless transfers between devices. Bluetooth and Wi-Fi are the driving forces at work, but as always, it takes a little effort on your part to facilitate things. Eager to get more done while cutting even more cables? You're in the right place.

CUTTING THE USB CORD

I have to wonder if even Apple knew that its proprietary 30-pin Dock Connector would end up being the barnburner that it has been. It's quite remarkable, actually. There's a USB port on one end, and a Dock Connector on the other, but you'd be hard-pressed to know which one was the "universal" of the two. Indeed, the proliferation of Dock Connector accessories and compatible peripherals is staggering, and these days, it's the devices that *lack* support for a Dock Connector that are considered anti-compliant. The iPod and iPad have become so prevalent that the Dock Connector has become standard fare on lots of audio-related gear, but it's now clear that Apple may be planning the funeral of its own socket.

> NOTE   The iPad, for all that it is, truly isn't stuffed to the gills with wireless modules. The 3G and 4G LTE editions have a leg-up on the Wi-Fi only variant, but really, they all rely on a combination of GPS, Wi-Fi, and Bluetooth. Forget about Infrared, keep dreaming when it comes to NFC, and feel free to write to Apple's nonexistent Suggestions Department when it comes to a wireless power solution such as Qi. But as you've seen with AirPlay, a tried-and-true Wi-Fi signal goes a long way (figuratively, not exactly literally), and, with few exceptions, the bulk of the iPad's wireless tricks are based around a protocol that engineers know best as 802.11b/g/n. So hey, don't say Apple never chose a well-established standard over a proprietary alternative. (But I'll understand if you insist.)

With the introduction of AirPlay and the many, many cloud features in iOS 5, it's becoming less and less important to have a Dock Connector cable nearby. Of course, until wireless power is implemented (remember the TouchPad?), you still need a cable to connect to the wall socket, but your goal after reading this chapter is to simply unplug the iPad from charging and leave the cable there. Believe it or not, it's feasible in a lot of situations.

Taking Advantage of AirPrint

What's most attractive about AirPrint is just how (relatively) easy it is to use. In typical Apple fashion, all of the functionality is baked right into the operating system, so there are no drivers to tinker with, no additional software to install and—most importantly—no cables to connect. You can see an example of just how integrated it is in Figure 8-1. AirPrint is actually capable of doing its thing in the background, too, so after you send out a print command, you push the dialog aside and get back to whatever it was that you were doing—sifting through e-mail, flipping through a slideshow, or engrossing yourself in that *X-Men* trailer.

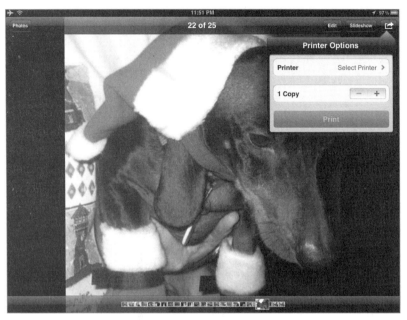

FIGURE 8-1: Who could resist printing this fellow out?

Getting started, however, requires a bit of elbow grease. And, on second thought, it may actually require a bit of hard-earned cash. You see, not every printer is designed to play nice with AirPrint. As nice as it would be for the iPad to be able to print wirelessly to any printer ever built, part of that "no driver" deal is the inclusion of software on the other end. And that means a new printer, perhaps. To date, only four major printer manufacturers are producing AirPrint-enabled printers: Lexmark, Canon, HP, and Epson. The list of compatible printers is certainly growing, though, and there are currently a few dozen options to choose from. The full (expanding) list can be found at http://support.apple.com/kb/ht4356.

▶ At first, only HP had AirPrint-enabled printers, and that company list has already grown by three. Expect more to join as the bandwagon forges ahead.

Overcoming AirPrint's Natural Limitations

If AirPlay was any indication, you may have a sneaking suspicion that there simply *has* to be some way around the inability to not print to every modern printer. After all, buying a new printer just to print a few documents per month from your iPad doesn't exactly sound ideal. Thankfully for us all, the third-party development community is coming to the rescue once more.

▶ Apple's Time Capsule ($299+) is an 802.11n wireless router and NAS backup drive that also has a USB port for your shared printing needs.

For those diehard Mac users, there's a phenomenal piece of software called Printopia 2 that enables your iPad (and any other nearby iOS device with AirPrint support) to send print commands to practically any printer in the known universe—assuming the printer is in your home and in some way affiliated with your Mac, of course. All you need is a printer of any description plugged into (and configured to work with) your Mac. Or, you can have a network printer plugged into a connected Time Capsule or AirPort. Check out the shot of Printopia 2's control panel (see Figure 8-2) to see how well integrated it is in OS X's Settings.

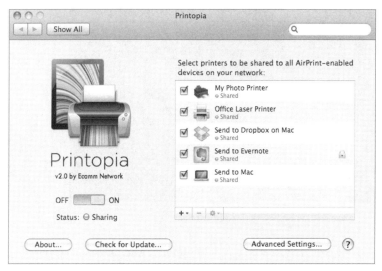

FIGURE 8-2: Printopia 2 blends right into OS X's Settings; no separate app required.

Printopia 2 even recognizes printers that are simply connected to the same router as the one your Mac is on, be it via wire or wireless. In case you haven't caught on, so long as you have a connected printer that's set up to work with your Mac, the installation of Printopia 2 creates the missing bridge that enables your iPad to view it as an AirPrint-enabled printer.

The software itself is freely available on a trial basis from www.ecamm.com/mac/printopia/, but the full version costs $19.95. It's important to note that this is software *for your Mac*, not for your iPad. There's no App Store download required, and no jailbreaking or other tomfoolery necessary. If the program is installed on your Mac, the printers show up in the exact same spot on your iPad with no configuration necessary on the tablet itself.

> **TIP** Perhaps the most impressive feature in Printopia isn't its printing abilities, but its virtual printing abilities. One of the most difficult things to do on an iPad is get a document, a photo, a web page—anything—from the iPad to a computer with little-to-no fuss. It generally requires some strange third-party app, or some mysterious series of clicks to e-mail something to yourself. By enabling your iPad to print to an unlimited amount of virtual printers, you're able to "print" a file directly to your Mac or even send files directly to a Mac app such as iPhoto and Evernote, as well as Dropbox. Talk about seriously cutting the cord on file transfers!

It's also worth mentioning that Printopia 2 works with a shocking amount of legacy Macs. Even Leopard (OS X 10.5) and PowerPC-based Mac users can download the utility and take advantage. Unfortunately, there's no Windows client to speak of, and the company certainly doesn't seem eager to change that in the near term. But, as you'd expect, there's an alternative for those who have Microsoft's OS running the house.

If you'd prefer a workaround with a bit more of a multi-platform vibe, there's AirPrint Activator (see Figure 8-3). It's a subtle, less sophisticated application that effectively does the same (basic) thing as Printopia 2. It enables non-AirPrint printers to be seen by one's iPad. Unlike Printopia 2, it sticks to rudimentary printing functions. On the upside, AirPrint Activator is absolutely free, though donations are obviously encouraged if it ends up suiting your needs. Installing it on a Mac is as easy as downloading the program and tucking it within your Applications folder. You can download it from:

FIGURE 8-3: Flip it to On. Do it!

```
http://netputing.com/airprintactivator/airprint-activator-v2-0/
```

For Windows users, things are (unsurprisingly) a bit more complicated. But if there's anything I hope you've learned thus far: "If there's a will, there's a way." If you want to enable AirPrint on a Windows XP, Windows Vista, or Windows 7-based machine (32-bit or 64-bit), you'll need to do a bit more manual labor. And by that, I mean manually creating a few file folders, mashing Okay through a firewall warning, and feeling extra proud about yourself in the end. The complete how-to guide is at:

```
http://jaxov.com/2010/11/how-to-enable-airprint-service-on-windows/
```

If you're concerned about your ability to follow instructions, or you'd simply rather pay someone $9.99 for the convenience of something simpler, there is *one other* Windows option worth mentioning. Collobos has launched its FingerPrint software—shown in

Figure 8-4—for both OS X and Windows platforms, and similar to Printopia 2, no jailbreak (or software installation at all, for that matter) is required on your iPad. You can download Fingerprint from `www.collobos.com/index.html`.

FIGURE 8-4: So many wireless print options with FingerPrint.

Finally, there's experimental support for printers working in conjunction with Linux. You can find the step-by-step at the following link, but even more than with any other OS, your miles may vary:

`http://forums.macrumors.com/showthread.php?t=1265049`

WI-FI SYNCING YOUR WAY TO CORDLESS FREEDOM

Thinking back on it, it's a little crazy that we ever had to connect our iPads to a computer in order to have very basic and essential information synced between the two. But, as with most things, it was probably easier said than done when it came to putting the necessary architecture for wireless connectivity between the two in place behind the scenes. With the introduction of iOS 5—according to Apple—you don't actually need a computer any longer in order to fully operate an iPad. Of course, what it isn't telling you is that it's still *highly* beneficial to have one tagging along, but at least you don't actually have to physically connect the two with a cable.

THE ORIGINS OF WI-FI SYNC

The introduction of Wi-Fi Sync was an uncharacteristically tumultuous one. If you're looking for a quick history lesson, here goes. Greg Hughes, a university student at the time, submitted an app called Wi-Fi Sync to Apple in May of 2010, where it was subsequently rejected for breaking a few rules in the developer handbook. But, as it turns out, Apple actually pinged Greg, asked for a resume and affirmed that it was "impressed" by the app submission. Nothing ever became of that relationship, but after Greg tossed Wi-Fi Sync into the Cydia App Store (for jailbreakers)—selling around 50,000 copies at $10 each—Apple soon launched a like-named service of its own. Curiously, this isn't the first time such a case has cropped up; a gal had an app similar to Apple's own iAds rejected, only to soon be aped by the designers in Cupertino themselves.

As it stands, Wi-Fi Sync isn't an app. It's an innate, built-in feature of iOS 5, and you see it just as soon as you start your iPad for the first time.

CROSSREF Specifics on enabling Wi-Fi Sync are discussed in Chapter 1.

How to Initiate and Handle Wi-Fi Syncs

Let me make it easy for you: You have two options when it comes to syncing your contacts, Safari browsing data, e-mail, photos, apps, and music. You can go the wired route, or you can do the wireless thing (as shown in Figure 8-5). A quick survey has confirmed that the latter of the two is what all "cool kids" are into. Jesting aside, here's what you need to do if you're interested in syncing things wirelessly.

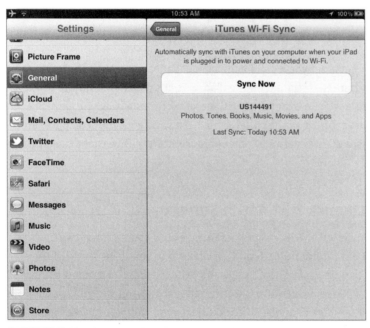

FIGURE 8-5: Here's your option to get things going without wires.

TIP I *strongly* recommend running your initial sync with a cable. That first one—during which you are most likely to push many, many gigabytes of audiovisual content onto your iPad—is arguably the most important. It's also the most likely to take the longest, given that so much information is being transferred. Trust me on this one: wired at first then go wireless.

After your initial sync is complete, you need to change something in your iTunes settings *while your iPad is connected* with the standard USB/Dock Connector cable. On the Summary page in iTunes, scroll down to the Options block and look for the Sync with this iPad over Wi-Fi box. Check it. Now, your iPad's set up to. . .sync over Wi-Fi! From there, you can disconnect the cable, grab your iPad and begin part two of this operation. (See Figure 8-6.)

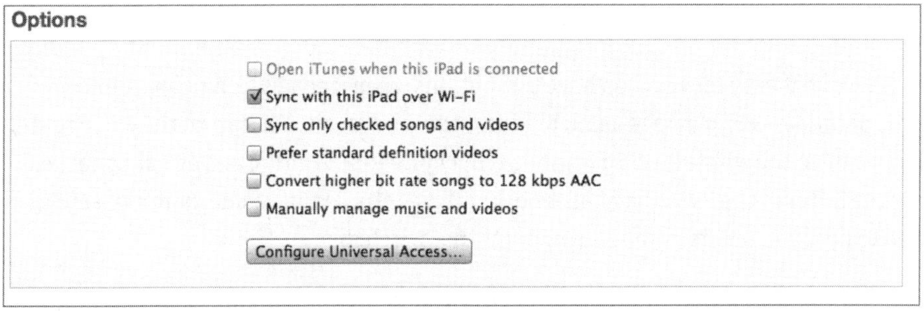

Options

☐ Open iTunes when this iPad is connected
☑ Sync with this iPad over Wi-Fi
☐ Sync only checked songs and videos
☐ Prefer standard definition videos
☐ Convert higher bit rate songs to 128 kbps AAC
☐ Manually manage music and videos

Configure Universal Access...

FIGURE 8-6: Find this option on the first pane of 'em within iTunes.

Because it's obvious that you won't be initiating iTunes syncs with iTunes, it *should* be obvious where to initiate it on the iPad. But, it's not. Here's how to initiate a sync from the iPad itself: Go to Settings → General → iTunes Wi-Fi Sync (see Figure 8-7). The button at the top of the pane—if your iPad and your host computer are both online on the same Wi-Fi network—should say Sync Now. Give that a tap, and the process begins.

Time Commitments with Wi-Fi Syncing

▶ make sure you have at least 10% battery life left before starting a sync!

A few words of warning with Wi-Fi syncs. First off, be sure you have got two or three bars of Wi-Fi signal before starting a sync. And make sure you have plenty of time, too. Depending on the amount of new data that's being shuffled around, it could take anywhere from 20 seconds to 20 or more minutes for a wireless sync to complete. If only a few files have changed since your last sync, you won't have to wait too long. If, however, you're hoping to add a gigabyte or two of new music, it could take a solid 15 minutes for it to complete.

In testing that I've done, particularly with larger syncs, Wi-Fi syncing takes between 8 and 15 times *longer* than a USB cable sync. That's fairly significant from a percentage standpoint, but when you're talking about 6 minutes versus 20 seconds— well, so long as you aren't in a hurry to make an exit, 6 minutes isn't too awful, particularly if you're in a different room than your host computer or you don't have immediate access to a USB/Dock Connector cable.

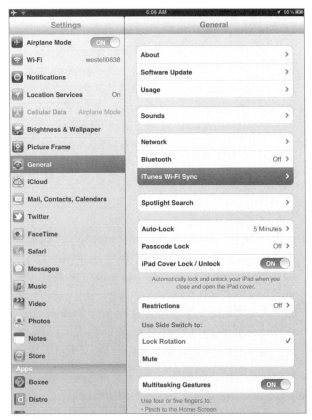

FIGURE 8-7: Sneakily hidden, but worth finding!

The good news, however, is that your iPad is fully functional while Wi-Fi syncs are ongoing. In other words, you don't have to sit around and wait for a sync to complete before you can browse the Web, send an e-mail, or enjoy a round of Angry Birds. That fact alone makes the idea of waiting 10 times longer entirely more palatable.

If your iPad is set up to sync over Wi-Fi, it automatically syncs whenever plugged into power (and iTunes is running), so you don't have to initiate it in that case.

MASTERING DEVICE-TO-DEVICE TRANSFERS

As I alluded to in earlier chapters, one thing the iPad is actually a bit weak on is file transfers. You can thank the innate limitations of a mobile operating system (compared to a full-scale desktop operating system, such as Windows or OS X) for that. But of course, just because your options are limited from the factory, that *doesn't* mean there aren't third-party solutions worth knowing about. With Bluetooth and Wi-Fi (and 3G/4G, for select models) onboard, the iPad technically has the hardware to pass files around sans wires; it all boils down to having the proper software in order to make it happen.

The iTunes ecosystem, in this sense, is really a blessing and a curse. While the rigidity of iTunes makes it fairly easy to keep your digital life squared away on both your host computer and iPad, it also makes doing anything outside of those invisible bounds a bit of a challenge. Apple hasn't even included native support for e-mailing each and every file type on the iPad, so you can imagine how difficult the transfer of material using any other method is. In this section, I offer up a few tried-and-true solutions for getting things to and from the iPad.

Using Dropbox

Dropbox: To all but the technologically misinformed, this term is probably one that's known well. It's a program that actually acts a lot like Apple's iDisk—a feature the company curiously killed as it phased iCloud into existence. But unlike iDisk, Dropbox is about as universal as it gets. The premise is fairly easy to *grok*: You sign up for an account, which gives you 2GB for free. This 2GB is available on pretty much any platform you can imagine, and so long as you log in to each account with the same e-mail address, you find mirrored views of your stash everywhere. The Dropbox iPad app is shown in Figure 8-8.

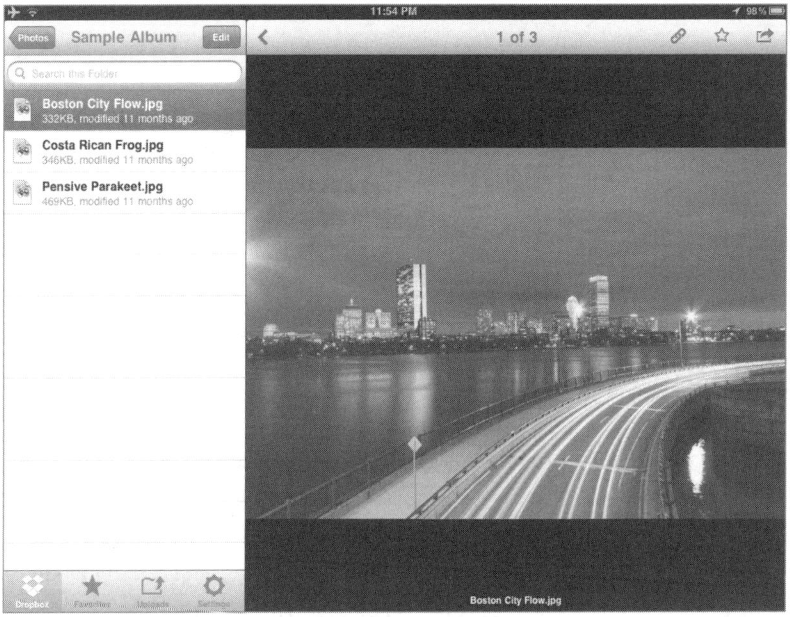

▶ If you need more storage, you can grab 50GB for $9.99 per month, or 100GB for $19.99 per month.

FIGURE 8-8: Say hello to Dropbox on iPad.

In other words, if you upload a document on your Windows machine to Dropbox, you can see it on your Mac, iPad, iPhone, and Android smartphone within seconds without any extra effort on your part. It's pretty fantastic, and it serves an incredible purpose on the iPad.

> **TIP** Be sure to tap the Settings icon while in the Dropbox app and then visit Local Storage and increase it to 1GB. That enables the vast majority of your loaded files to be stored internally on the iPad, so you have access to said files while offline. Have a look at the option in Figure 8-9.

FIGURE 8-9: Go ahead and select 1GB unless you're really pressed for space.

If you're hoping to send myriad documents, e-mails, and PDFs to your iPad for offline viewing—which is important when you travel overseas or into areas where you know that finding Wi-Fi will be a challenge—Dropbox is tailor-made to help you out. My suggestion is to convert (or Print to PDF) documents and messages into PDFs and then host them all in a named folder within your Dropbox account. After they're uploaded, your iPad is able to open them. After they're loaded, they repeatedly open without having to ping back to the Internet.

One of the biggest iPad limitations is the one-way street that surrounds cloud transfers. For example, if you open a text document, you can only view it. You can't edit it within Dropbox, and you can't even ask Dropbox to allow another application to open it, edit it, and then save it back to your Dropbox account. There's no universal

> ▶ Be careful not to assume that Dropbox will download your files automatically. You need to manually load each file once on the iPad while connected to the Internet.

solution yet, but in apps that support WebDAV (such as Apple's Pages), you can tap into the power of the WebDAV app, which is available on the App Store ($5.00 per month). DropDAV lets you interact with Dropbox files through a conventional WebDAV connection, which enables you to edit on the tablet and then save it back via the same unorthodox channel. It's a bit of a hack job, but it does the trick! You can read more here at www.dropdav.com.

If you're not interested in monkeying around with WebDAV connections, and you only need very basic text-editing capabilities, there are a few app options to consider. Elements ($5), iA Writer ($1), and Textastic ($10) are all beautifully seamless, and all are Dropbox-compatible.

Working with Box.net

The similarly named Box.net does many of the same things that Dropbox does, but it's geared more toward small businesses and IT professionals. In other words, it's a bit less simplistic, but the advanced feature set may prove useful for those who have money or resources on the line when it comes to file sharing. Aside from enabling all sorts of business collaboration features, it's also completely free to try.

What's more, Box.net's iPad app even taps into a few of Apple's most impressive built-in features. Using AirPlay, you can wirelessly stream Box.net content to an Apple TV for seamless projection of photos, videos, and presentations. It also supports video output via Apple's Dock Connector to VGA Adapter.

Multimedia Streamers

Make no mistake—iTunes facilitates the movement of audiovisual content from host computer to iPad. I'm guessing, though, that more often than not you'd rather just have content magically appear on your tablet, rather than having to touch base with iTunes. There aren't too many easier ways to get that kind of material onto your iPad itself, but it's important to think about alternatives here. Storing content locally isn't the only way, and in most cases, it's actually the least desirable way.

The concept's pretty simple, actually: "What if you could use some Wi-Fi device to just beam content to the iPad for easy viewing?" A lot of companies have had the same thought, and this section carves out the best of the best for more easily piping music, videos, and photos onto your iPad. Sorry iTunes—you're about to get circumvented.

CLOUD ALTERNATIVES

Although Box.net and Dropbox are the file-shuffling mainstays, you have *plenty* of alternatives. In fact, a new player seems to crop up every other month or so. Here's a short list of solid, oft-updated options should the big boys not tickle your fancy:

▶ **SugarSync**: This highly sophisticated file-sharing app doubles as a backup solution.

▶ **SpiderOak**: This option enables you to e-mail any file from the iPad's mail client and allows access to all of the data you have backed up across your various devices regardless of platform.

▶ **Wuala**: Although it accomplishes effectively the same thing as Dropbox, Wuala offers a native Linux client for those using Linux host computers.

▶ **Nomadesk for iPad**: Designed specifically for unlimited (yes, unlimited) storage and sharing, Nomadesk for iPad requires $35 monthly payment per file server.

PROJECTING WIRELESSLY

While it's highly specific, the free Panasonic Wireless Projector for iOS app (available on the App Store) enables consumers to send PDF files and JPEG images saved to an iPad, iPhone, or iPod touch to a Panasonic wireless projector over a wireless network. You can send PDF files transferred from a PC via iTunes to the Documents folder of this application, and JPEG images saved to the Photos folder of your iPad, iPhone, or iPod touch. You can also project websites with the built-in web browser, and photos taken with the built-in camera on your iPad, iPhone, or iPod touch. In addition, the application also lets you rotate the screen, enlarge or reduce the screen with a pinch operation, and flip through pages with a flick operation.

Granted, this only works with a certain class of projector from a certain company, but it proves that interest is there. With time, expect this type of functionality to be baked into more and more devices, enabling even more wireless power to be emitted from the iPad's antenna array.

ACCESSING VIA AIRSTASH

If you're someone who commonly shoots videos and stills on a camera that uses SD (Secure Digital) cards, you owe it to yourself to consider yet another $99 accessory. The AirStash looks like a beefed-up SD/SDHC card reader, and, in fact, it is. There's a USB plug on one end, and a slot for your full-size or micro SD memory card on the other. If you simply plug it into a PC, it functions as a card reader. But that's hardly what's magical about it.

The *real* pizzazz lies within. AirStash has a multimedia streamer, an internal battery, and a Wi-Fi module all tucked inside, which allows any audiovisual content on your SD card to then be transferred to your iPad over Wi-Fi. The accompanying app, not surprisingly, is completely gratis. After all, you need the $99 hardware in order to actually use the software. Said app enables users to wirelessly stream movies, view and import photos, listen to music and podcasts, and view documents stored on your AirStash. AirStash+ (that's the name of the app) is an enhanced alternative to the built-in web app adding features only possible with a native app; you can stream materials into the browser by directing your iPad to connect to the Wi-Fi access point created by the AirStash, but why bother? It's all about apps, at this point. The app's interface is shown in Figure 8-10.

> Don't try to stream DRM-laced files over AirStash. They won't work, sadly enough.

> For shooters that shoot RAW, you'll be happy to know that format is supported. In-the-field previews are a go!

FIGURE 8-10: The AirStash+ iPad app is laid out much like Dropbox.

HARD DRIVE-BASED STREAMERS

AirStash is a terrific device—*if* you have SD cards full of content. Although a multi-format card would probably serve a greater slice of the population, there is one more alternative to even AirStash. Both Kingston and Seagate have hard drive-based solutions, which enable you to use Wi-Fi to stream audiovisual content socked away on an external (and yes, portable) hard drive to your iPad. Both hard drive options also have batteries within, so a couple hours of wireless streaming is totally feasible. These devices are fantastic for kids on road trips; just load one up with their favorite movies before leaving, and let 'em stream at will in the back seat without any wires whatsoever.

Kingston's Wi-Drive starts at $130 for a 16GB model, while a 32GB model is $175. Seagate's GoFlex Satellite is far more sizable, but with 500GB of capacity at $200, it's arguably a far better deal than Kingston's alternative. It also streams to up to three devices at once, and that includes Android devices. The GoFlex Satellite iPad app interface is shown in Figure 8-11.

▶ Seagate's option is also capable of streaming directly to a Web browser, so pretty much any device is compatible.

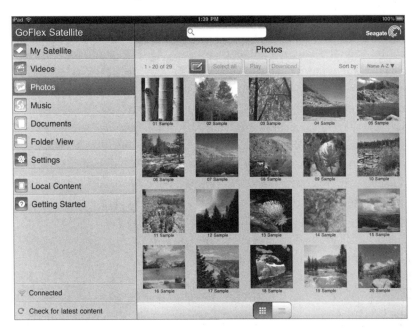

FIGURE 8-11: Seagate's GoFlex Satellite iPad navigation.

CAMERA-TETHERING SOLUTIONS

You have got a couple of options when it comes to transferring photos onto your iPad. For slow-pokes, there's the iTunes sync with your photo galleries on a host computer. For the technologically inclined, there's Apple's own Camera Adapter kit. For wireless aficionados, there's the AirStash method mentioned earlier. But there's an even *better* solution for all of the sects mentioned here, and it doesn't matter what camera you use or what kind of memory card is in your camera.

▶ Eye-Fi has stuck to SD cards, but CompactFlash users can always pick up an SD-to-CF adapter.

You need a few things in order to make the magic happen: your iPad, a camera with an Eye-Fi memory card, a wireless network and a $15.99 app dubbed Shuttersnitch. Never heard of Eye-Fi? That's a company that specializes in producing Secure Digital memory cards with built-in Wi-Fi modules. In other words, having one in a camera enables you to distribute images over Wi-Fi as soon as you capture them.

That's how the chain of events begins. You shoot a photo, and the Eye-Fi card is primed to send it. But to do so, you need a wireless network nearby. The easiest way to create one is to use a MiFi device—In Chapter 1, I discussed opting for an external 3G/4G device instead of buying an iPad with the network module embedded. Here's another example of that decision paying dividends. After a network is in place, you need to connect your Eye-Fi card and your iPad to it; having them on the same network is essential for the process to work as it should.

Now, you need Shuttersnitch (see Figure 8-12) running on the iPad. It's a highly specialized app that sucks down photos passed through an Eye-Fi card. Seconds after a shot is taken, you can see it right on your iPad's display. From there, you can browse, pinch, zoom, and evaluate, and your original shot remains on your camera's memory card. It also enables users to arrange shots in albums, lock private albums, resize or watermark shots before sharing (via e-mail, FTP, Flickr, SmugMug, Zenfolio, Facebook, or Dropbox), geotag incoming photos, add a caption and byline to the photos, and much, much more.

FIGURE 8-12: Shuttersnitch shows all sorts of useful metadata as images are sucked in.

▶ There are plenty of wireless tethering options that use a host computer in between, but the Shuttersnitch setup doesn't require a middleman.

If, however, you don't need an advanced program to watermark or significantly tweak the incoming photos, and you don't mind buying a new SD card, there's one more option you should know about. The Eye-Fi X2 (and only the X2) supports Direct Mode. That's a short way of saying that it's capable of sending photos directly to the iPad without a MiFi or other network in between. So long as your iPad has Wi-Fi enabled, and the free Eye-Fi app is launched, you're in business. In fact, it works even if the app is running in the background in iOS 5.

The app accepts full-resolution images, and it automatically sorts by date captured. You can also send over videos, and you can share select clips or shots via your favorite social networking program (including Facebook, Flickr, Picasa, SmugMug, and YouTube). Eye-Fi also has an Android app that enables Google-fied devices to accomplish the same thing, but you have to pony up $99.99 for an 8GB X2 card. You can learn more about the whole operation here:

www.eye.fi/how-it-works/features/direct-mode

Creating an iPad File System

One of my biggest gripes with the iPad—a gripe that is shared by many—is that there's no file system. That limits the functionality of the tablet in a number of ways, but not in a way that can't be at least patched over by third-party development. Air Sharing, a $7.99 app available on the App Store, enables you to wirelessly mount your iPad as a drive on your host computer. (Have a look at its interface in Figure 8-13.) From there, you can create folders and load it up with files—things such as Excel documents, PDFs, and so on. Better still, no cable is required; it mounts as a wireless drive, and you can drag-and-drop files as you would on any conventional flash drive.

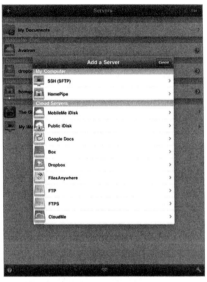

FIGURE 8-13: Air Sharing gets ready to share.

With OS X, the iPad is found automatically via Bonjour, whereas Linux users can connect via SSH. Windows users need only download the free Copy FTP desktop app. Beyond the conventional file sharing capabilities, Copy FTP is yet another facilitator of wireless printing, and it auto-detects Air Sharing on other devices for tablet-to-tablet (or tablet-to-phone, and so on) sharing.

▶ In other words, tell all of your iOS-using friends to download a copy of Air Sharing if you're looking to easily swap files.

TAPPING INTO BLUETOOTH

A decade ago, Bluetooth was the go-to protocol when it came to short-range sharing on phones. Everything from ringtones to photos were slung from friend to friend using some of the earliest Bluetooth stacks, but today, Bluetooth has slipped into the background when it comes to file sharing. By-and-large, most modern-day mobile devices have a Wi-Fi module built in, and given how much quicker Wi-Fi transfers are. . .well, there isn't much incentive to stick with Bluetooth.

▶ You can use Bluetooth to link headsets for Skype calls and to beam music to Bluetooth-enabled speakers, too.

Except, of course, that you may be dealing with devices that only have Bluetooth. You've got a few options when it comes to transferring files with Bluetooth, and the only ones worth paying attention to are those developed by third parties. For whatever reason, Apple includes no functionality whatsoever for Bluetooth file transfers directly from the iPad. Thankfully, it hasn't ignored developers who figured that some users may be interested in this very functionality.

Without question, the premiere Bluetooth transfer app for iPad is Bluetooth Photo Share by Nathan Peterson. It's completely free, and it doesn't require that you jailbreak your iPad. It works as advertised for sharing contacts and photos; better still, it doesn't compress images that are shared. The receiver not only gets the full-resolution image, but sees a thumbnail of the shot as it's being beamed over (see Figure 8-14). Just remember: You need to keep your iPad and the other iOS device close to one another. Bluetooth's pretty finicky, truth be told.

Need to transfer something other than a contact or photo? I figured you might. Bluetooth Share HD, available on the App Store for $1.99, allows two iOS devices to share files, photos, and contacts. You can also use your iPad as a USB disk to store files and transfer them between iPad and computers.

If you're looking for completely unrestricted Bluetooth file transfer capabilities, there's an app for you. But—and it's a big but—you need to jailbreak your iPad. If you're comfortable doing that, you can head to the Cydia app repository and download Celeste for $9.99. This app enables users to send and receive images, contacts, music, iBooks, and just about anything else (using iFile, which is also available on Cydia). But unlike the approved options, this one allows files to be transferred between iOS devices *and* between an iOS device and any other Bluetooth device that supports OBEX transfer capability.

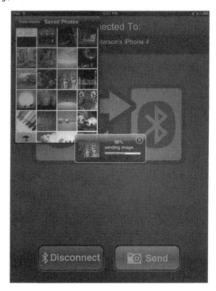

FIGURE 8-14: At least you're well aware of what you're receiving.

WARNING The vast majority of Bluetooth sharing applications in the App Store are of poor quality, and rarely do what they say they do. Even with the solid ones mentioned in this section, you are best served by keeping the transferring devices close to one another. Bluetooth transfers are (comparatively) sluggish, and if you stray beyond 20 or so feet, it's likely that your transfers will fail.

EXTENDING YOUR COMPUTER SCREEN WITH AIR DISPLAY

In almost every situation thus far, I've discussed ways to make your iPad the center of your digital universe. And indeed, there are plenty of ways to make the iPad into the ultimate dictator. But if we put aside any megalomaniacal tendencies, the iPad's a darn good friend to host computers, too. Apple never designed the iPad to act as any sort of dumb terminal, but why let a good screen go to waste? The 9.7-inch IPS panel is a real stunner, particularly on the new, Retina display-equipped iPad, and although you may figure that it's better off dark while your workday is ongoing, I have another suggestion.

A couple of years prior to the iPad's launch, a new product category began to take shape. It was loosely dubbed the world of "secondary monitors"—small, mobile displays that were generally powered by USB. In other words, you could plug one of these monitors into any notebook or desktop with a USB port in order to easily extend your visibility, and in turn, increase the amount of screen real estate available to you. What are secondary displays good for? Glad you asked!

I recommend using them for chat clients, secondary e-mail inboxes or websites or charts that automatically refresh throughout the day. For office workers who need to keep a close eye on stock trends as they move throughout the hours, it's great to keep a tracker open at all times on a secondary display. For those who continually scroll through a contacts list, you can now add a slice of display meant specifically for that. But instead of going out and dropping $200+ on a miniscule monitor, why not convert your iPad into one?

Believe it or not, it can be done for $9.99. For the price of a venti latte and a bagel, your iPad can become a secondary monitor. The secret is within an app (Air Display) from Avatron, which enables both Mac and Windows machines to treat an iPad as a secondary display. *Wirelessly*. Of course, those who plan on using the iPad as a display for an entire workday need to have it connected at least to a charging solution, but if you only need it for a hour or so, you can let the internal battery handle the heavy lifting.

First off, you should be aware that Air Display requires 10.5.8 (Leopard) or 10.6 (Snow Leopard) or later, on an Intel CPU. Both 32-bit and 64-bit systems are supported, and, if you're on the Windows side, you need Windows XP (32-bit only) or Vista or 7 (32-bit or 64-bit). Unfortunately, Windows 7 Starter is a nonstarter in this particular scenario. Furthermore, you need your iPad and the host computer connected to the same Wi-Fi network, as all of the display data is transferred over Wi-Fi. Due to this, you may see a hint of lag when loading movies or high-bandwidth scenes; I personally recommend using the iPad with as much 2D, static imagery as possible to

▶ If you're a hardcore Windows user, it's worth trying the DisplayLink app in the App Store (free for a limited time). It's a robust alternative that's tailored for Windows intricacies.

▶ You can find out more about new and incoming Air Display features at http://avatron.com/apps/air-display.

avoid disappointment. Tons of data is passed over when you're trying to send a video stream to a secondary display over Wi-Fi, but if you're just using it for standard web pages or chat clients, you see next to no hesitation in the handoff.

Now that you're familiar with the requirements, it's probably smart to clue you in on what's possible should you pony up for the app. Air Display lets you position your iPad next to your computer, drag windows onto it, and interact with those windows as you would on any other computer display. In its most basic form, your iPad actually becomes another monitor. Got that? Good. This app has been around since the launch of the original iPad, which means it's super ironed-out and phenomenally well-equipped at this point. When you disconnect and reconnect, your windows automatically reposition, so you don't have to drag them back onto the Air Display screen. Now, there's even keyboard support for iOS devices (both on-screen virtual keyboard and Bluetooth keyboard), and your iPad's battery level is displayed in the menu bar on your Mac. It works in both landscape and portrait mode, as well.

> ▶ You don't actually have to use Air Display if you're a hardcore DIYer; any VNC server allows computers to tunnel in and share screen space.

TIP If you're seriously considering the use of your iPad as a secondary display, I strongly recommend opting for a case that includes a built-in kickstand. There's nothing more frustrating (trust me, it's proven!) than having to line up a stack of books or use an old lunch pail to prop one's iPad up for Air Display purposes. If you know that you'll be using the iPad at the same workstation each day, I highly recommend Sanho's HyperMac Stand ($130), which not only offers two angles to hold your device, but acts as an external battery—perfect for those who have a highly mobile office.

One thing you might have noticed here is that all these suggestions rely on a Wi-Fi connection. In theory, wireless is always preferred. But the reality of the matter is this: Those using an iPad as a secondary display for any significant length of time will inevitably require a tether. If only to keep power running to the tablet, a cable of some description will eventually be involved. In fact, I'd love if Air Display had a "wired" option where you could simply plug your iPad into a host computer's USB port and allow both the video signals *and* power to run through that; it'd certainly cut down on imagery lag, and it would solve two problems with a single wire.

Unfortunately, the art of sending video signals over a USB cable is one that the iPad has yet to master. But that doesn't mean it's impossible. If you'd prefer to use a wired solution in order to both cut down on lag and simultaneously power or recharge your iPad, you need to turn to jailbreaking. (Taboo, I know.) You not only need a jailbroken iPad, but you also need the MyWi app or USB tethering installed, the Air Display app, Air Display for Mac, and an iPad USB cable. It's a remarkably simple process after you've got the ingredients, and you can view the step-by-step here:

```
http://hijinksinc.com/2010/06/01/use-air-display-over-a-usb-cable/
```

USING YOUR IPAD AS A WIRELESS INPUT DEVICE

Here's a thought: Given just how easy it is to touch the iPad, why not convert those touches to inputs on a computer? Apple doesn't offer a native way to do precisely that, but—as the record player continues to spin—there are a litany of third-party apps that enable that kind of magic.

It seems almost natural to think of the iPad's giant touch panel as an input device for a Mac or PC, and sure enough, there are a number of applications in the App Store that enable it. In effect, these apps turn the entire 9.7-inch surface of the iPad into an input device for a nearby computer that's connected via Wi-Fi. If you're having a difficult time envisioning what it acts like, think of Apple's Magic Trackpad. That's a far smaller surface, and it uses Bluetooth instead of Wi-Fi to connect, but the overall premise is the same.

WiFi Touchpad HD Free (see Figure 8-15) is the best gratis option, and I'd strongly recommend downloading this first just to see if you're comfortable using such a giant touchpad to control your notebook or desktop. It works with both OS X and Windows, and although connections can be finicky, it's oft-updated and continually improved. Splashtop Touchpad is a far superior app, but it's normally priced at $4.99. If you're convinced that using your iPad as a trackpad is something you're into, it's worth the investment. It plays nice with Windows and Mac machines, supports multi-touch gestures, and also works with any iPhones or iPod touch units that you have sitting around.

FIGURE 8-15: WiFi Touchpad HD Free gives you all sorts of input device options. . .for free!

TIP The iPad isn't really a suitable replacement for a legitimate Wacom tablet, but using one of these apps makes it darn close. Users who would prefer to use a touchpad to make subtle Photoshop tweaks or doodles could benefit from using an iPad over a conventional mouse, as the swiping actions are far more natural and closer to how one would truly operate a pen or paint brush.

SUMMARY

The iPad's wireless functionality doesn't stop with AirPlay. Given just how adept it is in creating and viewing content, tweaking it for an optimal wireless printing experience is a great place to jump in. After you've had a taste of just how much is possible without wires holding you back, the possibilities are then only limited by the imagination of the developers pushing apps into the App Store.

Tapping into AirPrint (or just tricking your existing printer into believing that it's compatible) is a great start, but syncing files without a USB cable is where the real magic begins. However, keeping the Wi-Fi Sync to yourself just seems rude. Device-to-device transfers are possible through both Wi-Fi and Bluetooth, though the speed and ubiquity of the former is making the latter less of a go-to solution. There's an entire stash of cloud-based apps designed to make hosting and viewing files a cinch, but I've got a few tricks that enable you to edit things on your iPad, too.

Finally, it's important to put your iPad to use even when you think it's time for a day off. There are no days off. If your iPad's sitting dormant, fire up Air Display and turn it into a wireless secondary monitor. If you need a makeshift Wacom tablet, install Splashtop Touchpad and get your doodle on—wirelessly.

PART III

DIVING INTO SOFTWARE

Game on with Game Center

In May of 2010, Nintendo of America's President,

Reggie Fils-Aime, said that Apple was Nintendo's primary "enemy of the future." That was stated shortly after Nintendo's CEO, Satoru Iwata, said that the battle with Sony was one "already won." A decade ago, Apple was the laughingstock of the gaming universe. The company's platforms were so underutilized by the mass market that the vast majority of developers wouldn't even bother porting their Windows and console titles to Mac. 'Twas a sad, sad state of affairs.

Now, iOS has completely transformed Apple's position in the gaming universe, and in many ways Apple is now the company to catch. Mobile gaming has shifted dramatically in recent years, with mobile phones and tablets becoming powerful enough to handle the gaming that was once reserved for portable handhelds. Game Center is Apple's first major foray into the gaming universe, but the company doesn't go to great lengths to publicize its features. This chapter discusses the ins and outs of Game Center and shows you the ropes to getting connected, staying engaged, and keeping tabs on your progress.

GETTING JACKED IN

Although Apple has received a stunning amount of praise and credit for its innovations of late, it doesn't do everything right. In fact, the company had a quite serious miss when it comes to social networking; its Ping music network went nowhere after popping up in iTunes. But unlike Ping, Game Center has traction—and all of the pieces are in place for it to see the kind of growth that people have grown to expect from Apple. Check out the app's understated design in Figure 9-1.

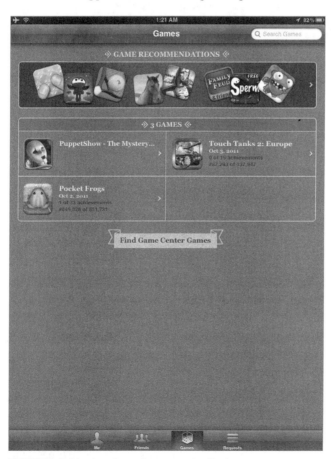

FIGURE 9-1: A look at Game Center on the iPad.

In a nutshell, Game Center is a gaming social network. If you're familiar with console gaming, it's most akin to Xbox Live or the PlayStation Network, but only for iOS devices. Game Center, in a way, is like Newsstand, acting as a unified portal for hosting all of your Game Center-enabled titles. Furthermore, it enables you to locate and track friends, start or join a multiplayer game, track achievement, see where you stand globally, and easily find new titles to try out and challenge yourself with.

NOTE Apple recently soared past 70 million Game Center users. For a service that just recently came to the platform, that's pretty impressive, and it's proof that iOS device owners are interested in gaming. It's also more than a Newsstand for games; instead of just housing your games, it's a place where your profile lives and thrives, your achievements are stored, and your next multiplayer game is just a click or two away.

You should know that while Game Center is a native inclusion on the iPad, it doesn't work with Apple devices using iOS 4.1 or older. Furthermore, it only runs on the second-, third-, and fourth-generation iPod touch, the iPhone 3GS, iPhone 4, and iPhone 4S, as well as each iPad model. That's the bulk of portable iOS devices, sure, but first-generation iPod touch users and iPhone 3G holdouts won't be able to join any of your games; they aren't ignoring your friend request, they just don't have the capability to accept it.

Understanding the Setup Process

Game Center is quite unlike any other built-in app on the iPad, or within iOS 5 as a whole. It's one of the few places where Apple actually asks you to register; for the most part, an iTunes ID is enough to get you around in iOS 5, and although I recommend using that very ID to sign up for Game Center, you can create a username that's different from the associated e-mail address, which is useful for privacy reasons. As you can tell, my birth name and my gamer tag (see Figure 9-2) are different in almost every respect.

Game Center—much like Mail, Music, Messages, Maps, and Safari—can't actually be "deleted" from the iPad. Even if you have no interest in using it, you'll be forced to file it somewhere that's not easily accessible in order to get it out of mind. I'd strongly recommend creating a username that's nothing like your e-mail address and reveals nothing about your personal identity. I've never been one to don a tin-foil hat, but there's just no compelling reason to let perfect strangers in multiplayer game sessions know precisely who you are.

▶ Friends can still find you via username or e-mail, even if your full name is kept private.

FIGURE 9-2: Choose a handle that fits you well (and hasn't already been taken).

After you've created a username, you can click the stock Photo icon to the right of your username in order to select a new avatar (see Figure 9-3). That's shorthand for a photo that represents your online profile; you can either select a shot from your image gallery, or use the iPad's camera to capture your mug on the spot. Of course, you could use the Change Photo button to do the same. Just above that, there's a space for you to input your status. Oddly, Apple provides no predetermined lines— things such as Online, Away, BRB, or Ready would make a lot of sense. At any rate, a tap of that button pulls up the iPad's virtual keyboard, where you can input any status you want. Folks that have you in their friends list can see your status as you update. See for yourself in Figure 9-4.

Navigating the User Interface

Apple includes but four main tiles to sift through: Me, Friends, Games, and Requests. I'll start with the first. There's an awful lot of blank, green space here, but the deluge of icons dotted about aren't just there for show. Tap 'em, and you go into a windowed view of the App Store page for the respective apps (see Figure 9-5). These tiles are live; in other words, they rotate in and out based on what games are on top in terms of ratings, play time, and so on. In fact, I believe that tapping these icons is the best way to start discovering titles you might like that are compatible with Game Center. Not every one is free, however, so be careful about jumping into each one and installing it.

FIGURE 9-3: You can choose a photo of your pup or a photo of your mug. Or anything in between.

FIGURE 9-4: Go on, customize your status. Tell us how you really feel.

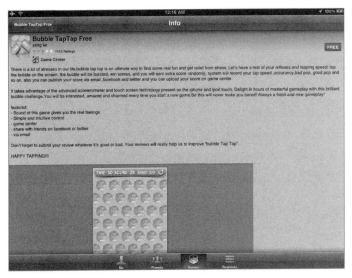

FIGURE 9-5: It's the App Store...inside of Game Center.

► It's highly important to have your Contacts in order. They affect more than just your daily forwarding list.

Moving right along, you should visit the Friends tab (see Figure 9-6) just as soon as you get a couple of titles in the stable that you're interested in playing. If you're online (and you're *always* online, right?), the iPad scours your Contacts list to find acquaintances that also have a Game Center account. Given that Game Center accounts are assigned by e-mail address, it's pretty easy for the system to put two and two together. This is even more reason to ensure that your Contacts app is stuffed with e-mail addresses, not just phone numbers.

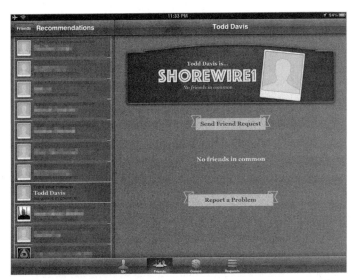

FIGURE 9-6: A list of possible friends (and a close-up of a great one).

The Add Friends button enables you to manually search for new pals via e-mail address or username. (See the interface in Figure 9-7.) Contrary to popular belief, this pane is actually useful for more than just *finding* friends. Just above the Recommendations banner, a single-finger down-swipe unhides a Search Friends box. For those with massive lists, this shortcut enables you to quickly and easily pull up a friend's profile, see if he's online, and peek at his status. Call it digital snooping, for gamers.

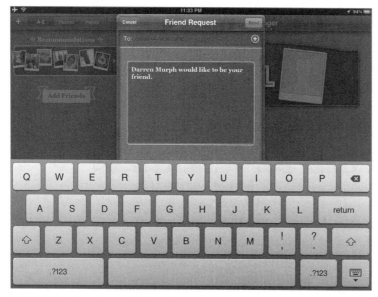

FIGURE 9-7: Got a friend? Add 'em!

NOTE Notice the A-Z button, a Recent icon, and a Points button at the top of the page? The latter showcases your friends (or enemies) in order of most points to least; naturally, this is the place to go if you need a little motivation in getting your scores up.

The Games icon is precisely what you think it is, but it's actually *more* than that. Aside from playing host to all of your downloaded games that are Game Center compatible, it's also a place to find game recommendations. Tapping that top Recommendations bar slides you into a hidden window with a grid of top apps, but you might be surprised at just how few are there. You can't just keep scrolling down or sideways, but you *can* initiate the addition of more apps by swiping away ones you aren't interested in. Swiping on any app title from right-to-left brings up a Remove button; tap it and a grid space opens up. After you've removed all that you're uninterested in, hopping out and back into the Recommendations portal enables those blanks to be filled once more with different options. Check out the grid in Figure 9-8.

FIGURE 9-8: That subtle Remove icon evaporates apps you aren't interested in.

The final main pane—Requests—couldn't be any simpler to use. You can respond to any requests from folks to add you as their friend. Easy!

KEEPING NOTIFICATIONS IN CHECK

Check out Android's pull-down notification window and then do the same in iOS 5. See any similarities?

With iOS 5, Apple completely overhauled its notification system. In fact, it was one of the most notable, visible, and fundamental changes to iOS since the platform's inception. Aside from taking a few cues from Google's Android, Apple has also enabled some fairly specific controls for notifications. Rather than just giving users the option of having them on or off, or giving users the option of customizing how they appear, Apple has enabled *both* of those for pretty much every major (and in some cases, minor) facet of the system.

Engadget Distro is a (free!) digital magazine that supports notifications for new issues. I contribute to it.

Regardless of how you have your Notifications arranged for other portions of the operating system—be it Messages, e-mail, FaceTime, Reminders, Facebook, Twitter, Distro (no shame), or Calendar—you can tweak your Game Center notifications to make them more useful and less annoying. How? Simple. Head to the Settings app within iOS and then tap the Notifications icon on the left rail. From there, you can toggle the Notification Center, choose how many notifications to show (I recommend five or ten unless you're a hardcore gamer), and Alert Style.

That final one is the most important. I recommend using Banners instead of Alerts. The three options beneath that (Badge App Icon, Sounds, and View in Lock Screen) are most useful if you leave them on, but if you'd rather disable Sounds you can certainly take a hint via the visual cues available in Alert Style. Have a look at what you should be seeing in Figure 9-9.

▶ Alerts are the typical pop-up notifications that troubled so many in earlier builds of iOS, interrupting whatever it is you're working on and forcing you to respond immediately in some form or fashion.

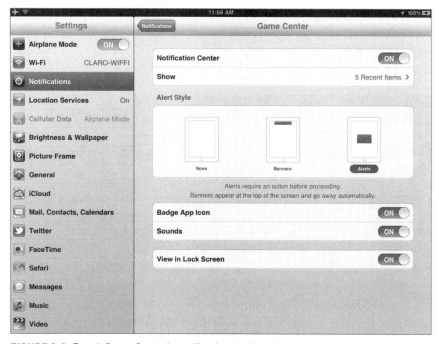

FIGURE 9-9: Tweak Game Center's notifications before they tweak your nerves.

NOTE My hunch is that Twitter and Facebook integration are coming soon to Game Center. Both social networking platforms are already well-integrated with iOS as a whole, and linking them to this makes gobs of sense for Apple. It'll also make it easier to find friends and gloat about your achievements, and it might make it impossible to put Game Center away for the evening.

If you end up amassing a load of friends—and given just how stunning you look, why wouldn't you?—notifications can easily get out of hand. In that situation, go to Settings → Notifications and turn the Alert Style to None and Sounds to Off. That leaves only badges on, which are the least invasive way to keep track of other events going on within Game Center.

DISCOVERING AND DOWNLOADING NEW GAMES

▶ Achievements are any number of accomplishments that toss "points" into your account once you reach a certain goal. The more you play—and the better you are— the more points you acquire.

Truth be told, Game Center is nothing without games that are compatible with it, and the functionality is severely limited without an Internet connection. Remember, this is a social network for games. Without the social aspect, it's just another hub for games. The Games icon along the lower edge is where I recommend you start and then tap Game Recommendations. The games that tend to be most addicting (and rewarding) are those with Achievements. Have a look at an achievements board for a single title in Figure 9-10.

FIGURE 9-10: Looks like I have a lot of work ahead of me.

▶ Take a deep breath: Angry Birds and Farmville are compatible with Game Center.

Not all Game Center games support Achievements. It's pretty easy to spot, though. When you click into any title in the Recommendations grid, you see a Leaderboard and Players tab; on occasion, you see an Achievements tab in the middle. By tapping there, you can see what goals lie ahead, and you know ahead of time what you need to strive for in order to rule the roost. As you play a particular game and hit those achievements, you see them "unlocked" in this panel. The great part about having your entire account tied to the cloud is that those achievements translate between iOS devices; so long as you're signed in with your iTunes ID, you have all of those statistics saved and visible.

Given the "social" aspect, it's no surprise that Apple provides a way to invite your best buds to download (and hopefully play) any title that you're fond of. But as of now, the suggestion feature is a bit spartan. Rather than being able to tap into your address book, invite via iMessage, or just send invites to folks who are already in your Friend list within Game Center, you're given the option to send an e-mail. Thankfully, you *can* pull addresses from your Contacts here, but an e-mail doesn't feel super personal. I'm guessing Apple will polish this up in future Game Center iterations, but you can see the current build in Figure 9-11.

▶ iMessage is an iOS-to-iOS communications protocol introduced in iOS 5. It's like BBM, but for iPods, iPhones, and iPads.

FIGURE 9-11: Let's see. . . who could I defeat at this?

In an effort to quell any confusion from hopping in and out of apps, I'd like to point out that downloading games from within Game Center isn't *exactly* the same as downloading one from the App Store. Let's say you tap the price (or Free) icon; from there, you slide into a windowed App Store, where you then have to tap the price or Free icon again. If you aren't signed in to your iTunes account, you need to punch in a password. Then, the app downloads to a home pane on your iPad, effectively exiting your Game Center session. When you hop back in, however, your new title should be sitting there, desperately longing for attention.

If the aforementioned grid of Recommended Games just isn't enough for you, it's worth tapping the Find Game Center Games banner. That switches you out of Game Center and into a specialized portal within the App Store, where you find a far more robust search engine. The top games are listed out already by category, but a quick search in the box in the top right enables you to pull up any app. After you've jumped into that app's Home screen, you can tell if it's Game Center-enabled by looking for a single icon: the Game Center logo just below the price (see Figure 9-12).

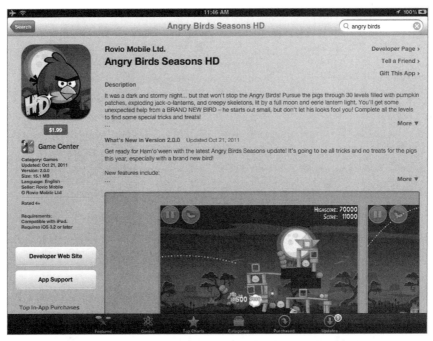

FIGURE 9-12: The Game Center icon is there in the left rail under the price button.

▶ You can easily wade through your games by using the Search box in the top right while in the Games pane.

If you're looking for a broader range of apps, or perhaps a more simplistic way to find games that the masses deem awesome, you can do so within iTunes itself. After you've opened the program, pay a visit to iTunes Store → App Store, and gaze over at the right rail. There's a box there entitled App Store Quick Links. A few lines down is the Games Starter Kit, an oft-updated catalog of the highest-rated, most-played Game Center titles on the entire App Store. If you're the type who prefers a higher power making decisions for you, this is absolutely the place where your discovery should begin. (And don't worry, it's okay to get ideas of what you may or may not like using a total shortcut like this.)

PROTECTING YOUR PRIVACY

Given that we live in a world full of connected devices, GPS hounds, and location-based deals, it's not surprising to hear of a privacy outrage related to this app, that program, or [*insert company here*]. Apple has certainly been at the center of a few of those, and although there's nothing tremendously worrisome about Game Center, I do want to point out one recommendation that most folks would probably never see without a fair bit of digging.

By default, your Game Center profile is made public. The upside to allowing this is that Game Center recommends you to other players using your real name, and your nickname is used on public leaderboards. Not surprisingly, I strongly recommend disabling your public profile. (See Figure 9-13.)

▶ What that really means is that your profile—including your real name—is made visible to other players.

FIGURE 9-13: Off equals less information floating around on the Internet.

To disable your public profile, hop into Game Center, visit the Me pane, and click your Account banner. After you enter your password, your full account pulls up; move the Privacy slider to Off, which disables your Public Profile. After this is complete, only your added friends are able to see your real name, though keep in mind that Game Center no longer recommends you to other players and your nickname isn't shown on public leaderboards. My opinion on this is clear: I'd rather not be on a leaderboard if it means my full name is widely available to the entire iOS universe.

▶ While we're on the topic of removing things, it's worth noting that you can't "remove" a game from Game Center unless you delete the app entirely.

KEEPING A HANDLE ON RESTRICTIONS

▶ In-app purchases can quickly turn a free app into a very costly one. Many new programs are using this free-then-fee structure.

▶ If it's flipped to Off, you and yours will be unable to ding your linked credit card from within an app.

Game Center's a joyful place, sure, but the fees can add up if your youngster gets in there and starts purchasing in-app additions at will. If you're planning to allow your children to tap into Game Center in order to pass the time (or keep 'em quiet on the long trip to grandmother's house), you should absolutely set a few boundaries beforehand.

I recommend going to Settings → General → Restrictions. From there, you need to create a Restrictions PIN code, allowing only the owner with that four-digit code to make changes. After you're in, you can scroll down to Apps in order to disable access to apps that are rated for a certain age category (or disable apps altogether), and beneath that, you can disable In-App Purchases altogether. Plenty of games offer in-app purchases; if you aren't careful, it's quite easy to slip a game update into your iPad with a subtle charge. (See Figure 9-14.)

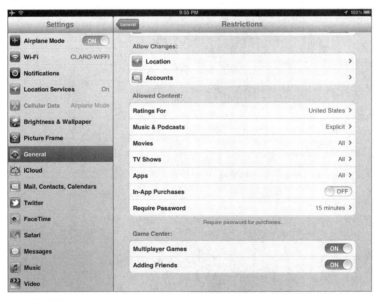

FIGURE 9-14: Plenty of security options to consider here.

▶ If you'd like to take things to the extreme and remove Game Center as a whole, you need to jailbreak your iPad and download an app called "Poof!"

If you'd rather your kids keep the gaming to themselves (but you still want to allow them to track achievements), you can glance down to the Multiplayer Games section and flip that toggle to Off. Not a bad idea if you're not keen on having perfect strangers play games with your offspring. (Yeah, this may sound extreme to some, but it's great that Apple has included the option here for the overly paranoid.) Taking things one step further, you can disable the Adding Friends option if you'd rather your kids not be able to accept unsolicited friend requests.

GOING BEYOND THE GAME

You may be wondering if there's a second level to Game Center, or if beauty truly is skin deep. Without getting into any deep, philosophical conversations, I'd like to point out that app developers are making Game Center into something much more robust than Apple likely intended for it to be. In fact, the name "Game Center" may not even be applicable if the trend continues. Fact is, there are quite a few titles in the App Store that tout Game Center compatibility, but in fact, aren't games at all. These apps simply tap into Game Center's use of achievements and social networking, but aren't "games" in the slightest.

One of my favorites is 100 Cameras in 1, a $1.99 app that acts as a cross between Instagram and Foursquare. In essence, this camera app enables users to add filters and tweak photographs taken on the iPad, but rather than letting the fun end there, certain achievements can be unlocked based on the location of your photos and what filters you use. It's quite the clever way to encourage the continual use of an app, and sure enough, it aids in the discovery of the app's sizable feature set.

The honest truth is that the vast majority of Game Center titles available today are indeed games, but there's a burgeoning market out there for non-games. Even if you aren't into gaming, it's worth keeping an eye on new apps that land with Game Center support. Every so often, one filters in with a category *not* named "Games."

ALTERNATIVES TO APPLE'S GAME CENTER

If, for whatever reason, you aren't satisfied with Game Center, there actually is another option for gaming-related social networking on the iPad. OpenFeint is a third-party network that serves a similar purpose, and there are a growing number of compatible games popping up in the App Store. Moreover, OpenFeint is also supported on Android, enhancing the potential for critical mass. It's worth checking into if you're a serious gamer. Visit **www.openfeint.com/**.

SUMMARY

Perhaps surprisingly, gaming has become not only an integral part of iOS, but iOS has actually become a leader in the portable gaming space. Companies such as Sony and Nintendo now have to pay attention to a new enemy, and the introduction of Game Center acts as proof that Apple is taking this initiative seriously. Setting up your account, establishing your privacy limits and setting restrictions on in-app purchases should be tackled before diving in too deeply. If the idea of downloading new, unheard-of titles to get going sounds daunting, it shouldn't. Apple's Recommendations help you ease into what'll likely become quite the addiction.

Unlike most other apps on iOS, Game Center is prone to tossing out dozens—if not hundreds—of notifications, particularly for those who have a significant number of friends. Calming that storm is fairly easy if you know how, though. Game Center is most beneficial (and enjoyable) when you take advantage of the social aspects: tracking achievements, watching your friends move up and down the leaderboard, and inviting contacts you haven't touched base with in a while to a few friendly bouts of Touch Tanks.

Game Center is primarily used for games today—not surprising given the title. But there *are* non-game titles being published with Game Center support. Even those with little to no interest in gaming can find something useful in Game Center, with 100 Cameras in 1 being an excellent example of how the functionality here could spread to other genres in the App Store.

Useful Productivity Apps

Apps. They make the world go 'round. And no matter the problem you have, "There's an app for that."™ It's pretty astounding to think that when iOS launched originally as iPhone OS, there was no App Store whatsoever. Trying to envision a successful iPhone today sans a market place for apps is nigh impossible, and it's clear that Apple's mobile stable of devices has seen skyrocketing adoption largely due to the creativity and determination of its third-party developer community. Today, apps aren't just a part of iOS, they are iOS.

Apple has done a phenomenal job making beautiful, desirable hardware, and it has also done a laudatory job optimizing its hardware and software in order to provide a world-class, rock-solid user experience. But the rest of the equation is filled in by people who aren't even employed by a company in Cupertino. Apple's biggest strength in the tablet market is its App Store. Tablets were actually on the market years before the iPad—most of them were based on Windows XP or some other non-optimized operating system. But Apple finally figured out that apps can transform the slate experience into one that's totally custom.

One of the first things that people ask me upon purchasing an iPad is this: "What apps should I download?" With well more than 100,000 iPad-specific apps on the App Store, it's a huge chore to wade through those in order to find a (comparative) handful that are worthwhile. In this chapter, I cover a wide array of genres and categories, dishing out my favorites and a few off-the-wall inclusions that you might not normally hear about through the proverbial grapevine. Everything from reading to traveling to learning is covered, and even if you're not a bookworm, there's no harm in using your iPad to increase your productivity.

CALENDARS AND TO-DO TOOLS

▶ An iPad is the perfect replacement to that pen-and-paper method you've relied on for way too long.

When it comes to being productive on the iPad, there are few tools more essential than a solid, trustworthy calendar. Apple has improved its built-in Calendar app quite substantially with the introduction of iOS 5—and those new notification options go a long way to making it more useful. But with more than 100,000 iPad apps at your disposal, you can rest assured that other options are out there. If you're planning to keep your iPad around on a day-to-day basis, using it to keep track of your upcoming appointments and events is a wise move.

Keeping those appointments tied to the cloud is an even wiser move. Self-contained calendars haven't been useful for years, but a shocking number of people still have their events tied to one single device, inaccessible to any other device (or even web browser). In the age of dumbphones and PDAs, that was forgivable; in today's world of hyperconnectivity your calendar needs to be everywhere at the same time.

Benefits of Using Apple's Calendar App

▶ In truth, even a $99 Garmin could be replaced by Google Maps Navigation on Android, or an inexpensive app on an iOS device.

I have to imagine that folks eying a brand-new vehicle ask themselves a similar question—do they opt for the built-in factory navigation system, or do they simply pick up a $99 Garmin unit to serve that purchase? The former is sleek, form-fitting, and beautifully integrated. Every morsel of it is able to interact with the vehicle's buttons and triggers, and no aftermarket tinkering is necessary. The latter, of course, is inexpensive. It's also more customizable—you can opt for any size or shape, with just about any feature set to serve your needs.

The choice is similar for having a calendar on your iPad: Use the built-in Calendar app or look for an alternative in the App Store. The two options are highly compelling, and in the end, both serve the core need. However, both options keep you abreast in very different ways. I recommend giving Apple's built-in option a go, at least initially. Not only is the layout quite pleasing to the eye (see Figure 10-1), but it's also fairly easy to tweak to work with any existing Google Calendars you may have.

FIGURE 10-1: Calendar: making an impossible schedule seem a bit less daunting.

Referring back to the "well-integrated" bit, there's no Calendar in the App Store more tightly integrated than the one Apple provides. In fact, this aspect is the strongest selling point for it. What does integration entail? Two things, primarily.

SPOTLIGHT SEARCHING IN CALENDAR

First off, the Spotlight Search feature I detailed earlier in the book only works with Apple's built-in Calendar app; no third-party calendar app can be added. It's unfortunate that Apple doesn't provide Spotlight APIs to developers in order to add that, but as of now, it's just the way it is.

▶ In fact, Spotlight won't search for anything in any third-party apps.

If you're wondering why this matters, allow me to queue up an example. Let's say you know you have a meeting with Alexander at some point this month. Your mother asks if there are any evenings coming up that wouldn't work for a surprise home-warming party. You immediately remember that you've blocked out a Thursday evening with

Alexander, but you've no clue which Thursday it is. Instead of glancing at every Thursday in your calendar, you can simply tap your iPad's Home button and type in **Alexander**. So long as Alexander's name is in that meeting notice, Spotlight pulls up the exact date and time in mere seconds. If you use any other calendar app, you won't get this kind of quick-search capability. Have a look at the results in Figure 10-2.

MAKING SENSE OF GOOGLE CALENDARS

One of the more frustrating things about the iPad's built-in Calendar app is the inability to recognize multiple Google Calendars. It has no issue recognizing the primary calendar attached to a Gmail account, but additional calendars (such as Google Calendars that were created by an admin and then "shared" with you) won't pop up without a bit of behind-the-scenes work. Here's how to do it:

1. Open your Settings app and then tap Mail, Contacts, Calendars.

2. Tap Add Account, and then select Microsoft Exchange.

3. In the Email field, enter your full Google Account e-mail address.

4. Leave the Domain field blank.

5. Enter your full Google Account e-mail address as the Username, followed by your Google Account password.

6. Tap Next, and be sure to tap Cancel if you see an Unable to Verify Certification box.

7. A new Server field appears; enter **m.google.com** here.

8. Tap Next and then select the Google services (Mail, Calendar, and Contacts) you want to sync. To receive and respond to meeting requests on your device, both Mail and Calendar need to be turned on, and New Invitations needs to be enabled in your Google Calendar settings.

9. Open the Safari browser on your device and go to **http://m.google.com/sync**.

10. Sign in with your account and select your device from the list of devices you've set up for Gqogle Sync.

11. Save the selections, and if you're online, you can choose those calendars from the iPad Calendar app within a few minutes.

For more information on this setup, visit:

www.google.com/support/mobile/bin/answer.py?answer=138740

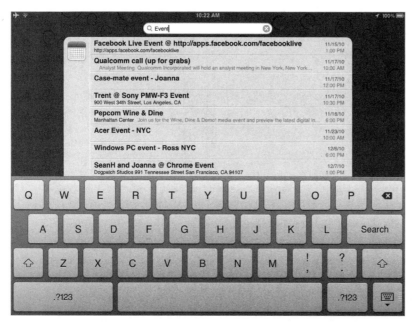

FIGURE 10-2: Lookie there—finding an appointment is just a search away.

Furthermore, Spotlight works *frighteningly* well. Even if you can only remember the first couple of letters in someone's name, Spotlight does its best to locate upcoming events that match whatever letter combinations you can muster. In many cases, it pulls up invites that you were searching for with a shockingly small amount of information. It works so well, in fact, that it has become my go-to way to search through my calendar events.

Apple's Calendar app does have its own search function; notice the search bar in the top-right corner. However, the integrated search function (see Figure 10-3) tends to disappoint compared to Spotlight. For one, Calendar provides a truncated view of its search results, and there's no way to drag the result box in order to enlarge it. However, I enjoy the built-in search box's ability to return results arranged by today's date forward, while giving you the ability to scroll backward for prior events; Spotlight starts with the oldest matching event and then forces the user to scroll to today's date. But here's the kicker: at least with Apple's Calendar, you have two great ways to search. No third-party calendar app can say the same.

CROSSREF You can learn more about customizing Spotlight for your needs in Chapter 5.

FIGURE 10-3: A look at Calendar's built-in search function.

NOTIFICATIONS AND DROP-DOWN REMINDERS

Apple is giving developers the tools they need to add notifications to apps within iOS 5. In other words, third parties can now create programs that allow for notifications to be pushed to users, and for those alerts to even show up in the new notification pull-down menu (shown in Figure 10-4). Of course, just because the APIs are there, doesn't mean all developers will use them.

As it stands, Apple's built-in Calendar app supports push notifications (which you can tweak and customize in Settings → Notifications). Whenever you set an iPad event or a synced Google Calendar event (as examples; other calendars work, too) to ping you before an appointment, you get a note that appears in and remains in your pull-down menu until you swipe it away. It's a fairly beautiful way to stay abreast of what's coming up in your day; just glance at the pull-down bar, and anything you've set to be notified of will be sitting there. On top of all that, there's no extra cost to using Calendar, and as easy as it is to chide Apple on this, you can't delete it, either. In other words, it'll be hanging around on your home pane regardless, so you need a really good reason to use a different calendar app.

▶ It's worth perfecting your notifications; without that pestering, your appointments go unnoticed.

FIGURE 10-4: You can clear out your drop-down notifications one by one, or all at once.

NOTE It's worth mentioning that Apple's built-in applications could become doubly delectable if (and more likely, when) Siri comes to the iPad. Apple launched Siri on the iPhone 4S as beta software, but it seems to me that the company's voice-recognizing starlet will be ported to its tablet group as soon as it's ready. If that occurs, you'll be able to simply tell your iPad to add an event, and it would do so on Apple's Calendar. Whether or not Apple will release Siri APIs to enable speech-to-action capabilities on third-party apps remains a mystery.

Third-Party Calendar Apps

Wouldn't you know it? There actually *is* a good reason to try something else. If you fit a certain set of criteria and you're willing to spend a little cash, that is. Apple's built-in Calendar app may be superb, but it's hardly a one-size-fits-all solution—particularly for hardcore Google users. As I've stated before, the iPad and Google's suite of applications don't always get along, and neither company is particularly inclined to help the other in making the compatibilities seamless. Thankfully for us all, there's a market outside of Silicon Valley that actually yearns for tighter integration, and the apps exist to prove it.

NOTE   Even grandmothers and infants have heard the term "app" by now. After all, that's half of the phrase "App Store." But what's in an app, really? Best I can tell, *app* is shorthand for *application*, but over the years, it's been slanted for use in the mobile realm. Recently, with the introduction of the Mac App Store and confirmation that a similarly styled shop will open in Windows 8, app has also been used to refer to desktop software. Apple actually doesn't hold a trademark on the term *app*; Google Apps were around in 2006, and the Amazon Appstore obviously uses it right in the title. But, Apple does own a trademark for "There's an app for that." The good news in all of this for iPad owners? When a company gets a trademark for something, there's probably some amount of truth behind it; sure enough, you'll have no issues finding more iPad apps than you'll ever have time to explore in Apple's App Store.

Following is a list of calendar apps worth looking into, and the reasons each is worth examining. Just search for each within the App Store to pull up its information and purchase page.

▶ **Readdle Calendar** ($6.99; also works with iPhone): What makes this option special is that it integrates with Google Calendars *even more tightly* than Apple's Calendar app. Readdle Calendar enables you to manage your calendars online and offline, and it supports the "drag-and-drop" functionality that has become a staple of using Google Calendar in a conventional web browser. In fact, the biggest selling point here is just how much the entire thing mimics the actual Google layout; if you're more comfortable staying in an environment you're familiar with, this is a great option. The real kicker is the support for Google Tasks; for those who make constant use of Tasks, losing them in Apple's default Calendar can be a serious buzz kill. In addition to all that, this app supports SMS alerts to upcoming events, the ability to search events and tasks, and the ability to undo additions you accidentally make.

▶ **Pocket Informant HD** ($14.99): Calling this "just a calendar" is probably doing the app a disservice. This is one of the most elaborate, sophisticated calendars available for the iPad, and, indeed, it does far more than just keep track of events in nondescript squares throughout the year. It's more of a digital datebook, with pages to flip and sections to comb. You can view year and month views simultaneously, with a detailed task and filter system helping you to keep tabs on what events and duties are coming due, which are overdue, which are in progress and which are completed. It's more like a life organizer, but the calendar function alone is truly exceptional.

▶ **Calendar+** ($2.99; also works with iPhone): It's drop-dead simple, and not nearly as full-featured as the others mentioned already, but it's also among the cheapest in the App Store. The primary selling point here is the multi-colored view and the automated syncing with built-in calendars that you've already set up. It also accepts new events while you're offline and then syncs them back to the cloud as soon as you're connected.

▶ **Agenda Calendar** ($0.99; also works with iPhone): The previous options generally add something *more* to what Apple's Calendar app offers. This one strips things away. It's aimed at consumers who don't want extras cluttering up their calendar, but there's a surprising amount of advanced functionality hidden just underneath the surface. It's designed to give you "at a glance" views at what's hitting you next—during your work day, that's what's most important, anyway. It works best if you set everything up in Apple's Calendar first and then allow Agenda to pull things in from there. This app also supports notifications in the pull-down Notification Center and on the Lock screen.

KEEPING TRACK OF MORE THAN JUST TIME

Naturally, the App Store is home to all sorts of alternative calendar apps, but what if you're in need of specialized calendars? To borrow a line from Apple's vault: "There's an app for that." Below are a few quirky, highly specialized calendars that just might strike your fancy.

▶ **Moon Calendar** ($0.99): View the phase of the moon for any month, in any location, as well as rise and set times for both the sun and moon.

▶ **Pampers Hello Baby Pregnancy Calendar** (free): Week-by-week guide of what to expect during weeks 4 to 40; great reference guide for expecting moms.

▶ **GW Calendar** ($4.99): A far snazzier interface than what's offered through Novell's stock GroupWise WebAccess portal.

▶ **WomanLog Pro** ($1.99): Yes, it's a menstrual and fertility calendar. No, it's not "a great gift idea" for husbands, boyfriends, girlfriends, or any other "friend."

▶ **Sports Cal** ($1.99): Perfect for keeping tabs on schedules from every major sporting league.

▶ **Baby Countdown** (free): Counting down the days to delivery? Don't get it wrong!

WRANGLING REMINDERS

There's a near-endless number of ways to keep tabs on what you need to keep tabs on, digitally. Some folks just create reminders in their calendar app, but if you're looking to keep appointments and your to-do list separate, there's a very real need to utilize Reminders. Clearly, Apple realizes this. It has included a dedicated app within iOS 5 (yes, named Reminders) that cannot be deleted—just like Maps, Messages, Calendar, and so on. There's definitely a good deal of value in using what's tightly integrated with the operating system, but for those yearning for more, the third-party world seems to have the to-do-list-app market completely satisfied. I'll discuss both sets of options below.

Benefits of Apple's Reminders App

▶ Despite your hunches, Reminders and Calendar are separate apps, and there's not too much interplay between them.

The usual lead-in applies here: When using a built-in app in iOS 5, you gain certain advantages that only apply to apps that are actually built into the fabric of the OS. Reminders is a fairly simple app, but it does what it purports to do. Upon launching the app, you're able to create or delete new reminder lists, as well as actual things you need to be reminded of. From there, you can sort them into the aforementioned lists, which is useful for keeping your repeating to-do items categorized somewhat. Have a glance at the interface in Figure 10-5.

FIGURE 10-5: Apple's Reminders app is simple. Maybe too simple.

You're able to gaze at your to-do list in both List and Date forms, and per usual, there's a search box in the top left where you can search for entries regardless of where they are, or how they're arranged. You can also sync them to the cloud—the iCloud, that is—if you enable it in Settings → iCloud → Reminders. (See Figure 10-6.) This might not strike you as particularly beneficial, but those who also carry an iPod touch or iPhone (or any other iOS device) will certainly benefit from this. The iCloud sync feature enables a reminder created on an iPhone to be immediately viewed on one's iPad, and vice-versa.

▶ iPad owners get the short end of the Reminders stick; iPhone owners can set up location-based reminders.

FIGURE 10-6: Toggle Reminders for Calendar on or off here. But mostly on, if you want to remember your appointments.

Considering Third-Party To-Do Apps

Truth be told, there's really only one third-party reminders app to be concerned with. That app, as you may have heard, is Remember The Milk. RTM is actually a full-featured website, which enables you to interact with your account and manage your profile from any web browser on any machine. There just happens to be apps to access the same service, with the iPad, iPhone, and iPod touch being supported. The app (shown in Figure 10-7) enables you to add and complete tasks on the go, while having it all synced to the cloud. You have access to priorities, due dates, time estimates, repeating, lists, tags, and so on, and you can even see tasks nearby and plan the best way to get things done. You can be reminded via e-mail, SMS, and instant messenger, and, amazingly, the basic version of the app is free. For $25 per year, you can upgrade to a Pro account, which unlocks unlimited syncs (instead of one per day), usage on multiple devices, and push notification reminders.

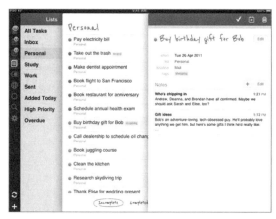

FIGURE 10-7: Don't forget to Remember The Milk.

▶ Try to get to-do/reminder apps that support push or SMS notifications. Without these alerts, you're apt to forget!

In the interest of expanding your horizons, I'm listing a few slightly off-beat alternatives that may be a better fit for your specialized reminder needs:

▶ **BugMe! Stickies Pro** ($1.99; also works with iPhone): If you're a fan of Stickies on OS X, you'll love this. You can craft alerts and pin them to a virtual corkboard within the app, and if the traditional reminder alert isn't enough, the visual board might be.

▶ **Due** ($4.99; also works with iPhone): This is a highly rated, frequently updated app that's overly simple in design and is engineered to handle short-term reminders with poise. I love the contrast with Calendar; use Calendar for long-term, repeating appointments, and use Due for the random to-dos that pop up during the course of the average day.

▶ **Task Pro** ($1.99; also works with iPhone): It does everything that Reminders does, but the multi-tiered approach to tasking makes it more flexible and easier to organize than most other options.

▶ **OmniFocus for iPad** ($39.99): Don't even bother diving in here if you aren't serious about organizing your digital life. At nearly $40, this is easily one of the most expensive apps you'll find in the App Store, but there's a ton of value here for those who need a sophisticated, robust to-do app for handling their personal and business lives. Cloud-based syncing is supported, and free e-mail and phone support is thrown in, too.

▶ **Corkulous** ($4.99): A clever name for a clever application. If you're coming from the School of Old where reminders were scribbled on scraps of paper and pegged to a corkboard, this app is most certainly for you. It enables you to place photos and notes on a virtual corkboard, and multiple boards are supported in order to help you segment your tasks and reminders.

▶ **Penultimate** ($1.99): There's no iPad stylus, per se, but I know some of you prefer the input of a pen over outright typing. If that's you, this particular app enables you to jot down notes on "paper." Though you write on a screen, the look and feel will likely ease your nerves if you're a digital holdout. After you've entered a note, the app enables you to e-mail each sheet of notes.

OBLIGATORY OFFICE APPS

You spent hard-earned money on the iPad, so it might as well pay you back in some form or fashion. It's true that most Office-style programs were designed for inputs from mice and keyboards, but now that the iPad has been out for a few years, app producers have had time to tweak programs to accept multi-touch inputs. There's no question that working on documents with the iPad is typically slower than using a full-fledged notebook or desktop, but toss a Bluetooth keyboard into the mix and the playing field levels somewhat. Of course, hardware's just half the battle. In this section I touch on a handful of world-class Office apps to handle documents, spreadsheets, and presentations.

CROSSREF Look for accessory and peripheral suggestions in Chapter 15.

Believe it or not, Microsoft doesn't make a version of its Office suite for iPad. Only heaven (or perhaps Bill Gates) knows why not. It'd clearly sell like hotcakes based on brand name and familiarity alone, but it's probably for the best. Instead, there are a number of third-party alternatives jousting for your bucks, and that intense competition makes 'em all better.

▶ **Quickoffice Pro HD** ($24.99): It's the preeminent Office-compatible document app for iPad. It takes full advantage of the extra screen space, masters the art of input via touch and boasts a multi-edit tool that enables users to quickly format text, numbers, colors, paragraphs, backgrounds, and cells, minus the multiple menus. It's also dead-simple to navigate to files, and the built-in integration with cloud services (Dropbox, Google Docs, Box.net, Huddle, SugarSync,

Evernote, and Catch) ensures that any files you create or documents you edit can be pushed back onto the Web as soon as you're done with them. Quickoffice Pro HD enables you to create, edit, and share Microsoft Word, PowerPoint, and Excel files, and the extensive amount of shared functionality (Find and Replace, as an example) makes it easy for Office addicts to adjust to.

▷ **Documents To Go** ($9.99; also works with iPhone): The primary advantages to this guy over the first option should be clear: It's cheaper, and it also works with the iPhone you probably own. It enables you to open, edit, and create Microsoft Word, PowerPoint, and Excel documents, not to mention RTF, iWork, PDF, text documents, and so on. The real kicker is the gratis desktop version that comes with your purchase, enabling users to two-way file sync with a Wi-Fi connection.

▷ **Apple iWork suite** ($29.97; also works with iPhone): Strangely, Apple doesn't sell a discounted bundle of its three homegrown Office apps, but you can still pick up Pages, Keynote, and Numbers separately for $9.99 apiece. These are Apple's document editor, presentation editor and spreadsheet editor, and not surprisingly, they're amazingly intuitive. Apple clearly built these specifically for multi-touch, and they're undoubtedly the most elegant, easy-to-use Office apps for iPad. Toss in tight-as-a-tick iCloud integration, and I'm finding a hard time not recommending this trio *strongly*.

▷ **Documents 2** ($1.99; also works with iPhone): Can you really go wrong? It's a full-fledged document suite editor for less than two bucks. It lets you store, manage, print and share all your photos, documents, spreadsheets and recordings in one place on your iPhone, iPod, and iPad. Furthermore, the user interface is very File Explorer like, so it should be quite familiar to anyone who has used a computer in the last decade. There's also the ability to view, edit, e-mail, and share (Google Sync, AirPrint, Wi-Fi, USB) whatever you open or create.

PRESENTATION IS EVERYTHING

First impressions are everything, and if you're pitching a startup or just showing off your analytical wizardry in a staff meeting, having a beautiful presentation setup can go a long way. These days, lasting through a conventional PowerPoint presentation is a feat in and of itself, but using the iPad to present with has been scientifically proven to both maintain interest while leading to higher projected earnings from future promotions. I confess, I made most of that up, but for anyone who stares at slides for a living, you'll probably understand the point. Not only does AirPlay give presenters an even sexier way to showcase their pitches, but the iPad as a whole is far easier to connect to a projector, far less likely to crash halfway through, and way more tailored to "present" than any work-issued laptop you have laying around.

CROSSREF AirPlay functionality is addressed extensively in Chapter 7.

Contrary to popular belief, presentation applications are actually useful for more than just business. Avid travelers can easily showcase trips with jazzed-up presentations, and parents who are entirely too active in their local PTA meetings could use this to petition for new band uniforms. Best of all, most of these apps make it possible to concoct a presentation right on the iPad itself, and even if you create a Keynote or PowerPoint presentation on a full-fledged computer, it formats beautifully for use on the slate. Here are a few of my favorites in the category:

- **Apple Keynote** ($9.99; also works with iPhone): Yes, I already recommended you pick this up in the earlier Office category, but in case you took that suggestion lightly, it's here again on its own. Keynote is a splendid iPad app—largely thanks to it being built in-house at Apple for use on its own tablet—and if you own a Mac with the desktop version of Keynote, all the better. The most outstanding aspect of this is that it was built specifically to be controlled 100 percent by touch. It's also worth pointing out that Keynote works with iCloud, so your presentations stay up-to-date across all your iOS devices—automatically. It ingests PowerPoint files with no fuss, and you can import files from Mail, the Web, a WebDAV service, or your Mac or PC using iTunes File Sharing.

- **Power Presenter** ($1.99): An inexpensive alternative with an educational slant, this option enables you to easily project presentations that have been converted to PDFs. Better still, it can fetch and open files stored on a website, so there's no need to have it locally accessible. It mirrors the presentation on your iPad display, so you can eye that while the crowd eyes the giant display behind you. You can also draw on or highlight text on the slides and send your drawing to e-mail. And you can embed videos along the way, too! Gone are laser pointers; in is your finger drawing on your presentation. It's the future, I tell you.

- **2Screens – Presentation Expert** ($5.99): This is the jack-of-all-trades option, doubling as a whiteboard, document manager, and viewer. It also plays nice with AirPlay and TV-out, but the real ace in the hole is a companion app. When a nearby iPhone has the $2.99 2Screens Remote app (and your Bluetooth radio enabled), you can use your iPhone to manage the flow of the presentation on your iPad, earning you major bonus points in the boardroom. The only bummer? Animation and transition effects within PowerPoint and Keynote aren't supported, so it's only truly attractive for those with an iPhone, too.

▶ **Wooji Presentation Remote** ($7.99; also works with iPhone): You're probably wondering why you'd ever consider paying $8 for a presentation remote, but if you've ever priced out dedicated presentation remotes, you understand that the price point here is actually a bargain. The only major downside is the incompatibility with PowerPoint, but for avid Keynote users, it works like a gem. You can tap anywhere on the screen to spotlight your slide, with a choice of graphics and colors.

▶ **Sadun's Whiteboard** ($2.99): It's not a presentation app in the traditional sense, but if you need to present on a whiteboard that doesn't exist, it's a perfect solution. This app supports multi-touch drawing inputs as well as TV-out, enabling you to draw right on the screen and have it projected to an external display. There's a litany of pen colors and textures, and you can even draw on top of images saved on the iPad. Your works of art can then be saved locally or shared via e-mail.

TRAVEL MUST-HAVES

There's just something about the iPad that seems tailor-made to travel. Maybe it's the wicked-thin frame. Maybe it's the ultra-long battery life. Or maybe it's simply a mobile device, and things that are "mobile" tend to "travel well." All joshing aside, most iPad owners that I've talked to purchased one with the intent to travel with it— have iPad, will travel, as it were. And it makes sense. It's smaller than any notebook you could buy, but it's more flexible than a smartphone. It's barely a burden, even in a conventional suitcase, and it's absolutely worth including in your carry-on.

CROSSREF I cover iPad travel accessories in Chapter 15. Hang tight!

Evidently, I'm not alone in that line of thinking, as the App Store is chock full of travel-related apps that make getting from Point A to Point B way easier than it should be. All hail technology, eh? Here's a look at my favorite iPad travel apps—

coming to you from a man who has proudly (and safely!) driven a motor vehicle in all 50 U.S. states:

▶ **Kayak HD** (free): Going somewhere? No? That's a problem. You'll know the travel bug has bitten when you can't rest easy if your next trip isn't somewhere on the calendar, and there's no better way to plan ahead than with Kayak. This app is a beautifully designed portal into the famed Kayak.com website, which searches hundreds of flights to find you the best prices, and even gives you the opportunity to expand your search backward and forward a few days in the effort of cost savings. Why use this? Airlines have a nasty, nasty habit of keeping track of your flight searches when you search directly on their websites; if they *know* you're interested on a certain route on a certain day, they'll jack the price up the second time you search for it. Kayak searches anonymously, helping you to avoid targeted price hikes.

▶ **TripIt Pro** (free app; $49/year service): Travel is complicated. It just is. But the journey is half of the fun, and keeping those journeys organized makes things even more fun. TripIt is a fantastic free service, and I'd recommend trying that first, but avid jet-setters will appreciate the $49 per year Pro service. TripIt monitors your travel-related e-mails and automatically builds and updates itineraries as changes fly in, and you can automatically share those details with folks who need to know. You even get flight refunds on fare drops, and it helps you find an alternate flight if something gets in the way of your existing one. (*Remember to avoid the ad-free $3.99 app if you're going Pro, anyway.*)

▶ **TripAdvisor** (free; also works with iPhone): TripAdvisor's website is still an absolute catastrophe of design, but the app is surprisingly *soigné*. It's worth signing up for an account. Within the app, you can search for reviews and ratings to nearby hotels, day trips, activities and attractions, and better still, you can access the highly valuable forums portion of the site. It's the easiest way to look for "top things to do" in any locale, but be warned: reviews aren't always what they seem. People *jump* at the chance to post a negative review, but the *vast* majority of satisfied customers never take time to leave a positive remark. (*In other words, always leave a good review for good experiences!*)

▶ **Travel Interpreter** ($4.99; also works with iPhone): Here's the thing—Google's language translate app is *amazing*, but it requires data. Not only is that tough to come by on iPads without 3G/4G, but you don't even *want* to use a data plan while you're overseas. International roaming—particularly on data—is impossibly expensive. To put it in perspective, looking up ten words using roaming data would probably cost you between $5 and $10. This particular app has popular terms and phrases for 28 languages, and all are available offline. More than 2,200 illustrated phrases and words with audio tracks are included per language, and although it checks in at a hefty 692MB, that's a small price to pay for offline access.

▶ **National Park Maps HD** ($1.99; also works with iPhone): If there's any place in America where you can count on spotty connectivity, it's in our beautiful National Parks. Having offline access to maps and trail maps is hugely helpful, and if you haven't been taking advantage of your parks, there's no better time than now. iPads love nature too, you know.

▶ **AllSubway HD** ($0.99): Hundreds of cities, thousands of subway lines. Tough to manage on your own, particularly if you don't speak the language. This oft-updated app provides a look at subway stops in the world's most popular city centers, and if you're able to grab an Internet connection, you can also look up schedules and revised fares.

FIDUCIARY RESPONSIBILITY

If you're looking for a way to justify your "investment" in an iPad (and in this book, while we're on the topic), you probably need an app or two. Good news for you—there are plenty to choose from. In fact, I've been downright shocked with how many finance-related apps are popping up in the App Store, and a handful of them are wonderfully polished. Steve Jobs spoke of a "post-PC world" shortly before his passing, and once you start doing taxes on an iPad (instead of a computer), you sort of feel like that future has arrived. Here are a few of my favorites for keeping your finances in check:

If you haven't already, creating a Finance folder to keep these apps in is a good idea.

▶ **Mint** (free): This app enables you to track, budget, and manage your money all in one place, so you can see where you're spending and where you can save. The iPad app is beautiful, and the web interface gives you another way to manage the same profile when your iPad is away. It's actually pretty astounding that this service is completely free. I'd highly, *highly* recommend this for college-age folk or users who are just starting to build their financial foundation. If you open an account, add your bank, credit, loan, and retirement accounts; Mint automatically pulls in and categorizes your transactions. Keeping things in order from the get-go makes record keeping all that much easier.

▶ **Compoundee HD** ($2.99): You might balk at the idea of toting around a financial calculator if you aren't a CPA, but in truth, a lot of financial calculations are best known by everyone. Money makes the world go 'round, and understanding how the decimal falls is vital to *grokking* mortgages, loans, and everyday negotiations. Best of all, it doesn't take a Masters in Mathematics to use it.

▶ **Expensify** (free; also works with iPhone): What's the first thing you think of when I say "expense reports?" Thankfully, the rest of this paragraph will still be here when you return from hurling. Managing expenses is one of the most dreadful experiences for avid business travelers, but having this app around makes it significantly less so. Not only does it pull in e-mailed receipts and keep 'em in a tidy list, but you can use your iPad's camera to snap photographs of paper receipts in order to keep track of new expenses as they happen (and before you lose said receipt). If your company allows it, you can even be reimbursed directly to a checking account.

▶ **iDonatedIt** ($2.99; also works with iPhone): Charitable donations are good. Fact. But keeping track of 'em is a massive headache. This app nixes a lot of frustration with that, enabling you to keep detailed records of thrift store drops and the like as they happen. A $2.99 app just made it easy to both help folks and whack a few dollars off of your taxes. That's progress.

▶ **Square** (free; also works with iPhone): This is easily one of the most innovative, game-changing applications in the past decade. The app itself is free, but you need to sign up for an account at https://squareup.com. A free card reader—which sits in your iPad's headphone jack—is shipped to you, and it enables absolutely anyone to start receiving credit card payments immediately. The fees aren't any worse than what you probably see in PayPal, and Square is a *far* more customer-friendly company. No monthly fees, no contracts. For small business users who simply have to accept credit cards in order to gain business, this is undoubtedly the best way. It even e-mails receipts immediately to those you do transactions with.

▶ **Time Master + Billing** ($9.99): Freelancers who need to keep track of billable hours should stop here. This is absolutely the most comprehensive time-keeping app on the iPad, and the real kicker is the included invoicing capabilities. Consultants, attorneys, and contractors (among others) can finally keep track of who owes 'em what, and yes, this tracks time right down to the second.

CALCULATIONS AND TRANSLATIONS

Look, math is hard. Scoff if you want, but even common multiplications are a struggle when the world's crumbling down around you, you're tired, or you're just feeling lazy. Thank heavens for calculators, right? The App Store is chock full of 'em, but finding the *good* ones is a challenge. There are also a slew of highly specialized calculators and translators, and I cover a smattering of my most trusted choices in this section.

▶ You can find calculators for nearly anything in the App Store: pregnancy, finances, weather, graphing, and so on.

▶ **Calculator for iPad Free** (free): With "Free" in the title, you probably had an idea of the cost here. It's kept gratis by including ads in the app, but for basic calculations (and even scientific ones), this app is plenty. If you aren't a power user, you needn't spend a dime to get a highly usable calculator.

▶ **Soulver for iPad** ($5.99): If you're still into the idea of doing math on paper, this app is a godsend. It's a masterfully designed program that enables you to use words alongside your numbers. It's ideal for comparison shopping, couponing, figuring out margins or just keeping track of what numbers correspond to what data.

▶ **Digits Calculator for iPad + iPhone** ($1.99; also works with iPhone): All of these basic calculators start to run together, but the one major standout of this option is the ability to enter a long series of calculations and then e-mail it all it to yourself for import into Numbers or Excel. You can also quickly calculate a few different scenarios by editing any previous entry to automatically update the total.

▶ **MedCalc Pro** ($4.99; also works with iPhone): It may only apply to those in the medical field, but having a full-on medical calculator at your disposal is a huge boon. Better still, this particular app is designed in a way that even the everyman could appreciate and use. Plus, it's cheaper than becoming an actual doctor.

▶ **Weight Watchers Mobile** (free; also works with iPhone): If you're already entrenched in the program, this is a full-featured app that works right alongside your program. The fitness calculator is the standout aspect, but having an app at your side could help you stay focused on reaching your goals—even while away from your desktop web browser.

▶ **Time Pad** ($1.99): It's definitely no conventional calculator, but if you're obsessed with tracking time, it's the one to get. It's designed mostly for use in sports and broadcast environments, featuring a central calculator section for performing various mathematical functions on time, as well as eight independent timers that you can use in three different ways: stop watch, countdown timer, or count-to timer.

▶ **Google Translate** (free; also works with iPhone): It's the quintessential translation app, supporting a staggering 60+ languages. It also translates spoken words into a foreign tongue, and you can actually listen to spoken translations for more than 20 languages. Best of all, it's totally free—the only downside is that a live Internet connection is required.

▶ **Jibbigo** (price varies by language): These guys started with just a Spanish/ English spoken translation app, but they're building out their language app library as we speak. Just search Jibbigo in the App Store and hope to find the language you need; it enables two people speaking different languages to speak into the iPad, and—*without an Internet connection*—it speaks aloud the translation. Pure magic.

READING AND RE-READING

Early on, pundits suggested that the conventional LCD on the iPad would render it near useless as an e-reader. As the market has unfolded, there's obviously still a niche being filled with E Ink-based products such as the Kindle, but many consumers have decided that a single iPad serves just fine as a digital reader when called upon.

The only major knock is the glossy display, which glares uncontrollably when placed in direct sunlight. That said, it's clear that Apple's positioning the iPad as a reading device; iOS 5 saw the introduction of Newsstand, and iBooks is another Apple-created app for fetching books. Outside of those two (which are included on the home pane of every iOS 5-equipped iPad), here are a few others that digital bookworms shouldn't miss:

▶ An anti-glare screen protector from BoxWave or Zagg works well to quell reflections.

▶ **GoodReader for iPad** ($4.99): There has been plenty of buzz surrounding this app elsewhere, but seriously, if you're attempting to open massive TXT or PDF files, there's no better option than this. It's also highly useful for things outside of just reading complex documents, making it a shoe-in for inclusion in your app library.

▶ **Kindle** (free; also works with iPhone): Funny, right? One of Apple's archrivals in the e-reading space actually has a highly sophisticated app in the App Store. The best part about the Kindle app for iPad is the cross-compatibility. You can buy an Amazon book on your Windows machine, open it where you left off on your iPhone, make a few notes in it on your iPad and lend it to a friend on your MacBook Pro. That's powerful stuff.

- **Nook for iPad** (free): It's pretty much the same story as the Amazon Kindle app, but works well for those already invested in the Barnes & Noble ecosystem. Cross-compatibility and sharing are both here, and the layout couldn't be finer.

- **Stanza** (free): If you're okay with having an app folder stuffed with e-reader apps, add this one to the pile. It doesn't hurt the wallet, and it offers better-than-average "sideloading" capabilities, meaning that you can load your own ePub, eReader, PDF, Comic Book Archive (CBR and CBZ), and DjVu books from your Mac or PC by dragging and dropping the files into the File Sharing section of the Apps tab of your device in iTunes.

NEWS AND REFERENCE MATERIAL

I confess: News is one of my passions. By day, I'm a news hound. I track and report stories, I investigate leads, and I bury my nose in the App Store looking for the sexiest, most seamless ways to consume the absolute torrent of news that flows from the Internet each and every day. Ingesting news on the iPad is one of the most lovely and enjoyable experiences of using the device. There's nothing quite like kicking back after a Hard Day's Night, grabbing a cup of Joe, and catching up on whatever it is you missed.

Many publishing companies assumed that the iPad was the second wind newspapers had been waiting for. But in reality, the form factor of a traditional newspaper and the dimensions of an iPad are very dissimilar. Instead, the iPad seems better suited to handle digital magazines and highly polished RSS readers; the iPad was designed to make the Internet look beautiful, and the following list includes a few of my favorite apps that exemplify just that:

- **Zinio** (free; also works with iPhone): This is a downright beautiful app that enables you to shop for and read a slew of great magazines—things that were seemingly built to be showcased on the iPad. You can read full-color, high-fidelity pages, or switch to enhanced text mode and resize text for simpler reading. It also supports offline reading, and you can buy subscriptions or single issues using your existing iTunes account—no extra sign-up necessary.

- **Flipboard** (free): Two things make this app great. One, the layout is stunningly beautiful. Two, it can ingest any content as it sits on the Internet right now,

> While I'm referencing The Beatles, I should note that those guys are finally in iTunes!

> I regularly contribute to a new iPad magazine, Engadget Distro. I'm biased, but it's worth a download. It's free!

so long as there's an RSS feed, and turn it into something gorgeous. In other words, you don't even need to find new favorites; simply pop the RSS feeds that you visit routinely into Flipboard, and it instantly converts those articles into magazine-like modules. It's really not doing much more than beautifying RSS content, but it does it *so well*. And, it's free.

▶ **Pulse News for iPad** (free): Pulse works in a similar fashion to Flipboard, but the layout is better suited to handle vast, vast quantities of news. In a nutshell, it takes your favorite websites and transforms them into a colorful and interactive mosaic. Not only does it do an excellent job of visually segmenting stories, but it also enables users to save particular articles for later reading across all platforms, or sync them with Instapaper, Read It Later, and Evernote. Sharing a story via Facebook, Twitter, and e-mail is as easy as two taps, and, truthfully, the hardest part is putting it down.

▶ **Reeder for iPad** ($4.99): In essence, this is an RSS client that syncs with your existing Google Reader feed. If you have your perfectly arranged RSS lineup already in Google Reader, you're ready to dive in right here. What makes this app particularly noteworthy is how it visually handles each feed; it's amazingly simple to parse, and it doesn't choke when handed an embarrassingly large number of unread items. You can star items, save 'em for reading later, share on popular social networks, and open items directly in Safari. There is a veritable smorgasbord of RSS clients out there for iPad; this is the one worth spending on.

▶ **Editions by AOL** (free): It's similar to Flipboard in its approach, but it takes an extra step by *actually* converting stories into magazine form. As in, you flip pages as you would a magazine. By-and-large, the conversion process is seamless and beautiful, and there's an enjoyable element of surprise as it customizes a new issue each day for you based on settings that you establish from the outset. (*Disclaimer: I work for AOL, but had nothing to do with the creation or distribution of Editions.*)

▶ **Instapaper** ($4.99): This is the de facto application for reading online articles at a later point in time when you're offline. It's tailor-made for underground subway rides, where you can load up a few longer articles in Instapaper and then read them when there's no connection available. Well more than 150 iPhone and iPad apps support direct integration with Instapaper already, and that list is growing by leaps and bounds. It does a commendable job stripping down complex articles to ones that are easily saved and read, and you can adjust a dizzying number of settings to make reading all the more comfortable for your two eyes.

> **The Daily for iPad** (free*): This may very well be the future of what we consider "the newspaper." It's updated faster than a traditional paper, but maintains the readability that you're used to. Individual issues can be purchased for $0.99, or yearly subscriptions can be procured for $39.99. It's bold, beautiful, and updates faster than most simpletons can appreciate.

WIZARDING WEATHER APPS

It's hard to explain, but there's something tantalizing about checking the weather on an iPad. Maybe it's the feeling of having your own "green screen" of sorts, or making yourself the meteorologist with those oh-so-easy swiping movements. Perhaps it's just the kid in me, but a super sophisticated, ultra-nerdy weather app just makes the iPad that much better. Googling forecasts for a certain area just feels boring; throw in interactive maps, webcam feeds, and historical data, and you have the forecast of the future. Here are a few of my favorites:

> **Intellicast HD** (free): In my estimation, this is the most fully featured, insanely detailed weather application in the App Store. There's support for high-definition radar views, push alerts for severe weather, and SkyTime, which is a visual indicator of the weather that has to be seen to be believed. No need to flip on the tube to catch the local weather—more than 50,000 locales have up-to-the-minute details on this.

> **Weather+** ($0.99; also works with iPhone): The only compelling reason to actually pay for a weather app on the iPad is the visual awesomeness baked into this one. The layout is simply stunning, and dare I say, looks a pinch like elements of it were borrowed from HTC's Sense Android overlay. It also offers full-screen video feeds from select locales, wind direction and speed details, and a plethora of customization options.

> **Living Earth HD** ($0.99; also works with iPhone): Half weather app, half Google Earth(ish), this app nicely mixes 3D simulations with up-to-date forecasts. It's less of a tool for figuring out your local weather and more of an exploratory app to discover weather patterns across the globe, but if you're in the education sector, it's a good way to get your kids to pay attention to a topic they may otherwise tune out.

> **Fahrenheit** ($0.99; also works with iPhone): There's really only one reason to consider this app over the others: the icon itself dynamically changes to show the current temperature, so you never actually have to enter the app

to know how warm (or frigid) it is in the area surrounding you. Should you do so anyway, you're greeted with a lovely user interface that shows forecasts, radar screens, and the usual complement of extras.

KEEPING THE KIDS OCCUPIED

Think modern technology is only for adults? Think again. Similar to how "child-proof lids" are only operable by children, iPads are remarkably easy for children to understand. In turn, there's an entire segment of the App Store carved out to serving the young folks, and it's definitely worth creating a folder or two of applications meant specifically for them. It's easily one of the most inviting, innovative ways to learn, and if you can't figure out a way to get your youngster to stop watching the television, just toss an iPad in front of his fingers. Oh, and make sure these apps are on there:

▶ **Star Walk for iPad** ($4.99): It's the next best thing to being shot up into space. . . maybe, anyway. This app is sure to educate both the young and old, enabling users to point one's iPad at the sky and see what stars, constellations, and satellites are above in real-time. It's a beautiful way of marrying augmented reality with education, and support for AirPlay mirroring and AirPrint make it even easier to use in group or classroom settings.

▶ **Fish School HD** ($1.99): Letters, numbers, shapes, colors, matching—just about anything you can think to teach your budding whiz-kid is here. It's an under-the-sea themed title that brushes up on the most basic of basics, aimed at "early learners" and chock full of activities. It's honestly one of the more elaborate learning titles for the iPad targeting this age bracket; I'm guessing your child will be spent long before she plows through every last game.

▶ **Math Bingo** ($0.99): It's inexpensive, and it teaches a tough subject using a game that just about everyone understands. You can select from addition, subtraction, multiplication and division, and push your youngster with three different levels of difficulty.

▶ **MathBoard** ($4.99): After your kids have outgrown Math Bingo, it's time to step it up a notch with this one. It's best used with an instructor, as the app mostly acts as a digital chalkboard. You can control the range of numbers you want to work with, the number of questions you want to answer, and even assign a time limit per quiz. It even supports VGA/HDMI output as well as AirPlay mirroring, enabling it to be used in groups or classrooms where a larger display is necessary to showcase the app to a wider audience.

▶ For loads of amazing reading experiences, search for "omBook" selections in the App Store.

▶ **Color & Draw** ($1.99): This one's probably fun enough for kids ages 3 to 103; it invites users to draw, color, and decorate drawings or photographs with voice over artistic invitations. In short, it's an interactive coloring book, and there are letter and number tracing tools to enhance learning as well. The only downside? Your offspring will never be excited about a conventional coloring book after experiencing this.

▶ **The Cat in The Hat** ($3.99; also works with iPhone): What would a kids' section about iPad apps be without a tip of the (cat) hat to Dr. Seuss? Not much. This particular app is a real standout, with its professional narration, background audio, and enlarged artwork for each scene. To promote reading in young children, individual words are highlighted as the story is read and words zoom up when pictures are touched.

▶ **Any app by PBS KIDS** (price varies): These guys have a model that just works; games are inexpensive, colorful and full of replay value. There's a variety to choose from to cover a wide array of ages, and I've yet to be let down by any that they've developed.

ALTERNATIVE BROWSING OPTIONS

Safari just so happens to be the web browser that Apple built (see Figure 10-8), so it stands to reason that it's planted front and center on the iPad. For years, developers of third-party browsers watched in vain as their handiwork was rejected from the App Store, but Opera Mini for iPhone finally broke that ice in April of 2010.

Since then, a handful of other finely tuned alternatives have filtered in, and some of them are even optimized for iPad. There's absolutely nothing wrong with Safari—particularly now that it has native tabbed browsing—but there's also nothing wrong with taking a look at what other options are out there. Following are a few of my recommendations.

Skyfire

▶ Did Apple catalyze the death of Flash on mobile? Let's just say Cupertino's non-support definitely didn't help matters.

Skyfire's a potent enough rival to deserve its own space, so its own space it has. The browser app itself can be purchased for $4.99, and although it certainly has a few laudatory features—things such as a robust bookmarking system, private browsing, and mobile/desktop view switching—there's one feature in particular that put this option on the map. Apple and Adobe have long feuded over the inclusion (or exclusion, I should say) of Flash on iOS products, and now that Flash development on the mobile side has been killed, I'm guessing it's just a matter of time before web-based video transitions entirely away from Flash. That said, thousands upon thousands of websites and web videos still use Flash, and not being able to view "the whole Web" on an iPad just feels. . . wrong.

FIGURE 10-8: Safari is simple and understated, but well-refined at this point.

Skyfire adds back that crucial missing feature with just a click. There's a built-in transcoding feature that converts Flash video to HTML5, and while it's a bit clunky when trying to stream over a cellular connection, it's certainly better than staring at a "This video requires Flash." error message. Any Flash video that shows up while using Skyfire can be initiated by clicking a small pop-up icon. A few seconds later, assuming the transcode goes smoothly, it starts playing back.

If, for whatever reason, you just aren't keen on the Skyfire browsing experience, but you love the ability to play iOS-unfriendly videos, there's a similar app worth downloading. Skyfire's VideoQ ($1.99; also works with iPhone) is a video-only app that enables you to browse with another browser, but still tap into Skyfire's video transcoding magic. It works as such: If you're browsing in Safari and discover a video that won't play, simply tap Safari's Mail Link to This Page icon and send it to video@skyfire.com. If you exit and then launch the VideoQ app, the video you shot over is waiting in your queue. It's not terribly intuitive, but it does the trick. Moreover, the Hot tab shows what the masses are watching—it's a direct line to the most trending videos, without any searching necessary on your part.

iSWiFTER

Skyfire is built for playing back Flash video, but entire Flash websites still need something extra. That "extra" comes in the form of an app called iSWiFTER. It's available for free, giving you a chance to try it out for 30 minutes; after that period expires, you can pony up $4.99 to keep it active if you're satisfied. Frankly, that's a business model I wholeheartedly support. As for functionality, this app is really another browser alternative, christened as "the world's first cloud-based Flash browser."

It's designed to work in place of Safari, but rather than throwing up error messages when surfing to Flash-based websites (portals such as Hulu, Vevo, and so on), it's able to render those pages on a server in the background, and then present to you—the iPad user—a perfectly materialized view of the site. The downside? The browser as a whole is less polished than Safari, so I recommend keeping this around only when you need to view Flash-enabled sites. Furthermore, it requires a Wi-Fi connection—largely due to how much data has to be exchanged in order to make this underhanded Flash support work—so 3G/4G users won't be able to indulge. Don't expect it to work seamlessly; there's still the occasional hiccup, but it's about as streamlined as one could hope to get for supporting a platform on iOS that Apple outright refuses to play nice with.

Opera Mini

It wasn't too long ago that Opera had its own fingers crossed, waiting and praying that Opera Mini would be accepted into the App Store. It was quite the precedent-setter when Apple allowed it in, effectively giving third-party developers the green light to produce and distribute apps that directly and unequivocally compete with software that was born and bred in Cupertino. Now, it stands as one of the best alternatives to Safari, and it's absolutely free to download and enjoy.

Not only is the interface polished (see Figure 10-9), but it includes an amazing compression feature that truly sets it apart. In a world constrained by data tiers, usage limits, and overage charges, the reality is that mobile Internet users have to be mindful of how much data they're consuming. It's a drastic change in mentality from even five years ago, where unlimited data was the norm and "usage" was never even considered.

Opera Mini takes web page requests and redirects them to its own servers, where pages are compressed by up to 90 percent before they're shot back to your iPad (see the Settings option in Figure 10-10). The result? Slightly lower-quality images, but huge data usage savings. Even if you're unconcerned with usage (those who are still

▶ Keep an eye on its Data Usage Meter to see exactly how many kilobytes you're saving. Take pride in frugality!

holding onto unlimited data plans, I'm looking your way), you're probably interested in faster browsing. Given that so much less data is transmitted when browsing with Opera Mini, pages load more quickly; on crowded networks, this could be the difference between a low-fi version of your favorite website loading or a page time-out. Furthermore, the Visual Tabs feature enables users to see all of their open tabs at once and hastily switch between them, while Opera Link enables those who use Opera at home to pull in their bookmarks with just a couple of taps.

FIGURE 10-9: Opera Mini is a bit flashier than Safari.

iCab Mobile

This particular browser won't do any zany Flash tricks or completely wipe the floor with Safari, but there *are* enough unique features here to justify the $1.99 price of admission. It enables you to search within web pages, save passwords and form-fills, and even use the customizable Filters function to toggle images off completely in order to save bandwidth. Fullscreen mode gets rid of the border and toolbar areas, and the homegrown Scrollpad function allows a three-finger tap to initiate an instant scroll to anywhere on a Web page. There's also native Dropbox support, which enables you to import/export bookmarks as well as transfer downloads, images, files, and web pages to your cloud account. AirPrint is naturally supported, and there's even a way to customize how multi-finger gestures control the browsing experience.

▶ iCab Mobile also supports page compression, similar to Opera Mini, to save you precious kilobytes while browsing.

FIGURE 10-10: Pick a compression option. Any compression option.

Dolphin Browser HD

▶ Heavy users can sync their bookmarks across the iPhone, iPad, and even Android versions of Dolphin Browser.

What if Flipboard and Safari got together on a wild, carefree evening? Don't bother envisioning the lovechild—it's right here. As one of the most highly regarded free (yes, $0.00) apps on the App Store, this browser is a surefire download for those who end up using their browsing sessions to consume news more so than anything else. The unique Webzine feature (see Figure 10-11) converts the news sites and blogs you read most into ad-free magazines, right inside the browser. Better still, it's all shockingly quick, and there's even the option to create your own gestures to access the sites you adore the most.

Duet Browser

▶ Duo Browser is a free, albeit infrequently updated, alternative to Duet Browser. It also supports two browser screens at once.

There's not a lot of special sauce baked into this $2.99 app, but the one killer feature is precisely that: *killer*. Tabbed browsing—which enables users to have multiple tabs of content open across a top menu bar—has become the norm, even on the iPad. But having two separate browser windows open at the same time, on the same screen, is pretty tough to accomplish. That's where this app comes in—divvying your iPad display in order to have two web pages loaded up alongside one another. It works in both portrait and landscape modes, and each window can also play host to four tabs. If you push that limit, however, might I suggest switching to an actual laptop? Kidding! (*Sort of.*)

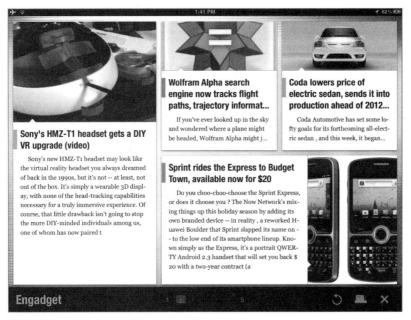

FIGURE 10-11: Webzine brings a magazine-style layout to conventional web pages.

SEARCHING FOR GREAT APPS

I'm closing by giving you a few tips on searching that tend to work quite well, regardless of what you're looking for. It's quite likely that you'll find yourself interested in related apps after diving into the laundry list given in this chapter. Question is, how do you even begin? Apple has segmented the App Store as best it can, but with well more than 100,000 apps designed *specifically* for the iPad, there's just no corralling them all.

I'd start by opening up iTunes, venturing into the iTunes Store, and looking for the App Store button along the top edge of the screen. Besides that, there's a drop-down arrow (see Figure 10-12). Give that a click, and a lengthy list of app genres and categories displays. Apple seems to be fine-tuning this list as the App Store blossoms and evolves, so you should definitely expect the list of categories to grow over time.

> **TIP** While in any section in an App Store category portal, you can find the iPad Hall of Fame in the top-right corner. That's a great overall place to start cherry-picking proven apps, and, in my experience, apps you find here are frequently updated. In other words, bugs are squashed nearly as quickly as they're found, as developers stand to lose a lot if their offerings aren't flawless.

FIGURE 10-12: Digging into the search functions within iTunes.

▶ In most sections, you can search by Featured or Name, whereas some sections add in Release Date.

From there, I suggest clicking into a category that you're interested in; you go to a portal page that features only applications from whatever segment you selected. From here, the search options really get useful. New apps are plastered across the top—this is a great place to hop into if you're religiously checking the store from week to week in order to see what new and exciting software has arrived since your last visit. If you're just looking for the best of the best regardless of age, the What's Hot and Top Charts sections generally have the highest-rated apps made most visible.

Best of all, a quick scroll down the page enables you to look only at paid apps, or only at free apps. I generally recommend a peek in the free section first; if you can find a suitable app for your existing need without having to spend any money, go for it. If you come up empty there, the paid section usually presents you with a far more robust, polished array of options. After all, the developers here know that they have to offer something quite exemplary to encourage users to buy their apps over free alternatives.

▶ Look for Great Free Apps in the right rail of any iTunes category portal. You should peek there weekly. It's like window shopping at the $0.00 Store.

If you simply have no idea where to get started, I suggest rereading this chapter on a day where your brain is a bit less frazzled. I *also* suggest visiting the iPad Apps Starter Kit, which is located in the App Store Quick Links section of the App Store in iTunes (see Figure 10-13). To get there, open iTunes, click iTunes Store → App Store and look in the top-right rail. Within is a stout collection of universally adored applications from just about every major genre. Tossing 'em all in folders is a mild nightmare, but it may be just the encouragement you needed to actually start that folder building project that I spoke of in Chapter 2.

FIGURE 10-13: Getting started with your app collection has never been easier.

Unfortunately, there's no *direct* way to force the Search box within iTunes itself to narrow a query to the particular segment that you're viewing. In other words, each search within iTunes scans the entire market place for results. You can, however, narrow these down somewhat. If you're on the hunt for apps—querying something like "biology app," for example—be sure to click Apps in the Filter by Media Type box that floats along the left edge after each search. If you're after something else—perhaps Music, Podcasts, Books, or Movies—you simply aim for the corresponding filter.

That said, there *is* a separate way to fine-tune your results. After you search, you can tap the Power Search button that sits atop the aforementioned Filter by Media Type box. The resulting box—assuming you already filtered by Apps—enables you to search specifically by keyword, developer, free or paid, and even by device compatibility (see Figure 10-14). It takes a bit of poking around to find this thing, but it's worth it for occasions when the traditional search just isn't finding what you need.

It's also highly important to peek into the iPad Apps section of results, not iPhone Apps. Although it's true that select apps are "universal" in nature and are coded to work with iPod touch, iPhone, *and* iPad, the only way to guarantee iPad support is to visit the iPad section. Any iPhone app runs on your iPad in a shrunken mode (or a "pixel doubled" mode that looks simply horrific), but it's worth aiming for programs that were designed specifically to take advantage of your tablet's screen space.

▶ If you snag a universal app such as Apple's GarageBand, one purchase gets you the app for your entire stable of iOS devices. Nice!

FIGURE 10-14: Power Searching—it does a body (and mind) good.

SUMMARY

It's an app-filled world, and the iPad's just living in it. In all seriousness, the iPad would be nothing more than a gorgeous paperweight without apps. Every ounce of its functionality is unlocked by the power of developers, and while many assume that the slate is simply a great way to consume entertainment, it's actually a potent productivity device if you have the right software.

Everything from highly specialized web browsers to educational and instructional apps are available, but wading through the more than 100,000 apps designed for iPad can be a huge chore. Apple has done a solid job in creating Best Of portals within iTunes, and I recommend that you frequent those weekly in order to see what's new and improved since your last visit. Digging into the productivity side of things is also the perfect excuse to finally buckle down and create a folder system that works for you, and generating a reliable and seamless workflow on one's iPad can end up creating a new world of free time.

It's important to remember that the apps listed here are surefire winners, but development is forging ahead each and every day. New coders are designing more intuitive ways to be productive on the iPad, and unless you develop masterful searching skills, you'll miss out on apps that are just around the bend. Keeping your toes dipped into the New section in the App Store is a great way to discover future hits before they hit the mainstream, and paying close attention to hidden gems that slip through the cracks is a great way to find, use, and promote programs that serve a given niche with poise.

CHAPTER 11

Most Effective Use of Time-Wasting (and Life-Improving) Apps

IN THIS CHAPTER

► Engaging in mindless flings
► Boosting your brain power
► Musical inclinations
► Playing with photographs
► Managing your fantasy league
► Finding your (fitness) stride

Chapter 10 focused almost entirely on iPad apps to make you more productive, or perhaps just more informed. But as any good foodie knows, the heart of the meal is only as good as the dessert that follows. The undisputable success of the App Store hinges largely on its ability to provide fast and cheap thrills (the legal kind), and if you're buying an iPad for play, this is the chapter to hone in on. Even the most dedicated of businesspeople need to blow off steam every now and then, and there's certainly nothing wrong with earmarking a Home screen or two just for non-business-related apps.

There's a litany of programs designed to do nothing more than kill time, but some of these actually pull double duty by mixing education and information into good old-fashioned fun. I'm guessing you can barely contain yourself at this point, so fire up the App Store, cancel all of your meetings for the next 24 hours, and let's get down to business. And by "business," I mean "everything but business."

MINDLESS FLINGS

Is there anything more fulfilling that opening up a folder's worth of apps that you know serve no purpose whatsoever outside of mindless entertainment? No. It's with that beautiful, wonderful fact in mind that I tackle one of the most difficult sections of this entire book. (Difficult in part because it's so hard to close the app shown in Figure 11-1.)

FIGURE 11-1: Angry Birds HD will undoubtedly make you less productive. But happier as a human.

NOTE *Productivity* is an interesting word. To some, it means inching ever closer to achieving a financial goal. To others, it simply describes the art of feeling accomplished. Most of the apps I discuss here aren't engineered to help you nail a boardroom meeting, but there's something to be said about firing up an app that brings a smile to one's face and gets the synapses firing. Unlike handheld gaming consoles, the iPad is able to wear multiple hats. The Nintendo 3DS is really only good at entertaining; the iPad, on the other hand, can entertain you for hours on end, but then you switch folders and it converts into a masterful pre-sentation tool. It's that multifaceted nature—and the truly unlimited potential in the App Store—that makes chapters like these so enthralling to write.

You laugh, but I'm actually tasked with narrowing down thousands upon thousands of incredible time-wasters into a subset that I feel best exploits the powers of the iPad. In truth, it's hard to go (*too*) wrong with time-wasters, but I'd encourage you to get your collection started with a few of my favorites:

▶ **Angry Birds HD** ($4.99): Cliché? Yes. But let's be honest—Angry Birds didn't reach its level of acclaim by simply being overhyped. This is easily one of the most addictive, rewarding, and interactive time-killers on the iPad. If you've somehow missed out on the craze, it's a (conceptually) simple title in which users fling birds at other objects and animals with the goal being to destroy all enemies with a very limited amount of flings. Despite its cleverly plain overview, it actually does a fine job teaching the effect and importance of angles, trajectories and physics. Fancy that!

▶ **Minecraft** ($6.99; also works with iPhone): This particular title took the long route to iOS, but it's having just as significant an effect here as it did on Android before it. It's a rather obscure-looking app; users take building blocks and construct "randomized worlds." You literally construct your own dream world, and if that's not a perfect method for killing time, I don't know what is. Furthermore, you can sync up with other Mincrafters on a local area network in order invite and play with friends in your own little world. Linguists may refer to this process as "extreme escapism." I prefer "awesome."

▶ **Tiny Tower** (free; also works with iPhone): Just in case you aren't getting enough building action in Minecraft (or you're hankering for a free alternative), this one absolutely fills whatever void is left. It's another low-fi construction game (see Figure 11-2), allowing iPad owners to erect a tower and then manage the businesses and digital citizens that live within. Game Center integration ensures that you know just how weak your tower is compared to the competition, and if you're sensing a bit of Sims inspiration here. . . well, let's just say you're probably onto something.

▶ **Cut the Rope HD** ($1.99): Let's set the scene: you're responsible for cutting a rope in order to drop candy into the mouth of a green alien. Period. This widely adored title epitomizes mindless entertainment, but the Game Center integration keeps you coming back for cut after cut. There's also a Lite version that costs absolutely nothing; you can try that one out before investing your $0.99, but I'll save you the trouble and confirm your greatest fear: You'll be unable to resist the full edition.

▶ **Fruit Ninja HD** ($2.99): More than ten million enthralled, totally occupied gamers can't be wrong, can they? This title is the top paid app in myriad countries, and I confess that it's a lot of fun for under three bucks. It's an action title that involves ninjas slicing fruit, with multi-fruit combos racking up major points. Throw in multi-player support through Game Center, and you've all the reason you need to exhaust your vacation days just to improve your overall rank.

FIGURE 11-2: Tiny Tower is ultra cute, and ultra addictive.

BRAIN BOLSTERERS

Looking for a few titles for which you actually need both eyes open and at least 20 percent of your brain active to enjoy? The App Store is actually home to a great number of exciting titles that also act as brain benders. Mixing education and entertainment takes a delicate development hand, but I have a handful of sure bets if you're looking to expand your horizons while passing the time on the tube.

- ▶ **Carcassonne** ($9.99; also works with iPhone): It's a classic board game title, but the execution on the iPad is just beautiful. Game Center integration enables users to play along with friends and family, or you can play with up to five locals by simply passing your iPad around. Make sure you stay sharp, though!

- ▶ **Contre Jour HD** ($2.99; also works with iPhone): This is one of the more challenging physics-based titles, and the otherworldly graphics and audio don't hurt its appeal. The game demands constant interaction, and there's Game Center integration to keep you pressing for more. As an aside, this is the perfect game to use with AirPlay mirroring; not too many titles look this good displayed on an HDTV.

- ▶ **Brain Challenge HD** ($4.99): In Brain Challenge HD there are 40 mini-games, all of which are designed to test your mental aptitude. Five different categories are covered—visual, memory, logic, math, and focus—and if you're into puzzles, you'll be at home playing this one.

- ▶ **Conundra** (free; also works with iPhone): Scared of mental commitment? I recommend starting here, given that noncommittal price. You're tasked with solving anagrams that are from six to ten letters long, with more than 1,000 puzzles to work through. The design isn't anything to write home about, but it's tough to kvetch given the gratis admission.

- ▶ **Brain Trainer Unlimited** ($49.99): Sick and tired of these other apps "attempting" to "challenge" your "amazing cranium?" Plop fifty bucks down on this one, and you have unlimited access to Brain Trainer's entire suite of scientifically designed exercises for life. Lumosity.com has worked closely with leading neuroscientists from Stanford, UCSF, and Berkeley to create a cutting-edge and clinically proven cognitive enhancement program, and that research is being brought over in this wildly sophisticated brain-training program. I can't promise that it'll improve your memory and generally enhance your life, but it'll certainly feel like a never-ending challenge, if that's what you're after.

PUZZLING PROGRAMS

Instead of reaching for the Sunday paper in an effort to get your synapses firing, you can reach for your iPad on any day that ends in "y." The App Store is chock full of mind bending puzzle apps, and I've included a few of my favorites below.

▶ **TanZen HD** ($2.99): Hailed as a game that provides "relaxing tangram puzzles," this app's good if you're looking to stretch those brain cells without stressing everything else (see Figure 11-3). More than 500 puzzles are thrown in gratis, and there's a fair bit of competition thanks to Game Center integration. Plus, there's a "Lite" version for absolutely nothing if you'd like a trial.

FIGURE 11-3: TanZen—it's a puzzle game, but with an extra dash of peace.

▶ **Unblock Me** ($0.99; also works with iPhone): If Jenga, Tetris, and that peg game at Cracker Barrel got together and decided to combine DNA, you'd end up with this. It's a beautifully simple puzzle game that requires you to get the red block out of danger in the most efficient way possible. With four levels of difficulty, the replay value is remarkably high. A free version is available for those terrified of buying anything without a trial.

▶ **World of Goo HD** ($4.99; also works on iPhone): One of the bigger, more immersive and thoroughly unorthodox puzzle games in the App Store. It's a monster of a download, but it'll reward you with hours on end of new game footage. You can compete in Game Center to craft the tallest tower of goo. Yes, I realize that sounds a bit nauseating.

▶ **Words With Friends HD** ($2.99): If you're Scrabble'd out, this is an excellent alternative for wordsmiths to get wrapped up in. The turn-based design lets you play up to 20 games simultaneously, and you're able to engage in multi-player games with friends or perfect strangers. There's even support for push notifications for alerting you when it's your turn.

▶ **Moxie 2 HD** ($2.99): It's one of the more relaxing word games, with no timer hanging over your head. You get five different game selections, a daily challenge mode, and a global leaderboard. Not like you care about *winning* or anything.

MUSICAL ENDEAVORS

There's nothing quite like using an iPad to enhance your musical aspirations. It's hard to imagine that Apple had in mind that the iPad would become a musical powerhouse, but I've seen dueling iPads used to DJ entire parties. And that's just the half of it. Third-party hardware dongles and adapters allow just about any instrument to be connected to the device, and there's an entire industry being created around music-related apps and peripherals. I touch primarily on applications in this section, but be sure to peek at Chapter 15 for recommendations on the hardware side.

Music Creation

One of the unheralded abilities of the iPad is to be an integral part of music creation and mixing. Legions of modern DJs have resorted to using the iPad as their primary source, and plenty of amateur musicians are relying on a single tablet instead of a floor full of pedals. It's actually never been easier (or more affordable) to start tinkering in the musical realm; if you've purchased an iPad, here are a few apps that'll have you humming along:

▶ **GarageBand** ($4.99; also works with iPhone): It's one of the few apps that Apple itself has designed, but this one's probably the most underpriced of them all. Anyone familiar with the desktop version of GarageBand will feel right at home here, and the iPad build is tailor made to take advantage of the enlarged touchscreen interface. Even if you're a musical newcomer, there's plenty of instrument sounds to tinker with here, and given that recording and tweaking tracks is so easy, it's the perfect way to blow off steam. Tap out drum beats, tickle the virtual ivory, mix up to eight tracks per song, and e-mail completed projects right from the app.

▶ **AmpliTube for iPad** ($19.99): What if you had hundreds of guitar effects in a pedal board that was less than two pounds and cost less than $20? In a way, that's precisely what this app is. Rather than spending hundreds (or even thousands) on multi-effect pedals, this one app enables connected guitars to have their input mutilated and tweaked to sound like just about anything—from an acoustic to a baritone metal axe. You need an iRig interface adapter (www.amplitube.com/irig) to connect your guitar or bass, but if you've been looking for an inexpensive way to track riffs, look no further.

▶ **A Noise Machine HD** ($0.99): This isn't your grandmother's music app. It's tailored for music geeks who salivate at the mere mention of "sequencing" and "bloops," but it's a wild ride in experimentation that will undoubtedly lead to the creation of music you never knew you had in you. You use your fingers to move dots to various spaces, with movements bending and tweaking outputs, rhythms, and tempo multipliers. It's a ton of fun, even if you have absolutely no idea what you're doing.

▶ **moxMatrix** ($4.99): If you're familiar with Yamaha's Tenori-on, you'll be right at home with this app. It's a bright, colorful sequencing app, enabling users to tap and un-tap in order to build interesting beats and rhythms. It's built with a matrix interface, with each track able to be customized with a sample set, transposition, scale and tone set, and mix volume.

▶ **touchAble** ($24.99): Pricey, yes, but powerful. If you're an Ableton Live user, you can now opt to use an iPad instead of a (even pricier) hardware controller. This app enables you to navigate around your Live set with the touch of a finger, tweak Live's mixer, instruments and FX with full automapping and unlimited tracks and parameters. It also enables Live users to walk away from their computers and perform Live from anywhere within Wi-Fi range while keeping latency at a minimum.

▶ **Korg iELECTRIBE** ($19.99): All of Korg's iPad apps are worthy of praise, but this one's a particular gem. It's a virtual analog beatbox that provides advanced Motion Sequencing, eight effect types, plus 64 new preset patterns. It probably best serves the advanced musical crowd, but even beginners should find plenty to tinker with.

NOTE SoundHound is a must-have for any iPad owner. It's completely free, and somehow hears songs (on the radio, from your pal who is humming in the corner, and so on) and then informs you of what the track is. After the song is identified, you also have access to lyrics and related YouTube videos.

Streaming Radio and Concerts

Remember when keeping track of your favorite artist required more than just a glimpse at their website? Now, it's even *easier*. You can both track upcoming concerts as well as use music streaming services to discover similar music you may like, all using the following handful of apps:

▶ **BandMate: Concert Tipster HD** ($2.99): Keeping up with which bands are playing in the multitude of venues near you is a royal pain; moreover, keeping up with non-local places where your favorite stars are playing is an even bigger hassle. This app solves both conundrums in one fell swoop, notifying you when a band in your iTunes library will be swinging by, and takes it one step further by alerting you to nearby shows from *similar* artists that you may like, based on what you already have on regular rotation. From within the app, you can listen to an artist's music, watch videos, purchase tickets, share via e-mail, Facebook, and Twitter, and view all upcoming shows at a venue. The only negative? Currently, it only works with major cities in the U.S., Canada, Europe, Australia, and Japan.

▶ **Pandora Radio** (free): This one needs no introduction, a fact that will simply have to serve as its introduction. It's the app that put streaming radio as we know it today on the map, enabling users to build out their own customized radio stations and hear music from related artists that they'd probably never discover otherwise. There are plenty of ads and limitations if you don't pony up a monthly fee, but some of those can be removed for as little as $3.99 per month. If you're already a Pandora subscriber on the Web, all of your stations show up when you log in on the iPad; if you create any stations on your tablet, they show up elsewhere. Thanks, Mr. Cloud.

▶ **Rdio** (free): It's an app that's quite similar to Pandora in most regards, but I tend to prefer the user interface of this one (see Figure 11-4); plus, for those into social networking, Rdio makes it remarkably easy to share what one is listening to on Facebook or Twitter. It's actually a social network itself, enabling users to follow friends and take suggestions from whatever they're

▶ Songkick Concerts is another fabulous app for tracking your favorite bands, but it hasn't been tweaked to take advantage of the iPad's display.

listening to. If you grow tired of ads and limitations, you can subscribe within the app for $14.99 per month. My suggestion? Subscribe on Rdio's website, where it costs only $9.99; the in-app subscription is presumably more to make up for Apple's cut of the deal.

FIGURE 11-4: If you haven't listened to Rdio, it's worth a listen. You never know what you'll discover.

▸ **Kazaa** (free): Most of you probably thought this name went under years ago when piracy music sites seemed to all take a hit, but it has somehow managed to find religion and slip into the App Store to offer legitimized music streaming. The interface on this app is surprisingly great, and although the $9.99 monthly fee is expected, the week-long trial that comes with every download is most certainly worth checking out.

▸ **Slacker Radio** (free): This one has been redesigned from the ground-up to look beautiful on the iPad, and yes, it's eerily similar to both Rdio and Pandora. I will say that those who prefer to put less effort into music discovery should admire Slacker, as it has more than 150 expert-programmed radio stations alongside the ability to craft your own. Per usual, a $9.99 monthly subscription fee unlocks the full potential of it. Slacker Premium Radio subscribers can cache stations, playlists, and albums to their devices to listen without a network connection, which is probably this guy's biggest strength.

TIP If you're willing to queue up an iPhone app on your iPad and deal with the non-optimized view, you have even more options to try. Last.fm, Turntable.mf, and Spotify are all in constant rotation on my iPod touch, and all work (albeit in a smaller window) on the iPad.

PHOTOGRAPHIC PLAYTIME

The camera on the iPad line (the original model notwithstanding, of course) is pretty lacklusters, and the new iPad's upgraded 5-megapixel rear-facing camera is still no replacement for a standalone camera. Additionally, taking photos with a tablet isn't exactly "widely accepted." All jesting aside, the iPad is actually quite capable of editing photos you've already taken, or photos that you pull down from your online Picasa or Flickr galleries. You could argue that the iPad's 9.7-inch panel is the ultimate canvas, and there are plenty of applications to prove that. In this section, I recommend a handful of my favorites; I leave it to you to determine whether or not photographing your next vacation with a tablet is a good idea.

▶ **Looking to get a little editing done on an upcoming flight? Sync over a recent photo gallery from your PC before you leave.**

▶ **Adobe Photoshop Express** (free): Free? Really? Sure enough, you can get a pinch of one of the world's most highly acclaimed photo-editing programs for absolutely nothing on the iPad (see Figure 11-5). You can choose from a variety of one-touch effects or simply drag your finger across the screen to crop, rotate, or adjust color. A few filters are here as well, and if you have a Photoshop.com account, you can upload your finished masterpieces.

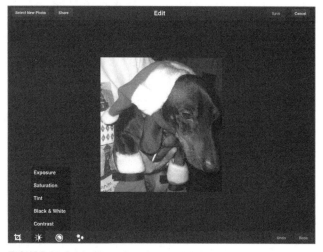

FIGURE 11-5: It's Photoshop, but on the iPad. And it's free!

▶ **PhotoPad** (free; also works with iPhone): With a price like this, it's hard not to recommend having a secondary editing application around. It's a bit simpler, but the red eye reduction tool does well when tweaking photos from cameras with harsh flashes.

▶ **Camera for iPad** ($0.99; also works with iPhone): Talk about ingenuity. If you already own a camera-equipped iPhone or iPod touch, it'll cost but $0.99 to add a camera to your original iPad. This app—when installed and run simulta-neously on two nearby iOS devices—enables the camera of one device to wire-lessly send results to another. Better still, the connected iPad actually sees what the iPhone is seeing, and you can control zooming and focus with multi-touch gestures. Just make sure your Wi-Fi and Bluetooth radios are active on both devices and be prepared for a slight bit of lag upon bootup.

▶ **iSwap Faces** ($1.99; also works with iPhone): I can't actually think of too many more ways I'd rather kill time than this. Put simply, this app makes it easy (way *too* easy) to crop and swap faces from people in a photo. Feel like tossing Marcus's mug on Jane's face? Here's your app, and I'm guessing the belly laughs you'll get from it will more than justify the entry price.

▶ **FaceGoo HD** ($2.99): Think of this as the perfect complement to iSwap Faces. It enables creative users to stretch and distort mug shots of whatever photos they take or pull in, putting a whole new spin on airbrushing someone's face "in post." The only downside? You can share your creations immediately on Facebook or Twitter, leaving plenty of opportunity for regret.

▶ **Photogene for iPad** ($2.99): This is one of the more sophisticated photo-editing apps available for iPad, and while it's obviously more of a financial burden than Photoshop Express, if you plan to heavily edit images on your tablet you will likely find the additional filters and RAW support worth the money. It also enables you to export several photos at once, and it supports a wide selection of export destinations, including Flickr, Dropbox, Facebook, Twitter, Picasa, FTP, and e-mail.

▶ **100 Cameras in 1** ($3.99): As one of the few *non*-games in Game Center, this is absolutely the paid camera app to get if you're only splurging on one. Not only can you add a hundred effects to photos you take, but you can actually "compete" on a global leaderboard based on photos taken, filters applied, and so on. Making a game out of mobile photography? It's more intriguing than you may think.

▶ **Home Decorator Pro** ($0.99): Looking for a practical approach to augmented reality? This app enables you to take a photo of any surface or wall (presumably within your home or office), and then paint the background in order to see what hue would look best. It's fairly great at avoiding objects in front of said wall, but you might have to snap it from a few angles in order to get a clean imprint.

▶ **PhotoShake!** ($1.99): Got a few photos? Got a few minutes? Then you have a collage. This app enables users to work a half-dozen or so photos into an impressive-looking collage print, and the actual construction couldn't be more enjoyable. Just select the photos you're after, shake the iPad and watch how it all . . . erm, *shakes out*. It also supports Wi-Fi import and export, social network sharing, and image filters. "Shake it like a Polaroid" has officially taken on an entirely new meaning.

SPORTING GOODS

You can definitely find your fair share of sporting news in one of the News apps listed earlier in the book, but the sophistication of sporting apps in particular warrant a breakout section. From following scores in real-time to streaming events right to your iPad's display, there's a plethora of options to keep you locked into the sporting world. I will say, however, that most of the more spectacular sports apps are limited in functionality unless you have a pay-TV subscription that includes ESPN. Cord-cutting comes at a cost, but you can square up by installing the following apps.

News and Viewing

Using the iPad to view and consume news is a very pleasant experience. In fact, it's probably more enjoyable than watching the tube, given that the entire ordeal can be customized to focus on bits you're interested in, while filtering out the noise. The following are a few of my recommendations for soaking up the latest right on your tablet:

▶ **WatchESPN** (free; also works with iPhone): Here's the good news—this app provides access to live streaming feeds from ESPN, ESPN2, ESPN3, and ESPNU. *Impressive*, no matter how you slice it. Here's the bad news—you need a pay-TV subscription on Bright House Networks, Time Warner Cable, or Verizon FiOS TV. There's no way to simply "pay" for access through the app. It's an awful ploy to keep people locked into an arcane, outdated pay-TV ecosystem that people are peeling away from, but until à la carte programming emerges in America, we're stuck with two options: Pay up or don't watch.

▶ **ScoreCenter XL** (free): The best part of this app is the newer, lower price tag, which is $0.00. ESPN has proven to be a go-to source for breaking sporting news as well as up-to-the-minute scores across just about every league you can imagine, and all of the web-based content is wrapped up here in an easy-to-digest format (see Figure 11-6). Better still, no pay-TV subscriptions are necessary to enjoy any of the material here.

FIGURE 11-6: ScoreCenter XL keeps you in every game. Especially NC State games. (Go Pack!)

▶ **Sports Illustrated** (free*): There's no charge to download the app, but you need a paid subscription to the print edition if you want to actually access the issues digitally. If you don't, you can still use the in-app purchasing functionality to buy single issues. The benefit? For one, an iPad is a lot easier to tote around than a stack of paper magazines, and furthermore, each digital issue includes more photos than the print edition, as well as slideshows, videos, and social media sharing through Facebook and Twitter.

▶ **Yahoo! Sportacular Pro** ($1.99): If it's not ESPN breaking sports-related stories, it's Yahoo!. I simply prefer the layout of this app when digging up game scores and following moment-by-moment updates on the fly, and there's a nice array of push notifications that you can enable, too. As for your fantasy teams? If you set 'em up with Yahoo!, there's a delightful amount of integration to be found.

▶ **Insert Your Favorite Team Here:** *Most*, and I emphasize "most," major professional teams have a dedicated iPad app available. Some of them are nothing more than schedules, while others have news updates, player profiles, and message boards. It's worth a search in the App Store for your team's name. And if your team's app isn't up-to-snuff, it's probably about time to reevaluate your loyalty.

Sports Games

To think that a tablet is suitable for gaming—let alone sophisticated sporting titles— is impressive in and of itself. But the truth is, many of the mainstays in the development world are investing massive resources in producing spectacular sports titles for iPad, complete with honed controls that work beautifully on the unit's touch panel. If you're a sports enthusiast, here are a few can't-miss apps:

▶ **Madden NFL** ($9.99): Every year a new Madden comes out, and every year it's worth a purchase. This game, if nothing else, takes full advantage of the iPad's touch panel and graphics processor. It looks amazing, and the controls are shockingly accurate. And for just $9.99, it's markedly cheaper than the console variants.

▶ **Tiger Woods PGA TOUR for iPad** ($4.99): It's the de facto golf title in the App Store, and Electronic Arts has been improving accuracy in the controls. Bonus: It's cheaper than a round of nine at your local club.

▶ **NBA JAM HD** ($4.99): BOOMSHAKALAKA. KABOOM. HE'S ON FIRE. One of gaming's classics is back and better than ever on the iPad, and if those three capitalized remarks didn't convince you already, it's definitely one of the best basketball games around. Just don't forget your headphones; the audio is half the fun.

▶ **Real Tennis HD** ($4.99): Perhaps more so than any other sport, tennis is just built for the iPad. Swiping and swinging go hand-in-hand, and even if you're not the biggest fan of the sport on television, it's a pretty exciting title to pick up for less than five bucks.

> **TIP** Sports games are a dime a dozen in the App Store, but if you're going to pay for any, I'd recommend looking to Gameloft and Electronic Arts. Both of those development houses have excellent reputations for producing polished, robust games.

FITNESS AND TRAINING APPS

For as long as the iPod has been around, runners have been strapping them to their arms in order to keep music rolling with each passing step. Soon, Apple realized that there was an entire niche waiting to be served by something more official, and over time, a partnership with Nike developed. The Nike+iPod arrangement has led to all manner of peripherals, sensors, and trackers, and although the iPad is obviously far too large to be taken with you on fitness assignments, it's still a useful tool for tracking runs, managing your goals, and keeping track of statistics. Here are a few surefire downloads for those who can't wait to put this chapter to bed and start another set of quad lifts.

▶ If anyone figures out how to strap an iPad onto an average bicep, please contact me immediately.

▶ **Fitness for iPad** ($2.99): This one won't do the sit-ups for you, but it'll handle just about everything else. It's pre-loaded with more than 700 video clips that demonstrate ideal exercises; think of it as a personal trainer, without the obscene monthly fees. You can find exercises for men and women, Yoga activities, a calorie counter, and the ability to tap into live support from real humans should you need to up your level of devotion. A free version is available as well; feel free to try that one first before committing.

▶ **MyNetDiary** ($9.99): It's pricy, but it's wildly comprehensive. If you're using your iPad to monitor every single calorie you decide to ingest, this is the program to have. It can store data offline, and when an Internet connection is available, you can sync data to MyNetDiary.com. The real power here is the overwhelmingly large food database, which is updated daily; just punch in what you're having, and the calculations handle themselves.

▶ **WebMD for iPad** (free): The good news here is that the app is free; the bad news is that you need a live Internet connection to access most of its features. The app is more of a website wrapper than a self-contained knowledge program (see Figure 11-7), but if WebMD attempted to shove all of the information on its site into an app, the iPad probably couldn't hold it. Still, the fitness and medical database here is world-class, and it's amazingly easy to browse using the iPad-tailored interface.

▶ **White Noise Pro** ($2.99): If you've been having trouble sleeping, and you're tired of embarrassingly shopping for those ambient nature sound albums at your local Target, this is a far more private (and way less expensive) way to get the sounds you need to rest well. The app includes 40 ambient sounds, multiple sound shutdown timers, and alarms. It enables users to create a custom playlist of sounds with different time durations. Nighty night!

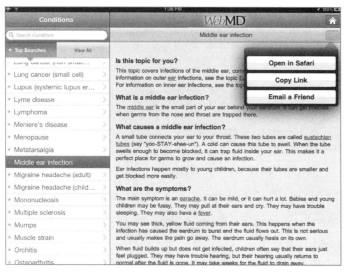

FIGURE 11-7: Oh, look—your iPad just made you a doctor.

▶ **Pocket Yoga HD** ($3.99): Thinking of starting up your own yoga routine? Not keen on heading to the park and breaking it down in front of tourists? Fret not—this one's able to give you workout tips, showcase different difficulty levels, and guide you through 27 different workouts. You even get detailed voice and visual instruction that guides you through every pose, including each inhalation and exhalation. Toss in AirPlay support, and you can pipe everything to your HDTV, making it even more useful for living room workouts.

ELEMENTS OF ENTERTAINMENT

Despite the iPad's inability to play Flash videos (natively, at least), there's a cornucopia of content available for it. Essentially, the iPad has proven to be such a force in the market that content overlords and programming providers have had little choice but to make the necessary changes in order to support distribution on the device. Streaming is clearly the way of the future when it comes to video distribution on mobile platforms, and the iPad handles a dizzying number of options. Rather than continuing to spin uncontrollably, regain some control by focusing on the apps in this section:

▶ **ABC Player for iPad** (free): Unlike a slew of other apps, this one doesn't require you to be a pay-TV subscriber to access full-length shows. So long as you're willing to watch ads, you have access to full-length episodes of

▶ Movies and YouTube are excellent apps, but both are already included in iOS 5—no separate download necessary.

Modern Family, Grey's Anatomy, Desperate Housewives, 20/20, and so on. There's also a built-in schedule, an episode guide, and a viewing history pane, and for whatever it's worth, the user interface is about as nice as they come. (See Figure 11-8.)

FIGURE 11-8: ABC Player has a UI that's so easy to navigate, a Desperate Housewife could do it.

▶ **Hulu Plus** (free*): Need I say more? The platform that largely started the modern-day Internet programming revolution has a gorgeous iPad app, but it's not worth much if you aren't paying $9.99 per month for a Hulu Plus subscription. If you are, however, a full season pass grants you access to every current season episode of top TV shows from ABC, Fox, and NBC.

▶ **Netflix** (free*): Similar to how Hulu Plus operates, you'll need a streaming account at Netflix (currently running around $8.00 per month) in order to actually view any of the content within the app. Best of all, video out is supported, so you could technically load a movie on your tablet and enjoy it on the big screen. That's the future, folks.

▶ **Movies by mSpot** (free*): It's the first major Netflix competitor worth a mention, doing effectively the same thing as the mainstay but relying more on a rental model than a subscription one. Movies rented on your iPad can also be watched on other platforms, and yes, 3G/4G streaming is supported if you have the bandwidth to burn.

▶ **i.TV** (free): You can't actually view content within this particular app, but it's a lovely TV guide program that'll clue you in as to what's coming on the tube. Moreover, it shows what's available on Netflix, Hulu, and iTunes, and it gives you the power to schedule your TiVo DVR and look up show information on IMDb and Wikipedia.

NOTE Vudu is another popular movie streaming service, but it has yet to introduce an app. Why? Because it doesn't want to share revenue with Apple, which is required with an app. Instead, it has created a beautifully appointed web app (`www.vudu.com/setup_ipad.html`), accessible via Safari, to stream high-quality movies to the iPad. Of course, you can always use the iTunes app to rent movies directly from Apple and play them back on your iPad.

HIGH-END GAMING

Traditional hand-held game consoles are certainly reeling at the thought of touch-screen-based devices (yes, like the iPad) eating their lunch. Games are easier to get (they're just a download away), they're cheaper (most are $9.99 or less), and they work on a device that folks are already toting around. There's the obvious limitation of not having a physical game controller, but Apple has done a magical job of making the touch response on the iPad worthy of praise. And, in fairness, app developers have done an incredible job developing programs with impressive control mechanisms.

The iPad's graphical engine is fairly potent—especially on the new, Retina display-equipped model—and although apps like Angry Birds HD look just fine, there are a few higher-end titles that *truly* show off its prowess. If you're looking to see just how far your jaw can drop while gaming on the iPad, pop these into your Games folder:

▶ **Mirror's Edge for iPad** ($9.99): Shockingly enough, this was a *launch title* for the iPad. But even today, it stands as an impressive example of what the tablet is capable of. It's an action title with a slew of levels, and, although the controls are challenging at first, it's an engaging and rewarding title to get wrapped up in.

▶ **Rage HD** ($1.99): It's incomprehensible that this game is only $1.99. Developed by the same company responsible for Doom and Quake, this action-shooter is widely regarded as having the most impressive graphics of any app in the entire App Store. Just try to avoid playing it while you're alone in the dark.

▶ **Infinity Blade** ($5.99; also works with iPhone): If you're looking for an epic action adventure title with drool-worthy graphics, this is your safest bet. It was built on the Unreal Engine—a platform well-known for producing visually stunning titles on PC—and the fact that it even runs on a device as mobile as the iPad is almost unbelievable.

▶ **Real Racing 2 HD** ($6.99): Not only is the iPad perfectly made for racing games (*thanks, accelerometer*), but there's something extra baked into this one that makes it worth a purchase. There's split-screen multiplayer support via HDMI or AirPlay, so if you have friends with iPads (and an HDTV nearby), you can actually bypass the whole "game console" thing. If you play online, it supports up to 16 gamers at once—no small feat for a tablet.

▶ **Dead Space for iPad** ($9.99): It isn't for the faint of heart, but if the idea of blasting through zombies that look entirely too real interests you, this app's well worth the $10. The graphics alone are worth seeing, and the storyline is engrossing regardless of platform. It might just push you to put off that impending console purchase, though.

▶ **Broken Sword: Director's Cut HD** ($5.99): It's a classic title re-envisioned, and while it's not as graphically impressive on a technical level, it's one of the most astonishingly artistic titles available. The storyline is also gripping, but it's probably not worth picking up if you're fearful of gaming-related addictions.

▶ **Pocket Legends** (free*): It's the prevailing choice for an MMO-like (Massively Multiplayer Online) experience on the iPad, and although it's free to download, you need to pony up $4.99+ via in-app purchases to pick up elements that enable you to move through the game. Have a peek at it in Figure 11-9.

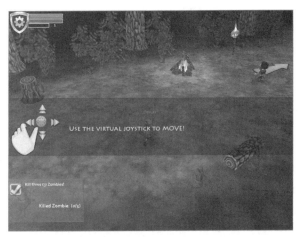

FIGURE 11-9: Pocket Legends: it starts out free, but that Platinum ain't cheap.

NAVIGATIONAL ASPIRATIONS

Due to the iPad's sheer size, you aren't apt to use it as a pure navigational tool in the way an iPod touch or iPhone would, but on the flip side, its enlarged display is primed for showcasing maps. The great news is that many of the navigational apps in the App Store function on all iOS devices, so if you're already buying one for your iPhone, you can squeeze a bit of extra utility from your slate.

- ▶ **iNavX Marine Navigation** ($49.99; also works with iPhone): One area where an enlarged display really makes sense is on a floating vessel. Pop a waterproof casing around the iPad, and it turns into a well-appointed marine navigation tool. $50 for this app probably feels steep, but if you've ever ventured into a sporting goods store in search of a boating GPS system, the price feels like a veritable bargain. It also supports waypoints and routes including KML (Google Earth) and GPX import and export, track log, measuring bearing and distance, GRIB weather forecast, tides and currents, anchor alarm, and port and navaid search.

- ▶ **MotionX GPS HD** ($1.99): A huge benefit with this app is the ability to download full maps before heading off on a trek, in turn enabling offline access to routes and trails. It can display your position and do worldwide tracking at all times on street, topography and terrain, satellite, or hybrid maps. If you're going to be using this a lot, you might want to consider a Wi-Fi + 3G/4G iPad; the GPS chip in the latter sure comes in handy when tracking waypoints in the wild.

- ▶ **TomTom U.S. and Canada** ($59.99; also works with iPhone): TomTom's stand-alone GPS interface is markedly less desirable than Garmin's UI, but the iPad interface is actually quite nice. The price of admission also includes daily free map updates, advanced lane guidance and background navigation instructions. You need an iPad Wi-Fi + 3G/4G model for the GPS chip, or else you have to pair an external GPS receiver to a Wi-Fi model.

- ▶ **BACKPACKER Map Maker** ($9.99): Although you might not be likely to use an iPad as your primary navigation tool within a motorcar, having one in your backpack while hiking is probably a smart idea, anyway. This app helps you plan backpacking and camping outings, and it's chock full of detailed, interactive topographical maps and aerial photos. You have access to nearly 70,000 of those maps throughout the U.S. and Canada, and adding and editing waypoints is as simple as touching the display. Better still, you can save trips to the cloud in order to access them from anywhere, on any machine.

SUMMARY

If you're overwhelmed by just how many apps are available to turn your iPad into a productivity powerhouse, you'll be floored when you start peeling back the other side of the proverbial onion. When it comes to gaming, entertaining, and just goofing off, the iPad has thousands upon thousands of choices. Of course, the cream of the crop can be tough to find, so in this chapter I segmented my top choices in a variety of non-business related categories.

It's important to note that productivity and wasting time aren't necessarily mutually exclusive. Many of the iPad's best games have some sort of learning aspect to them, and the built-in accelerometer adds a pinch of physics into otherwise mindless titles. More impressive than that, however, is the iPad's ability to act as a digital cutting board; there's a wealth of audio-, video-, and photo-editing programs out there, and being able to touch the content that matters to you most adds a personal feel to perfecting your work.

It's an iPad. It's fun. And it's worth spending time (and a bit of money) selecting a library of non-business apps that keep you coming back. After all, you just purchased a product that can kill time, enhance your brain, help you plan a backpacking excursion, and remove red eye from your birthday party photos. Might as well take advantage of it!

CHAPTER 12

iMessage and the Wide World of Push Notifications

A decade from now, I have to wonder whether the world will remember BBM or iMessage? BBM is short for BlackBerry Messenger, and since early 2008, it has been the crown jewel of RIM's software suite. Even today, there are millions of RIM loyalists who refuse to jump ship from BlackBerry, and routinely, I hear "BBM" as one of the primary factors for their dedication.

If you aren't familiar, BBM is effectively a supercharged SMS system. But rather than simply enabling two people to send short bursts of text to one another, BBM allows for group conversations, picture messages, voice note messages, read receipts, and a wide variety of emoticons. And trust me, the world would be a much :-('er place without those. The biggest reason for using BBM, however, just might be its ability to function over any flavor of data: 3G, 2G, 4G, Wi-Fi, you name it. The downside? It's a closed network, and only those with devices that link into BlackBerry Internet Service can indulge.

Three years later—up pops iMessage. There's no question that Apple's following the lead of services before it—BBM most notably—but iMessage has one thing going for it that similar services don't. And that thing is hundreds of millions of installed users. When looking at the iPad, iMessage delivers a service that was previously unavailable via any means. This chapter explains how short-burst messaging fits into the iPad's usage profile, how to manage multiple users, and how to put conventional text messages (mostly) to bed.

WHAT IS IMESSAGE?

Now that Apple has hundreds of millions of iOS products in the hands of users across the globe, it has a wide enough audience to launch something as closed as iMessage. Without critical mass, this service would be nearly useless. But given just how many people already own an iPod touch, iPhone, or iPad, it's markedly useful. With the introduction of iOS 5 came an all-new messaging service. It's built right into the Messaging app in iOS 5—don't bother looking for an app dubbed iMessage—and seamlessly integrates with standard text message threads that already reside there.

> **NOTE** In a world suddenly fixated on the cloud, it's becoming more and more apparent that data—not conventional voice communications—will be the leading protocol of the future. Already, VoIP services are seeing skyrocketing usage, and iMessage does a fantastic job of stealing the thunder of SMS by eliminating the requirement of a voice plan. iMessages are sent and received using data bursts— regardless of whether you're using cellular data or some other form of Wi-Fi, your messages can be sent. Even in areas where no traditional cell coverage is available, all you need is a coffee shop with a wireless signal that you can borrow, and the doors to communicate can be opened.

> ▶ You can send an iMessage to a cell phone number attached to an iPhone only. Trying to send to a non-iPhone results in futility and tears.

In addition to being able to send text-based messages as you already can through SMS (to iPhone owners), iMessage supports the sending of photos, locations, contacts, and videos (see Figure 12-1). As with BBM, this service also offers optional read receipts and delivery receipts, and as with AIM chats, you can see when the person you're corresponding with is typing a message back to you. I dig into the specifics of accounts in a bit, but for now you should know that because this is all tied to a single e-mail address, you can actually start an iMessage chat on your iPod touch, and pick it up on your iPad.

FIGURE 12-1: There goes a video—looks like the lighting was a little poor, though.

So, if iMessage is so much like BBM, why the fuss? Put simply, SMS-style notifications haven't really been possible on the iPad without using third-party services. Messaging is clearly possible through Skype, Google Voice, and other non-core apps, but you still have to be engaged in an app to communicate. iMessage is built into the fabric of iOS. It's always on, and it's always able to send and receive messages (via Push) so long as an Internet connection is present. And because it uses data exclusively, non-cellular products such as the iPad (which cannot make voice calls in the way an iPhone can) are capable of "texting" other products.

The other huge boon here is how much it can save those who are still paying for text messages. Sending out iMessages to those with iPhones can drastically cut down on how many texts are billed to your data plan. Friends don't let friends text when iMessage is available, you know?

▶ Don't bother looking for iMessage in iOS 4 or earlier; it's available only in iOS 5 and newer.

▶ iMessage works regardless of carrier or data source; if you can load Apple's homepage on a connection, you can send an iMessage.

> **TIP** Sharing is caring, is it not? Back in the day, Bluetooth transfers were all the rage, with the short-range wireless protocol called upon often in order to beam images and ringtones from one handset to another. That's still possible, mind you, but using iMessage is a drop-dead simple way to share photos and videos between iOS devices. Sure, you could do the same with e-mail, but if you're already living your life one iMessage at a time, why not spread a little visual love, too?

CROSSREF VoIP apps on the whole are described in frightening detail within Chapter 6.

UNDERSTANDING THE DEPTHS OF IMESSAGE

On an iPad, the messages you receive in the Messages app are all sent over data. The sheer omission of a voice module makes this Messages app infinitely simpler than the one on the iPhone. But still, it's a bit daunting to those who never considered that their tablet could be a communication tool, and it's worth digging into the specifics of sending and receiving messages.

▶ Remember, you can split or merge your keyboard at any time within Messages by grabbing it and pushing or pulling with your fingers.

First off, you'll need to ensure that you're connected to the Internet in some form or fashion. On an iPad Wi-Fi + 3G/4G, you can just flip on your cellular data radio in order to make contact; otherwise, you need to find a Wi-Fi signal to latch onto. From there, you need to actually ensure that iMessages are enabled. Just pop into your Settings app and then head to Messages (see Figure 12-2). That top icon (iMessage) has a toggle to the right of it; flick that to On and the journey begins.

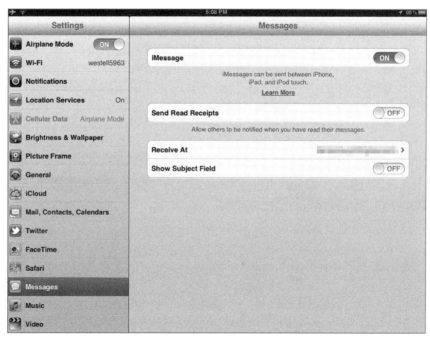

FIGURE 12-2: iMessages are active. Your social life can now commence.

TIP Crazily enough, you actually *can* send an iMessage to a phone number from within the Messages app on your iPad. In other words, if you compose a new iMessage—which requires a tap of the "pen on paper" icon to the right of the Messages banner—you can punch in an iPhone's cellular number in order to start a conversation. No extra fees are incurred on your end, though your recipient is obviously charged for receiving a text message. It's worth noting, however, that any iPhones in your household (or in your friend circle) should tweak their "Receive At" settings so that any subsequent messages use one's Apple ID—an e-mail address that takes the place of a phone number in the back-and-forth, and also keeps the conversation in sync across any iOS device that's registered with that same Apple ID.

While you're in the Settings pane, we might as well discuss those other three options. I recommend leaving Send Read Receipts off; if you flip that on, others are notified when you read their messages. Or, when looked at through a slightly more negative tint, this enables obsessive texters to know that you've read a message but haven't replied yet. *Tsk, tsk.*

Beneath that is perhaps the most important field. It's the Receive At field, and in it should be your Apple ID, *or* the e-mail address at which you want to be reached. Your life will be made infinitely simpler if you align these two, but I recommend popping in there and adding any alternate e-mail addresses that folks may think to ping you at (see Figure 12-3). For example, although your primary e-mail address may be known by many, your work e-mail address may be known by those who matter most. If you add that as an extra Receive At address, you'll be able to receive iMessages from peers that write to you at either address. Think of it this way: The more e-mail addresses you put down, the more likely it is that someone can contact you. Of course, those who'd prefer *not* to be iMessaged by colleagues can casually ignore this otherwise heartfelt advice.

▶ Yep, FaceTime also uses an e-mail address to register and verify. If you've done that, iMessage verification is no different.

Finally, the Show Subject Field should be toggled if you plan on using iMessage as more of a rapid-fire e-mail service than a short messaging service. It simply adds an extra field to each message sent, giving you the opportunity to preface whatever you're about to write with an overarching subject line. (My personal suggestion is to leave it off; if you really need a subject line, you need to head to your nearest e-mail app.)

NOTE If you'd like to add a photo or video to a message, just tap the circular camera icon to the left of your iMessage text box. From there, you have the option of capturing a photo or video (assuming your iPad has a camera), or choose an existing shot from your Camera Roll or synced photo library.

FIGURE 12-3: Add as many addresses as you have...if you want people to find you on iMessage.

Switching Accounts

Apple never seemed entirely devoted to MobileMe, and the sudden announcement of its death when iCloud hit the scene all but confirms that it never really had staying power. But if you and your family picked up a couple of MobileMe e-mail addresses, yet you share an Apple ID for iTunes purchases, things are a bit complicated. Since the launch of iCloud, those accounts were spun off into separate ones, but there's still a way to automatically download accounts that were linked by legacy. Just go to the Settings app on your iPad and find the Store option. In there, you can toggle Automatic Downloads for Music, Apps and Books. Off means that you manually sync whatever content you want to a device, though you still have access to materials in iTunes that were purchased in the family. On brings any purchase that your wife makes onto your iPad, or vice-versa. Have a look at Figure 12-4.

It's probably worth explaining why Apple had to break this out. If it didn't, family members would have each other's contacts, e-mail, Photo Stream, and calendars thanks to iCloud syncing. Naturally, that would end in tears—*or worse!*—so the Settings app was equipped with the Store option (mentioned earlier) and iCloud, where you can toggle what you want shared. Be careful when flicking those toggles mindlessly, though. If your iPad is only ever used by you, it's safe to flip any of these to On. But, if your significant other has a thing for grabbing it, signing out of your account and into hers, and then picking up her own iMessage conversations, make sure you leave all of those switched to Off. Why? If you toggle 'em on, the Apple ID is locked to your device for 90 days (chalk it up to anti-piracy measures), and furthermore, sharing across a family of devices is now restricted to only five.

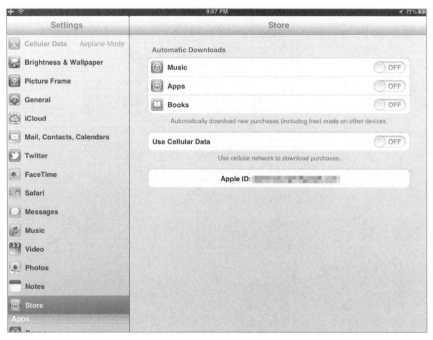

FIGURE 12-4: Keep these off unless you're okay with your Apple ID being locked to your iPad for 90 days.

NOTE In case you weren't aware, Automatic Downloads were created in order to make it easy to avoid the "conventional sync." Any app, book, or music track you download on iTunes would be automatically downloaded by your iPad so long as it was near an Internet connection. The problem, of course, is that you aren't apt to get all of your content from iTunes, so you'll almost certainly revert to that "conventional sync" in some form or another.

If you're all-in with iTunes, and you know your iPad will only ever be used by you, activating Automatic Downloads across the board might make sense. I recommend against it; Wi-Fi Sync is simplistic enough, and keeping your iPad free from 90-day locks is a huge boon if a pal needs to quickly log in to his Apple ID on your device.

Assuming your iPad is more of a family device than a personal one, it's important to know how to log out of your iMessage session and into a new one. Curiously, there's no direct way to switch accounts from within the Messages app itself. To do that, you need to visit Settings → Messages → Receive At → Apple ID. Click that, and a pop-up emerges giving you an option to Sign Out (see Figure 12-5). After you're out, another person can sign in from the same screen, and when he enters Messages, his conversation list appears. Magic, I tell you.

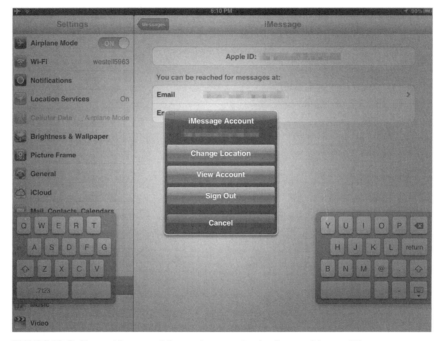

FIGURE 12-5: Sign out here, and the next person to sign in sees his own iMessages.

WARNING   If you have decided to enable Automatic Downloads (it's okay— we're all allowed to be lazy when technology enables it), you could end up in quite the pickle if a friend needs to use your iPad. After you enable Automatic Downloads, your Apple ID is "locked" to your iPad for 90 days. That's a pretty big hassle, in my opinion, and there's no overriding it without a jailbreak.

▶ Yes, you can hold a group message session with an iPod touch, iPhone 4, iPad 2 or newer, and an iPhone 4S. So long as everyone has iOS 5, you're golden.

Group Messaging

Sure, going back and forth with that cute someone you met the other day on the sub-way is enjoyable, but what if you're looking to converse with a gaggle of your besties?

Ahem—a group of colleagues all assigned to the same project. Either way, iMessage can make easy work of linking up on the fly, without everyone having to be near a computer and able to jump into an AIM conference room or the like. So long as everyone in your group has an iOS device (the mix matters not), you can start up a group conversation by simply starting a new message within Messages and pressing the + button in the top right for as many folks as you need to add.

WARNING You need to ensure you choose the right folks from the start, though. After a conversation gets underway, you can't bring a new party into it without starting an entirely new thread.

MAINTAINING YOUR CONTACTS LIST

As mentioned earlier, you can start iMessage conversations by shooting a note to someone's iPhone number, and if she has Receive At set to an e-mail address, the conversation then moves between two e-mail addresses. The easiest way to manage your contacts is to ensure that each and every one of them registers their Apple IDs as the e-mail address that you're familiar with. Of course, that's not apt to happen, so there's a trick to figuring out if someone is or isn't ready to receive iMessages based on the addresses you have stored in your Contacts.

By default, hitting the + button in Messages in order to add a recipient pulls up your Contacts list. When you select an individual with multiple contact options, you have a choice of which number or e-mail address to choose. After you select one, Messages immediately pings a back-end server to see if the method you selected has ever been activated for iMessage use. If so, it appears as a nondescript bubble with the name (see Figure 12-6), and you're free to send. If it hasn't been activated, a highly noticeable red exclamation point displays to the right of the name, letting you know ahead of time that sending your message to them will result in a non-delivery.

▶ If you try a friend's work e-mail and it shows as unregistered for iMessage, try the personal account. If that fails, call and ask. Nicely.

TIP After you've successfully initiated an iMessage conversation, you can keep returning to that thread to avoid having to remember which e-mail address was the correctly registered one. If, for whatever reason, you need to delete a thread, it's as easy as swiping right on a message thread and tapping the Delete icon that appears. Be careful, though—once a thread is gone, it's gone!

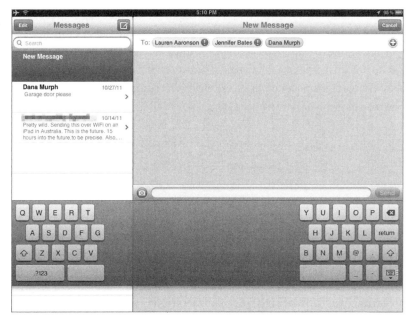

FIGURE 12-6: Two outta three ain't bad, right Meatloaf?

KEEPING NOTIFICATIONS UNDER CONTROL

One of the beautiful aspects of using iMessage is the built-in notification factor. True, you can activate similar messages for Skype and other communication apps (and I encourage you to do so!), but it's important to select the right notification options for you with any app. *Particularly* an app that specializes in back-and-forth messaging. iMessage is really only useful if you check it religiously (not recommended) or mind your alerts (recommended). Here's what I recommend.

> Try setting different alert mechanisms for FaceTime, Skype, and Messaging to help you differentiate between messages.

Visit Settings → Notifications and then tap into Messages. Make sure that Notification Center is toggled On, and in the option pane just below it I suggest you select to show 10 to 20 items. That way, older replies won't be thoroughly buried by new ones. I'm a huge fan of Banners as the Alert Style. One of my biggest gripes with iOS builds prior to iOS 5 was those pesky pop-up Alerts, which are still available as an option for those who'd prefer to keep tradition.

If you're actively using an app, a banner-style alert simply emerges at the top of the display (see Figure 12-7), shuffling the pixels just enough to momentarily grab your attention, but not completely sidetrack you from whatever it is that you were doing. As for the other options? Tweak 'em to best fit your needs; if you need the alert to repeat itself forever on end, so be it. I also strongly encourage you to flip the View in Lock Screen option to On. If you do, you can see who is messaging you even if your iPad's display is off. It's mighty handy, and you can see it in Figure 12-8.

FIGURE 12-7: Oh, look—it's the not-so-subtle iMessage hint.

FIGURE 12-8: Lock screen alerts emerge even when your iPad display is off.

SUMMARY

iMessage brings an entirely new method of communication to the iPad. It's nothing that hasn't already been done in some form or another by Skype and other VoIP applications, but the built-in nature of the program—and the fact that you have more than 200 million potential friends to chat with—makes iMessage a juggernaut in a world that's clearly in love with real-time chat. For all intents and purposes, iMessage is Apple's version of BBM, a closed messaging service made wildly popular by the maker of BlackBerry handsets.

The key to getting contacted is to add multiple Receive At e-mail addresses in Settings, and although there's no way to scan your entire Contacts list to see who is or isn't registered with iMessage, the app (which is simply titled Messages, oddly enough) is smart enough to check with Apple's servers each time you add a new recipient. If you see an ominous red exclamation point, you know that the message won't be delivered. And yes, adding multiple recipients is all that's required to start a group chat, which is great for working on group projects.

After you've started to use your iPad as a chat tool, your life is nearly complete. All that's left to reach pure and unadulterated nirvana is to set up notifications to best suit you. Thankfully, Apple provides a fair number of options, and with each beautiful bloop, you can take pleasure in chipping away at the price-prohibitive SMS market. It's the small things, you know?

Part IV

BECOMING A DIGITAL GENIUS

Social Networking Savvy

Prior to iOS 5, there was no core integration of social networking within Apple's mobile OS. There were plenty of third-party apps, sure, but nothing tied into its fabric in the way that Messages, Maps, and Twitter do now. To say that Twitter's 140-character microblogging site has become a worldwide phenomenon is a laughable understatement, and even Apple knows that it isn't apt to rival Twitter with anything of its own. (Yes, this is my gentle jab at Ping.)

With the introduction of iOS 5, Twitter became not only a recommended app, but an app with links to just about everything else in the system. If you're aiming to share anything whatsoever, Apple has made it easy to share via Twitter. It's as natural as e-mailing with the company's own Mail app. In fact, Twitter saw sign-ups increase threefold when iOS 5 was launched, as people found it convenient to register for the service that was most integrated.

Unlike Windows Phone, there's no "native" Facebook integration in iOS 5. . . yet. I suspect it's just a matter of time, and unlike with Adobe's CEO, I've seen no reason for Apple to hold a grudge with Mark Zuckerberg. That said, the iPad is a highly social tool, and there's *plenty* to be done with it in the world of sharing and networking. From learning the ins and outs of Twitter to diving into the rabbit hole of location-based deals, this chapter breaks down everything you need to know about "handles," "check-ins," and "Likes."

TAPPING INTO @TWITTER VIA iOS 5 #HOWTO

▶ Twitter trouble? Keep a check on statuses and iOS change-logs at https://support .twitter.com/.

If you're scratching your head wondering how that header got through QA, you're in the perfect place to learn. Twitter is not only an entity of its own, but it encourages a jargon and language all its own, too. It's both simple and impossible to explain. You're given 140 characters per tweet in order to make your point, and the sheer nature of that restriction forces you to get creative when thinking about how to best disseminate information.

> **TIP**   The Tweet command is always tucked within the generic iOS Share icon, which looks like a rectangle with an arrow emerging and pointing to the top-right.

As a casual browsing tool, built-in Twitter integration makes sharing stories, images, or videos with your "followers" as easy as tapping one or two icons. Interested? Getting started is as simple as opening your Settings app and visiting the Twitter banner (see Figure 13-1). From there, you can find a shortcut to download the official Twitter app (*do it!*), and beneath, you can enter your Twitter handle or sign up for one. Better still, you can add multiple accounts here, which is useful if you're the social media manager for a brand or a company. Check out the form to add an account in Figure 13-2.

> **WARNING**   Make sure you're very clear on which account is sending tweets; a business tweeting about "Bieber Fever" might not go over well. Each time you tweet from iOS, you can tap on the From field—assuming you have multiple Twitter accounts programmed—and select which one you want each tweet to be sent from. It's hard to miss, but admittedly easy to forget.

▶ When tweeting at someone, just type his name; if he's in your Contacts, the app auto-fills the Twitter handle.

I also recommend tapping the Update Contacts button. With a simple tap, your iPad uses the phone numbers and e-mail addresses in your Contacts to associate Twitter handles and profile images with your existing list of cohorts. It's worth noting, however, that this feature does *not* scour your Contacts list and then automatically follow them on Twitter. Phew.

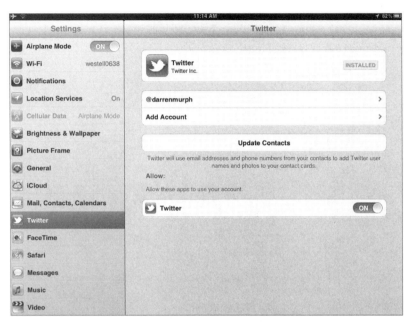

FIGURE 13-1: Setting up Twitter couldn't be easier. Doesn't even take 140 characters to explain it.

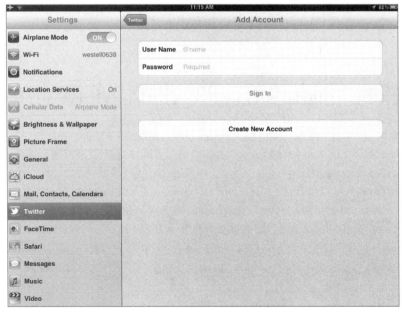

FIGURE 13-2: Punch in your Twitter credentials to add as many accounts as you need. Split personalities are welcome.

Beneath Update Contacts, still in the Settings pane, is an Allow section. What's curious about this is that a great number of Apple's own apps support Twitter, including Maps, Photos, Safari, YouTube, and Camera. But it's not until you actually open one of those apps, click the Share icon and tap Tweet that they show up in the list of apps to allow or disallow access. See Figure 13-3.

FIGURE 13-3: Not interested in enabling Twitter in certain apps? Flip 'em off! Er...switch them off.

> **TIP** If, for whatever reason, you ever need to delete your Twitter account from iOS (if you're quitting the business that owns a Twitter account that you manage, for example), it's easy to do so. Just go to Settings → Twitter, tap on the account that needs to be yanked, and touch Delete Account while waving goodbye with your free hand.

DISCOVERING THIRD-PARTY APPS THAT LOVE TWITTER

▶ Short for "application programming interface," which is code that allows app makers to build certain features.

One of the major ramifications to having an app become "native" to iOS 5 is what it means for app developers. And soon after, what that means for you—the user. With Twitter supported at an operating-system level, developers can now program their apps to support the Tweet function that Apple already includes in Maps, Safari, and so on. In other words, every single third-party app now has access to APIs that enable developers to build in a Tweet function, routing inputs through the official Twitter application.

Of course, not all apps will add support—it just doesn't make sense for some genres— but now that Apple is onboard, the floodgates here are officially open. Have a look at Twitter integration at work in Safari in Figure 13-4.

NOTE The notion that Apple thinks Twitter integration is so core to the usability of iOS 5 is proof that the devices will become increasingly less useful without an Internet connection. I've stated already that many of the iPad's best features cannot be tapped without a live feed to the World Wide Web, and it's exemplified here. All of this chapter assumes that you're online. If you're offline, Twitter can't help you. And it's a sad, sad state of affairs to boot.

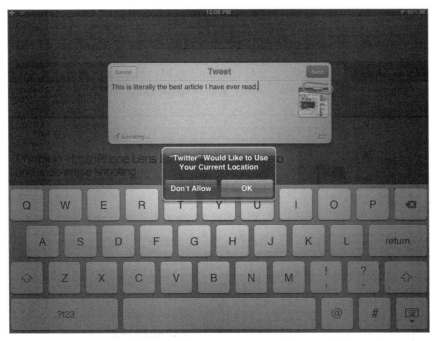

FIGURE 13-4: Tap OK if you're fine including your location with your tweet.

Developers are still working furiously to add Twitter integration to their programs, but a few choice ones are already trickling out. Here are a few of my favorites:

- **Flipboard** (free): This magazine-style reader that I recommended earlier in the book is one app that makes perfect sense for Twitter integration. As you're kicked back, reading, catching up on the day's news, having one-touch access to tweet out a link you love is brilliant. One of Twitter's biggest strengths is its ability to spread news; in turn, it works wonderfully here.

- **LivingSocial** (free): If you haven't caught on to the social networking + deals craze, you should. I discuss these types of apps as a whole in more detail later in the chapter, but suffice it to say that being able to tweet out your favorite deal could make you a local hero.

▶ **Groupon HD** (free): Same story as LivingSocial; but if you're in the mood to grab apps, go ahead and get this one downloading.

▶ **MadPad HD** ($2.99): This app is a real breath of fresh air in the App Store. You're encouraged to capture sounds from anything around you—a trash can lid, a bouncing ball, and so on—and then convert that into listenable tracks with the app. After you're ready to share your creation with a broader audience, built-in Twitter integration makes it a cinch.

▶ **PopSugar HD** (free): OMG! This is probably *the* perfect app for Twitter integration. Read the latest celebrity gossip, tweet about the latest celebrity gossip. It goes hand-in-hand, really.

▶ **Showyou** (free): If you ever doubted the power and utility of social sharing, this is the app that'll win you over. With just a single tap to sign in via Twitter, this app shows you the videos that are being viewed and shared by those you follow. It's like getting the scoop, without ever having to ask, "What are you guys talking about?"

If you're wondering how to keep track of what apps do and don't support native Twitter integration (Twitter itself is shown in Figure 13-5), there's one last app you should download. It's a freebie called Chomp, and although it's designed for use on iPod and iPhone, it serves the same purpose on iPad. After you've installed it, you tap an icon that clues you in on a Top 100 list of Twitter-friendly iOS 5 apps.

▶ The same gentleman, Jack Dorsey, created Twitter and founded Square, both of which are amazing iPad-friendly products.

Sifting through here could tip you off to socially inclined apps that you might otherwise never discover. If you're looking to see if apps you already own have been updated, just use the aforementioned Share icon and look for Twitter or Tweet to be an available option. Check it out in the Camera Roll in Figure 13-6.

WHAT ABOUT FACEBOOK?

To date, Facebook hasn't found a native home in iOS in the way that Twitter has. But to be fair, Facebook is a *far* more complex product than Twitter. The functionality list of the latter can be summed up in two or three bullet points, whereas Facebook seems to be growing into new arenas every other week. In a nutshell, it's not possible to share stories and multimedia over Facebook the same way you can with Twitter. You won't find any Share with Facebook banners popping up under a Share icon—at least not on Apple-developed apps.

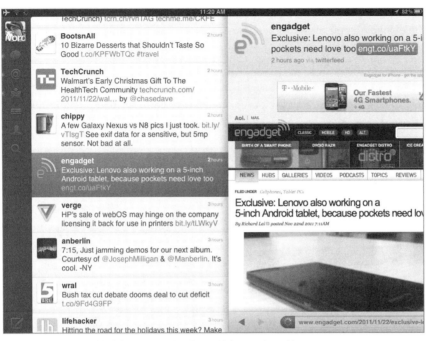

FIGURE 13-5: The iOS 5 Twitter app loading a link mentioned in a tweet.

FIGURE 13-6: His name is Pedro. How could you *not* tweet about him?

The exception to that rule comes into play when looking at third-party programs. Taptu, for example, supports both Facebook and Twitter login profiles (see Figure 13-7). So when you're skimming through news directly in that app you get Post to Twitter as well as Post to Facebook options underneath its Share icon. Third-party apps are free to integrate Facebook sharing (not to mention e-mail, LinkedIn, and a whole host of others), so if you have an app that lets you log in with your Facebook credentials, there's a better-than-average chance you can share there as well.

FIGURE 13-7: Taptu is one of many independent apps that support native Facebook sharing.

That said, Facebook finally (and when I say "finally," I genuinely mean *finally*) produced a bona fide iPad application (see Figure 13-8), and it's definitely one of the more elaborate, useful, and polished free apps in the App Store. It's gratis, so I heartily recommend that you download it, and while you won't be sharing much with it without a copy and a paste, at least iOS 5 makes even that process fairly painless.

On the plus side, the Facebook iPad app does integrate with iOS 5's Notification Center, so you can customize alerts, see how many unread messages you have by just looking at the app icon, and get alerts of incoming wall posts and the like right on your lock screen.

FIGURE 13-8: Facebook's iPad app—as useful as it is beautiful.

THOSE OTHER SOCIAL NETWORKING APPS. . .

Facebook and Twitter are mainstays, for sure, but you're selling yourself short if you stop there. The App Store is home to dozens upon dozens of other social networking and sharing applications, some of which far outclass the official Twitter app that iOS 5 relies on for integration. A few of the apps below also weave in some of the more esoteric chat protocols—fading, but not forgotten.

> ▶ **IM+** (free; see Figure 13-9): You could opt for the $9.99 Pro version to add Skype chat, but there's really no need. Download Skype for free if you're interested in doing that. IM+ has a few advertisements, but they're easy to swallow given the immense amount of functionality that's here. Rather than being a standalone app for one chat or social networking platform, IM+ enables you to punch in your credentials for Windows Live/MSN, Facebook, Yahoo!, Google Talk, AOL, ICQ, MySpace, Twitter, and Jabber—among others.

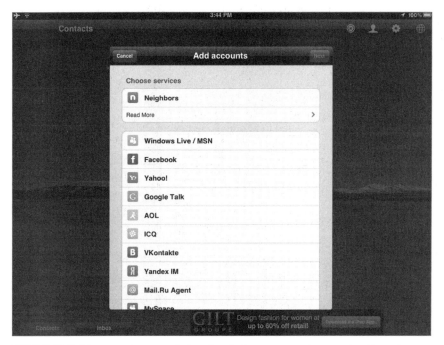

FIGURE 13-9: IM+ supports more chat protocols than any sane human should need.

▶ **GetGlue for iPad** (free): This isn't your everyday social networking tool. So long as you have a Facebook account, you can log in to the app and then "check-in" with whatever you're doing. Unlike Foursquare, which focuses on location, this app focuses on activities—listening to a certain song, watching a certain show, and so on. Then, your actions are immediately pushed out to your Facebook account, where your friends can Like your statuses and comment on them. Of course, Facebook holdouts (all six of you) can sign up for a dedicated GetGlue account.

▶ **Twitter** (free): The reason for this inclusion? Even if you have no interest in iOS 5 integration, Twitter is the most polished Twitter app for iPad. If Twitter wouldn't have purchased TweetDeck, I suspect TweetDeck's iPad app would have hung around. As it stands though, one of the best social networking apps on the iPad has been removed from the App Store following the company's acquisition by Twitter. If you're a diehard TweetDeck user on the desktop, www.tweetdeck.com still renders beautifully on Safari or Opera Mini.

▶ **Yelp** (free): Looking for a place to eat? Something to do? Real reviews from real humans? This app has it all—by the truckload, I might add. Furthermore, you can converse about your decisions through the Facebook and Twitter integration, and the iPad-specific layout makes finding things through the embedded Google Maps a cinch.

▶ **Taptu** (free): It's almost as sexy as Pulse News for iPad, but there's a social networking flair here that you shouldn't overlook. Similar to how Showyou displays videos that your friends and colleagues are viewing, this app can show you news based on what's being shared by both your Facebook *and* Twitter friends. It's a great way to engage and keep track of what your inner circle is (and isn't) paying attention to.

LOCATION-BASED NETWORKING

It's true—you aren't as likely to use an iPad over a smartphone for 100 percent of your navigational needs, but you're also highly likely to turn in new places with your tablet in tow. Location-based networking has boomed in the past few years, likely due to the growing ubiquity of mobile broadband and the rapid emergence of group-based couponing sites such as Groupon and LivingSocial (see Figure 13-10). But even if you aren't interested in saving money (or better still, *spending* money), you have plenty of options to keep yourself on the map while traveling with your iPad.

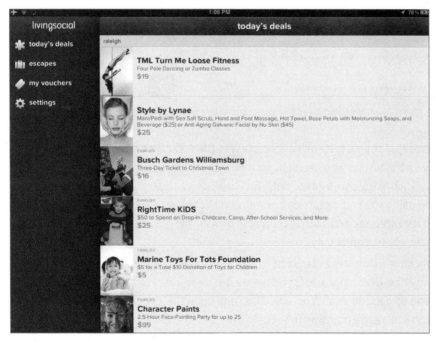

FIGURE 13-10: Just a small taste of the deals likely surrounding you right now.

iPad Check-ins

When you hear "check-in," one entity primarily comes to mind. Foursquare has yet to concoct its own iPad-specific app (an iPhone version is available, though), but the upside is that its web view is remarkable (see Figure 13-11). Simply surfing to foursquare.com using your iPad web browser of choice results in a request for your permission to share your current location. Naturally, you should grant it. Otherwise, you won't be able to share your current location.

FIGURE 13-11: If you didn't know any better, you'd swear it was an app.

> ► Gowalla, a Foursquare rival, includes travel guides to great nearby locales at gowalla.com. Its iOS 5 app should be available by the time you read this.

Foursquare supports its own proprietary login or Facebook logins, and even if you rely on the former, you can visit your Foursquare settings on any web browser in order to "link" your check-ins to both Facebook and Twitter. For example, whenever I check-in using the Foursquare app or website, those alerts are immediately published on both my Facebook and Twitter profiles, enabling me to take the conversation to two places where a great majority of my friends are.

"Checking-in" serves a couple of purposes. For one, it enables your friends and family to know where you are. If you have a few co-workers in a certain area, you might end up getting a call from one if you end up in their neck of the woods. It's also becoming a more realistic way to socially network. Prior to the check-in movement,

Facebook status updates would consist of your location details. With the advent of GPS and mapping IP addresses, you can add credence to those claims. Foursquare and its contemporaries make no bones about it—the digital badge of honor received when checking into a wild or exotic place is very real.

FINDING YOUR FRIENDS WITH FIND MY FRIENDS

It's not quite the same, but Apple's gratis Find My Friends app is a must-download for any iPad owner. It uses your contact list to sift through people you actually want to keep in touch with via location, and if your requests are granted, you soon see fellow iOS owners (and Find My Friends users) popping up on a map within the program. The major downside is that it's iOS-only, so it won't track check-ins from Foursquare, Twitter, Facebook, or elsewhere. Plus, it requires an Apple ID to sign in, so families using the same one won't be able to easily track one another unless they each sign up for a separate account.

Facebook's Move into Location

Recently, the mainstays in the check-in business have been challenged by a lurking giant: Facebook. Now that Facebook has a native iPad app, it enables users to check into nearby locales from within the app, and, of course, those check-ins can also be forced to Twitter if you'd like.

Facebook's iPad app has quickly become my go-to app when looking for friends in my area, and for check-ins in general. I suggest loading the Facebook app, tapping that three-lined icon in the top-left, and surfing to the Nearby section (see Figure 13-12). If you're connected to the Internet, a map loads showing your current location, as well as the location of friends that are near. It's a frighteningly painless way to see if any of your colleagues or childhood pals are near, and if they are, sending them a Facebook message is only a tap away.

If you'd prefer to check yourself in while you're at it—and put yourself on the visible map of those who may also be looking around for friends to ping—you can tap the Check In icon in the top-right corner (see Figure 13-13).

▶ You can also check-in while in the standard News Feed; the Check In icon is just right of center along the top bar in the app.

TIP If you pinch-to-zoom out on the map, you can get a global view of where all of your Facebook friends are checked into at the moment. For argonauts, it's a pretty amazing view, and it's exceptionally easy to access.

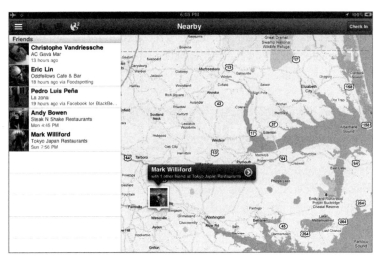

FIGURE 13-12: Facebook's Nearby section clues you in to who is where.

FIGURE 13-13: Facebook automatically pulls up nearby places where you may be, assuming you allow it to access your location.

Checking-In for Deals

Impulse buyers with a goal to stop burning up their credit cards should probably look away, or better yet, flip on over to the next chapter. Over the past couple of years, a handful of "deals" sites has cropped up with location as the focal point, and "group buying" has been fleshed out in a major way. A decade ago, the only way you were getting a bulk discount was to be a major corporation with a direct line to a major supplier, or on a smaller scale, you shopped at Sam's Club. The trouble there—outside of needing a significant amount of money to take home individual discounts—was the sheer quantity of product that you'd end up with.

Thanks to Groupon and LivingSocial (among many, many others), the cost savings of group buying have been delivered to the everyman. If you've been tuning out the noise, it works as such: Every day, both Groupon and LivingSocial work with companies small and large in major (and, increasingly, minor) areas in order to promote deals to their users. In short, these deal outlets convince companies to offer up a certain service or product at a ridiculous discount, with the understanding that hundreds—if not thousands—of people will flock in to take advantage. Some might say it's making money on quantity instead of margin; others would say it's underselling in order to build a larger, more loyal customer base.

Either way, both outfits have beautifully designed iPad apps that are most effective when you're looking for deals in proximity to you. (Groupon HD is shown in Figure 13-14.) If you show up in a new place with a bit of time to kill, firing up either of these apps can enable you to find local activities, services, and food on the cheap. It immediately takes the legwork out of discovering coupons in a new locale, and even when you're home, the coupons come to you.

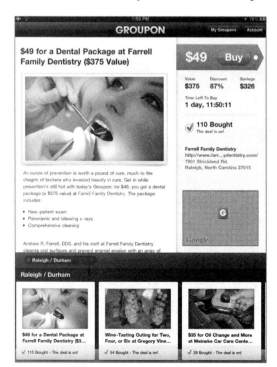

FIGURE 13-14: Groupon HD puts deals in your face. And occasionally, in your mouth.

MAKING APPS OUT OF THOSE WEB APPS

I allude to it in earlier chapters, but the iPad seems particularly primed to help those who really want to get social on the go. Gowalla, Foursquare, and a host of other fantastic services have shunned the iPad in recent years in favor of the iPhone. From a resource allocation standpoint, I get it—more people are apt to be checking in from an iPhone than an iPad. But even if no app exists for iPad, all hope is not lost.

There's generally not too many good reasons to use Safari's Add to Home Screen shortcut, but web apps are the one exception. When a company invests time in sprucing up an iPad-specific web portal that you can access via a URL within Safari, it's useful to turn the shortcut to said URL into an app icon (see Figure 13-15). To do with Foursquare, as an example, simply navigate to foursquare.com on your iPad (using Safari) and then tap the familiar Share icon just to the left of the URL address bar. After you tap Add to Home Screen, you can customize its name as it appears on your home pane. I actually went a step further and tucked the resulting icon into my Social Networking folder that I created, right alongside Groupon HD, LivingSocial, Facebook, and Twitter. (See Figure 13-16.) It's not quite the same as using a native app, but it sure beats loading up Safari and then poking around for a buried bookmark.

FIGURE 13-15: Add a web app to your Home screen if you'll be accessing it frequently.

FIGURE 13-16: Neatly organized social networking apps. Quick, tweet a picture of it!

SUMMARY

Fact is, you can find entirely too many amazing things on your iPad to not share them. Apple knows it, and deep in the back of your mind, so do you. With the introduction of iOS 5, Apple unveiled a deep level of Twitter integration, enabling a swath of its core apps to share activities on Twitter. Though Facebook was shunned, there's still an API out there that allows third-party app developers to enable easy posting to either social networking site, and Facebook's bona fide iPad app is one to be reckoned with.

Not only does it allow you to do everything you can on the desktop version of Facebook, but it also enables easy check-ins. Aside from letting you place your mug on the map, the Nearby feature elegantly shows you the most recent location of your Facebook friends. On the topic of location, Foursquare addicts are best served by creating a web app, whereas deal hounds will surely spend (and save) a small fortune with the Groupon HD and LivingSocial apps.

iCloud Integration and iTunes Match

IN THIS CHAPTER

▶ Understanding how the cloud operates
▶ Keeping your digital life in sync
▶ Managing multiple Apple IDs
▶ Comprehending compatibility
▶ Implementing iTunes Match

I've tiptoed around the cloud issue throughout this book, mentioning it here and there as a means to an end. This chapter dives headfirst into the relatively new, unexplored, and unpublicized world of consumer cloud use. In years prior, cloud services were mostly reserved for enterprise users—companies where VPN access was a requirement due to remote or traveling employees. But as the world itself becomes more mobile, there's an obvious need to jack mere consumers into this same model. Without all the headaches involved, of course.

Apple's iCloud not only takes the place of MobileMe, but it adds an entirely new layer of sync capabilities. Beyond that, iTunes Match might just be the most galvanizing creation from Apple since the iPad itself. It, along with Google Music across the way, has turned the music world on its ear, and aside from keeping your music safe from deletion and accessible wherever an Internet connection is available, it has also pushed the industry as a whole closer to the "rent, not own" model. Turns out, Apple isn't the only one piping consumers into the cloud, so I also discuss the best cloud storage iPad apps and how to best manage your iPad files across hard drives you never actually touch.

WRAPPING YOUR HEAD AROUND THE CLOUD

▶ Lots of clouds are accessed via VPN or FTP. iOS disguises the tunneling and makes it an extension of what you see locally.

What is the cloud, exactly? It's ambiguous. It's everything and nothing all at the same time. It's always online, but it's only useful when you too are online. I've probably driven you even further from what the definition of the cloud really is, but so far as the iPad is concerned, here's what you need to know. The *cloud*, as it's loosely explained, is an offsite storage location for any type of file; the trick is that the offsite locale is constantly connected to the Internet, able and willing to accept new files or upload existing ones on command.

In a sense, having access to a cloud storage device expands the amount of content that a product has access to, oftentimes exponentially. As I discussed in the opening chapter, you can't buy an iPad with more than 64GB of local capacity onboard. Because there are no expansion slots, the only way to add more material to an iPad is to either delete what you have on there to make room, or reach out to the cloud.

> **NOTE** The cloud is actually breathing new life into the iPad. As it stands, iOS 5 isn't a "true" desktop operating system. There's no file system, so storing and retrieving files is a very real challenge. The solution, it seems, is to use an Internet-accessible hard drive whenever an iPad user needs to access, edit, save, or send a file. Years back, the original iPhone OS skyrocketed to a new level of fame with the launch of the App Store; now, people can't imagine using an iOS product without having immediate access to apps. I suspect that iCloud and iTunes Match are the two new facets to Apple's mobile strategy that'll catapult iOS to the *next* level of stardom. Other platforms will "do cloud," no doubt, but the seamlessness that comes with using it within this ecosystem will be tough to match.

▶ This state is amazing. You and your iPad should go. Maybe we'll bump into each other!

Obviously, the latter is preferred, and Apple has spent years perfecting what we now know as iCloud. In fact, the company spent more than a *half billion dollars* building a monolithic data center in the mountains of North Carolina simply to make possible what it has enabled with iCloud (see the setup screen in Figure 14-1) and iTunes Match.

Outside of extending the amount of accessible content to your iPad, the cloud also serves another monumentally important purpose. It keeps your digital life in sync, across a litany of devices, without you ever having to intervene. Imagine this: You have contacts, e-mail accounts, photos, music, and videos that all matter to you. Some of it gets created and uploaded from your iPad; other stuff is created on your work PC, and more on your Mac at home. Just last year, it was an absolute nightmare attempting to keep content in sync across devices, let alone information. "Did I add this contact in my phone, but not my tablet? Does my PC need its address book updated, too?" Have a look at the initial moment of iCloud glory in Figure 14-2.

FIGURE 14-1: iCloud selection screen; seen during the initial iPad setup.

TIP Thankfully, Apple enables users to use different Apple IDs for different services; this is hugely beneficial when you'd prefer to sync music and app purchases from one "family-owned" Apple ID, but still have separate Apple IDs for programs such as FaceTime, Contacts, iMessage, iTunes Home Sharing, and Game Center. Nothing is more frustrating than your son getting your FaceTime call due to a bungled Apple ID setup. Where it's *vital* to use your own Apple ID is iCloud. If not, you'll have family members' appointments, contacts, and all manner of content overlapping your own.

FIGURE 14-2: The iCloud journey begins.

If you ensure that each computer or mobile device is linked into the cloud via the same username (or Apple ID, for the purposes of this book), "the cloud" can ensure that information uploaded from Device A is shot down to Devices B, C, D, and E without ever needing your input. Suddenly, completely disconnected devices are connected, and information that was once siloed is now readily and immediately available across an entire portfolio of products. If you need another example still, envision an e-mail being sent on your iPhone, and then needing to reference that material on your iPad moments later. Simply visit the Sent folder in the Mail app, and it's there. Now, on to setting things up so you're maximizing the effect of the cloud on your digital life. . .

WARNING While you can enter a separate Apple ID in iCloud and in the Store (where family-owned content can be shared), you *can't* place separate Apple IDs in individual iCloud services. In other words, your entire iCloud portfolio must be connected to a single Apple ID. That's fairly frustrating for families who would love to program their suite of iOS devices to share a Photo Stream, but still want to keep calendars separate.

SETTING THINGS UP

So, you're sold on using iCloud to make your life easier. Congratulations. And because I haven't already mentioned that it's 100 percent free, now is probably the time to do it. I start with explaining the setup process on the iPad, which is where you're apt to setup your contacts list, calendar, e-mail, and so on. After you've completed that setup (described in detail in the first two chapters), you need only to go to Settings → iCloud. From here, you can flip toggles to On for items you want to keep synced across devices (shown in Figure 14-3). I'm having a tough time thinking of a reason why you'd prefer to not make any of these available elsewhere, aside from perhaps Notes, which forces you to create a separate @me.com e-mail address to enable it.

► If you attempt to toggle On a section to sync with iCloud and it detects that it's too large, you get a notification right away.

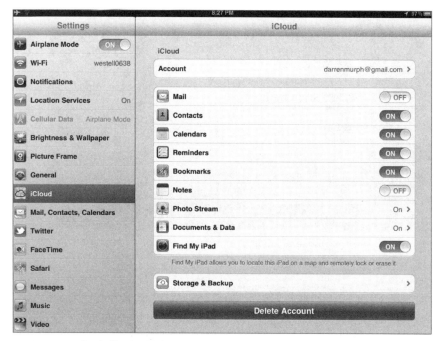

FIGURE 14-3: Don't flip that Mail switch unless you're ponying up for extra storage, or you rarely send messages.

iCloud is free for anyone that registers for an Apple ID, which you've already done when setting up your iPad or punching in payment information within iTunes to download apps. You get 5GB at no cost, and Apple even excludes your purchased music, apps, books, and TV shows, as well as your Photo Stream, from counting

► If you don't want to pay extra for more storage, make sure you only buy media from Apple. Simple solution! (Wink, wink.)

against your free storage. If you have a bulging e-mail account or gobs of music that you didn't purchase through iTunes, however, 5GB is almost certainly not enough for you (bonus storage sizes are shown in Figure 14-4). In my example, I've disabled the syncing of Mail simply because my inbox alone tips the scales at 19GB, and I haven't ponied up the extra to send it all to Apple yet. (For what it's worth, it's synced with Google's servers.)

FIGURE 14-4: Extra storage, anyone? Pony up!

NOTE As for those extra pricing options, you can buy an *extra* 10GB of iCloud storage for $20 per year, whereas another 20GB costs you $40, and an extra 50GB sets you back $100 per year. For clarity, you get to keep your initial 5GB with each of these plans.

You need to be in range of a Wi-Fi signal in order to initiate an iCloud sync. Why? You probably don't want up to 5GB of your data flying over the Internet on a 3G/4G connection. Even on so-called "unlimited" data plans grandfathered in from the earliest of iPad sales, you'll probably get a stern phone call if you push 5GB to the cloud over a cellular data network.

By default, your iPad backs up to iCloud whenever it's plugged in, locked, and connected to Wi-Fi. If you'd like to override that little list of requirements, just surf to Settings → iCloud → Storage & Backup, and tap the Back Up Now icon at the bottom. I strongly recommend that you have a strong, non-flaky connection when doing so, and if you're on a relatively slow or limited connection, I suggest backing things up overnight as to not consume the lion's share of the upload capacity. Nothing is worse than killing a friend's upload rate when you're crashing on his couch.

▶ Nothing kills the cloud buzz like a spotty connection or sluggish download rates. Time to upgrade your Internet service!

If you're wondering why Music, Apps, and Books aren't listed in the iCloud section of the Settings app, there's a perfectly good explanation for those omissions. Recall from Chapter 12 that there's a seldom-visited section of Settings called Store. Within, you'll find the missing toggle switches to the aforementioned trio, as shown in Figure 14-5. From here, you can enable any tracks, books, or apps purchased (or just downloaded, in the case of freebies) on your computer's iTunes library to be automatically pushed to your iPad. Why separate 'em from the rest of the group? If you toggle these three to On, you lock your Apple ID to this iPad for 90 days, thwarting future efforts of pals to log in—even briefly—on your iPad. In other words, think long and hard before automating those three. As beautiful as iCloud syncing is, it might be worth it to manually sync those three things in order to keep your iPad available to any and all Apple ID logins.

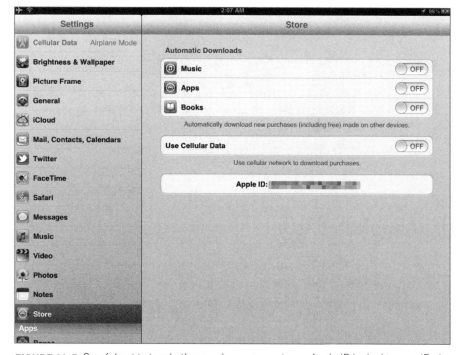

FIGURE 14-5: Careful not to toggle these unless you want your Apple ID locked to your iPad.

▶ In many cases, a single iCloud backup would generate overages on AT&T's entry-level iPad data package. Ouch.

If you *do* decide to enable them, and you own an iPad with a 3G/4G radio within it, I'd also recommend leaving the Use Cellular Data option flipped to Off. Data's expensive, particularly on the iPad, and it's a rare occasion that you'd absolutely need to suck down a song or book over the cloud when you couldn't wait for either Wi-Fi or a traditional system-to-iPad sync. Of course, the best course of action is to leave it Off by default, and then trigger it On only for occasions when you specifically want certain content purchased on another device with your Apple ID to appear instantly on your iPad.

MANAGED BACKUPS

For the control freaks in attendance (it's okay, I'm in that crowd), you might be wondering if there's any detailed mechanisms for backing up only certain aspects on your iPad to the cloud, even beyond the traditional options. Turns out, there is, but it's not particularly simple to find the options. First, go to Settings → iCloud → Storage & Backup. When you're there, the journey continues. *Exciting*! Tap Manage Storage and then your iPad, and the third bar from the top informs you of the backup size for your next backup. It's not atypical for a backup to weigh in at over 400MB. On a conventional broadband connection, that could take anywhere from a few minutes to a couple of hours, depending on your upload capabilities.

Beneath, you can tap a Show All Apps button that gives you a highly detailed look at what apps are pushing data into your iCloud, and exactly how much each app is responsible for. It's arranged to show the heaviest hitters at the top. If you're looking to lighten the load of a particular backup, you can actually toggle individual apps Off, while still backing up the data associated with the others; sure beats having to decide between backing up app data with an all-or-nothing approach.

WORKAROUNDS GALORE

As I suggested earlier, Apple IDs can be tricky to manage. The most vital thing to keep constant when you're looking to share music, app, and book downloads with family members is the Apple ID entered in the Store section of your Settings app. I recommend creating a universal family e-mail address that's used for all of your purchases, and then sharing those login credentials with your kinfolk. Remember, however, that sharing is—in theory, at least—restricted to five iOS devices per Apple ID.

This might mean that you'll be setting up a new Apple ID (see Figure 14-6) to share among family, but here's what I recommend. If your own personal ID is tied to years of purchases, make that the family ID. Then, use an alternate e-mail address of your own (a work one, perhaps) to use with your new personal services—things like FaceTime, Contacts, Calendar, and iMessage. This way, you aren't splintering iTunes purchases between an old ID and a new one. That kind of fragmentation undoubtedly introduces needless headaches into your sharing setup.

▶ If you start crafting multiple Apple IDs, make sure you keep a running list of usernames and passwords in a safe place.

FIGURE 14-6: You can enter various Apple IDs depending on the application.

If you need even more control over what's connected to what ID, you can do a number of things. For starters, you can head to the Mail, Contacts, Calendars pane within Settings and add additional iCloud accounts, toggling differing inclusions for each account. The rationale here is that one iCloud account—which syncs only Contacts and Calendars—could be shared with your children, whereas another iCloud account is used strictly to sync your e-mail, which you don't want anyone else reading.

▶ Keep in mind that only your main iCloud account can use Photo Stream, Documents & Data, and Backup.

WARNING Careful with setting up multiple devices to use the same Apple ID associated with Photo Stream. Those raunchy shots you took last night at the bar might just end up on mum's iPad. Can you say, "embarrassing?"

An important point to mention here is one that often helps basic users get around the pesky 5GB iCloud limit when involving e-mail. It's not uncommon for inboxes to exceed 20GB themselves these days, but if you're a Gmail user, you can use that service for e-mail and iCloud to back up everything else. Google keeps all of your e-mail messages in its cloud, enabling you to access them from practically any device or browser, so there's no actual need for iCloud to waste space duplicating the effort.

For those who'd rather bypass the ordeal of setting up multiple iCloud accounts, there's another card to be played if you're using Apple's @me e-mail. First off, you'll need to setup a family @me account—you can easily find that prompt in Settings → iCloud and flip the toggle on Notes from Off to On. When that's arranged, head to www.icloud.com and visit the Mail portal. Visit Preferences → Rules → Add a Rule. From here, you can create very specific forwarding rules that allow a single @me e-mail account to be tied to all family devices, but only the messages forwarded to you show up on your iOS device.

DRAGGING AND DROPPING ICLOUD DOCUMENTS

By default, Apple hasn't enabled automatic iCloud document syncing between Macs, but thanks to a handy workaround that requires only a small amount of rooting around within Lion's file system, it's completely possible.

As it stands, Documents in the Cloud doesn't allow you to do much more than upload iWork files for use with iOS products. If you'd like to use those documents on another iCloud-enabled Mac, you have to actually reach out and download the file manually using the `icloud.com` web interface. It's definitely not what I'd call "smooth" or "seamless." The solution to that—which converts Lion's file system into a Dropbox-like experience—begins with locating a Documents and Data option within iCloud preferences. When that's selected, head to ~/`Library/` `Mobile Documents`. In order to get the `Mobile Documents` folder to appear, you have to use iWork and have synced documents before over iCloud. Depending on how many iWork apps you've used, you could see a different quantity of folders here. Regardless, dropping a file into the ~/`Library/Mobile Documents` abyss automatically pushes it into that same folder on another connected Mac, effectively creating a Dropbox-like transfer. I caution you that files transferred via this method won't show up on the web interface, and I've seen reports that some files never actually arrive at their destination. When it works, it's a magical thing, but your miles may vary.

▶ The Library folder is hidden by default in OS X Lion, but there are a multitude of ways to find it. Choose your method here: www.macworld.com/ article/161156/2011/ 07/view_library_folder _in_lion.html.

TEAM PLAYERS

Any iOS 5 device is able to run iCloud, so newer iPads, iPhones, and iPod touch units should be fine. But what about the computers that run alongside of them? Apple had to make a few tough choices with iCloud—namely, that it wouldn't bring support to any OS X operating system outside of the latest. For those with OS X 10.7 (Lion), iCloud is neatly tucked within the System Preferences, under Internet & Wireless. If you peek in there, you can toggle the same expected list of programs to be synced to the cloud—Mail & Notes, Contacts, Calendars, Bookmarks (applies to Safari only), Photo Stream, Documents & Data, Back to My Mac, and Find My Mac. If enabled—for example—any contacts you add in your Mac's Contacts app automatically appear on any other iOS product (such as your iPad) and any Windows-based PC that's also tied into the ecosystem.

Yes, I said Windows. Apple threw the millions upon millions of Windows users a bone years back with the unveiling of iTunes for Windows, and it's extending the olive branch once more with iCloud. If you're using Windows 7 or Vista with Service Pack 2 installed, a 40MB download (entitled iCloud Control Panel for Windows) brings iCloud support to your machine. Believe it or not, Microsoft's *last*-generation operating system supports iCloud, but Apple has blocked all but its latest desktop OS from indulging. Make of that what you will.

> If you're using OS X 10.6.8 or earlier, you can't utilize iCloud. Sadly, you'll need to upgrade to Lion.

MAXIMIZING THE CLOUD

Think the cloud is just for keeping your contacts in order? Think again. An entire subsection of apps are emerging in order to take advantage of the iPad's iCloud and iTunes Match functionality, and none are more astounding than djay for iPad. It's a $19.99 app that enables one's iPad to be the life of the party. It's iCloud-enabled, so that tracks you build on your Mac, iPhone, or iPad are all kept in sync, with a tweak on the iPad shown immediately—in real-time—on your iPod touch. After you've spun up the tracks over the week and downloaded them from the cloud onto your iPad, you can hook it up to any number of DJ controllers in order to get the crowd moving. Learn more at **www.digitaldjtips.com/2011/10/cloud-djing-is-here/**.

> If you update to Lion for iCloud, you'll lose Rosetta support for legacy apps. Rock, meet hard place.

After the add-in is installed, Windows users can cruise to the Windows Start menu and choose Control Panel → Network and Internet → iCloud. Similar to Lion, you are then able to toggle the services you want synced with iCloud. For Mail, Contacts and Calendars & Tasks, you need Outlook 2007 or 2010 installed; Safari 5.1.1 or Internet Explorer 8 or later is required for accessing bookmarks. To enable automatic downloads for your music, apps, and books, open iTunes and click Edit → Preferences → Store. You can find more details at www.apple.com/icloud/setup/pc.html.

ICLOUD WEB APPS

I'm pretty sure you'll never leave home without your iPad, Mac, or PC, but in the unlikely event of a catastrophic brain fart, there's actually *another* way to access the information you've gathered in iCloud. Believe it or not, it's. . . *the Internet*. Apple realized that not everyone would have access to their iOS device or a compatible machine at all times, and in turn, launched icloud.com. Surfing here in any web browser prompts you to log in with your Apple ID and password, so that you can easily look at your e-mail, contacts, calendar, iWork (Pages, Numbers, and Keynote) and Find My iPhone (see Figure 14-7).

FIGURE 14-7: The icloud.com interface; clean, simple, useful.

▶ Anything you add or change on the icloud.com portal is also synced to your other iCloud devices. It's not just a read-only service.

While it's certainly convenient be able to access iCloud portals through the web, it's the Find My iPhone functionality that's truly mind-blowing. If you've enabled the awkwardly named Find My iPhone on your iPad (*do it!*), and you've logged into icloud.com with the same Apple ID as the one used on the iPad, you soon see its location emerge on a Google Map. Sure, it's an excellent way to find a tablet that accidently slid between your couch cushions, but it's an even better way to find a highly coveted product that "mysteriously vanished" on the streets of Dodgyville. After it's located, you can send a message to it (I recommend a plea to call your phone number) or make it play a sound (great for those who've simply misplaced it in the house). Have a look at the interface in Figure 14-8.

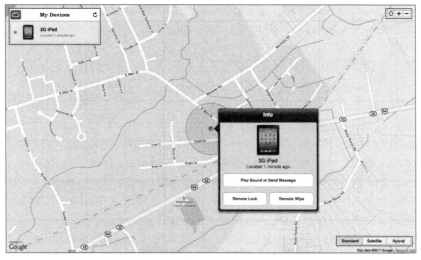

FIGURE 14-8: Hope you never have to use this, but if you do, be thankful it exists.

If things get a bit more serious, you can actually remotely lock or remotely wipe your iPad right from the web browser. Of course, you need your iPad to be connected to some form of Internet in order to get the signal across, but it's fairly unlikely that an iPad thief would yank it and never once hop online to boast about his misdeeds on Facebook. (Or just hop online, period.) If any of your requests are successful, you immediately receive an e-mail from Apple saying as much.

▶ If your iPad has been stolen and switched off, Find My iPhone displays its last known location.

There aren't too many bummers concerning iCloud's web apps, but as of now, you can't access music, photos, or videos on the web portal. It's doubly depressing when you consider that Google Music is not only fully accessible via a web browser, but Google actually optimized a portal for Safari's web browser on the iPad. That said, this may be all the reason you need to also sign up for Google's rival service—after your account is set up and your music is synced, just navigate to https://music.google.com in Safari. It automatically detects your browser type and formats accordingly.

▶ You can add Reminders from icloud.com; it's on the right rail within Calendar.

IMPLEMENTING ITUNES MATCH

Now that iCloud is squared away, it's time to make a choice. For the music you've purchased in iTunes over the years, iCloud automatically backs it all up and enables you to stream it on other iCloud-enabled products—free. But the compact disc has existed far longer than the iTunes ecosystem, and if you have many, many gigabytes of digitized music that you didn't procure from iTunes, you need iTunes Match to bring those into the same fold. Apple describes the cloud-based iTunes Match service as one that brings "the benefits of iTunes in the Cloud" to music that you didn't buy from iTunes.

Indeed, it's built right into the iTunes app on your Mac and PC, and it enables you to store your *entire* iTunes library in the cloud for $24.99 per year. Let me break that down a bit further. If you enable iTunes Match, your computer scans your iTunes library and "matches" tracks that it understands with tracks already hosted on Apple's servers. This serves a couple of purposes. For one, the version on Apple's side is a high-quality 256-Kbps AAC DRM-free music file; even if your version was ripped a decade ago at a pitiful bitrate, you can stream a version with higher fidelity.

Secondly, this *dramatically* decreases the time it takes to upload your music gallery into the cloud. I'd guess that most folks—save for those who relish the opportunity to listen only to the most obscure of tracks—can find well more than 75 percent of their music libraries automatically matched. The remaining tracks are uploaded to Apple, with your upload rates being the limiting factor. For vast, unsung libraries, it could take a week or more to get your entire library uploaded, but that's probably at the extreme end of things. Thankfully, you don't have to upload all of your tracks at once, and the upload manager intelligently resumes if the connection breaks.

> ▶ Apple's matching library currently has 20+ million songs it in. In other words, "a few."

> **TIP** Curious to know what tracks are matched and which are to be uploaded? Eager to know how your uploads are progressing? Within iTunes itself, visit the View option pane within Music, and select View Options. Tick the iCloud Download and iCloud Status selections. After you tap OK, you see a status beside each and every song, and if you want a higher-resolution version of any track on your local hard drive, just click the cloud icon beside it.

SUMMARY

Syncing is a necessary evil, even if you sync wirelessly, but Apple's taking a huge step in the direction of effortlessness with the introduction of iCloud. Setting it up is crucial for those with multiple iOS devices, and even those with Macs and PCs can take advantage of keeping their e-mail, contacts, calendars, and documents in sync. Gone are the days of manually moving files, forgetting what is stored where and never truly knowing what copy of anything is the most recent. For times where you can't access an iOS device, the `icloud.com` web interface suffices; plus, it offers an easy way to find your iPad if you misplace it.

Tackling Apple IDs can be daunting for families, but it's worth putting in the effort to segment appropriately. Careful about enabling iCloud downloads for apps, books, and music, though; enabling those locks your Apple ID to your iPad, disallowing friends to log in on your device and have their content synced, even if temporarily. Backups only apply to your main Apple ID, so if you use it across multiple devices, only those services that are using that ID are backed up. Apple's take on cloud services may be seamless to the end user, but it's not without its fair share of setup complexities.

iTunes Match takes your music library to an entirely new level, and a whole slew of devices. There's no web interface (yet), but if you pay $24.99 per year, all of your tracks are available to stream instantly from any iOS 5 device or iTunes-equipped computer. Apple even grants you access to high-resolution files, and because you can download DRM-free copies of them, this enables you to replace poor-quality rips with superior alternatives.

CHAPTER 15

Ace Accessories for Your iPad

Companies not named Apple—such as Kensington, Belkin, Case-Mate, OtterBox, Apogee, and countless others—have to love Apple. The iPad itself is but one tablet of many, but its commanding lead in terms of market share has enabled an entire industry of accessories to sprout up around it.

Make no mistake—no iPad owner will be hurting for options when it comes to peripherals, and in fact, you'll probably have to put the credit card away long before you run out of items to buy. The iPad is quite the extensible platform. With Wi-Fi and Bluetooth, you can connect a plethora of devices; everything from input products (mice and keyboards, namely) to guitar adapters.

This chapter also covers the best protective apparatuses—after all, your iPad is only as good as its overall health allows it to be. I discuss tools that are aimed at bolstering productivity, doodads that simply serve to make owners smile, and widgets that no self-proclaimed iPad addict should travel without. It's a wide, wild world out there in the land of Made for iPad products. I pinpoint the standouts for you in the pages to come.

DECIDING ON A KEYBOARD

The iPad's virtual keyboard is undoubtedly one of the best in the mobile realm, and iOS 5 even enables it to be split for easier typing with just your thumbs. But sometimes, that's just not enough. Certain keyboard commands and button combinations are nigh impossible to hit on a software keyboard, and for those actively seeking to use the iPad as a productivity tool, having a physical keyboard around certainly makes things easier. iPad-compatible keyboards come in all shapes and sizes, aimed at all sorts of different solutions.

> **NOTE** Apple designed the iPad to operate on its lonesome. The multi-touch capabilities are second to none, and in reality, you could absolutely get away without ever touching a peripheral. But you'd also be missing out on an entirely new world of possibilities. The 30-pin Dock Connector, 3.5mm headphone jack, Bluetooth radio, and Wi-Fi module might seem pretty ordinary—forgettable, no less—but these seemingly prosaic ports and protocols make it possible for the iPad to become a part of the whole, rather than the star of the show.

For example, under normal circumstances, copying and pasting requires a number of long presses and icon taps. But with a keyboard around, it's as easy as mashing Cmd + C to copy, and Cmd + V to paste. Keyboard shortcuts are a huge time saver, and those who invest the time to learn about them can enhance their efficiency greatly. For a wildly comprehensive list, bookmark this link: www.danrodney.com/mac/.

Desktop Options

Are you using your iPad in an office or another stationary setting? If so, it's probably not a bad idea to invest in a solid, more full-featured keyboard. The iPad will never truly be a replacement for a bona fide laptop, though it may work as a suitable substitute for more casual users. If you find yourself replying to e-mails or drafting basic documents more and more on your iPad while at home, here are a few options that positively improve your input efficiency.

▶ **Apple Wireless Keyboard** ($69): It's the home-crowd favorite, but there's a reason. Apple's own Bluetooth-enabled keyboard is stiff, sturdy, rigid, compact, and spun to function beautifully with OS X and iOS. The keyboard commands that make sense in a Mac world are all here, so there's no befuddling key remapping to worry over. Keyboard shortcuts that you've grown familiar with in OS X almost universally translate here, and it's certainly one of the most roomy and most comfortable options out there. To boot, those with Mac machines elsewhere can easily pair this up for use with a desktop or notebook using OS X 10.6.8 or higher. Of course, not *all* of the functions translate to the iPad—there's no Spaces or Expose function, for example—but at least Apple throws in a couple of AA batteries. Sweet, right?

▶ **Apple iPad Keyboard Dock** ($69, if you can find one): Apple made a keyboard for its first-generation iPad that included a handy docking port and stand. It's tailor made to work with the original iPad, and if you've recently picked up a used model, this one's worth searching for on eBay and in secondhand shops.

TIP Pretty much any Bluetooth keyboard suffices; if you already own one at home, pair it up and see how it works out. You may miss out on having no iPad-specific hot keys, but it's always best to make the most of what you have before spending extra on something new.

Compact and Travel-Worthy

You might say that an all-in-one case + keyboard combination is the slimmest overall option, but if you've already sunk money into a particular case, you have a healthy number of travel-worthy keyboard options to complement it. For those looking to type for multiple hours, I suggest stepping up to a desktop keyboard or a keyboard that's built into a case. But for short bursts—sessions where finger cramping isn't too likely— these pocketable alternatives are worth a look.

▶ **Bluetooth HID Wireless Keyboard Mouse Control** ($31): Hard to say who actually manufacturers this unit, but the device that won the Worst-Named Product of the Past Decade is also one that's highly useful for jet-setting iPad owners. It's barely longer than the average human hand, it's light as a feather, and should fit snugly in the rear of most pant pockets.

▶ **IOGEAR GKB601B Bluetooth Keyboard** ($44.99): It's somewhat larger than the aforementioned alternative, striking a nice balance between a full-sized option and a handheld keyboard. It also works just fine with any other Bluetooth machine you have sitting around, so it'll get exercised even when your iPad's taking a breather.

▶ **Jorno Folding Bluetooth Keyboard** ($99): It's the folding keyboard of the future. In fact, it folds up on itself, and when closed, none of the keys are exposed to the harsh, outside world. It even features a Dock Connector stand, capable of hoisting an iPod touch, iPhone, or iPad.

Keyboard Cases

Without question, the most popular form in which iPad keyboards appear is the keyboard + case combo. And for good reason. Any iPad owner with a mind to protect her investment is probably considering a case (a section that gets its own attention later in this chapter), and tucking a keyboard into a product many folks were already planning to purchase provides quite the value proposition.

In fact, I strongly recommend looking into a keyboard case over a case alone; even if you have no interest in having a keyboard at your side right now, they tend to become invaluable the more you use the iPad. The obvious downside is that most of my suggestions *do* add a bit of bulk to your overall package, but in my estimation, the boost in functionality more than makes up for the extra millimeters in thickness. Speaking of, the new iPad is marginally thicker than the iPad 2. Apple has confirmed that most iPad cases will still fit, but it's worth double-checking with each individual manufacturer before purchase.

▶ **Crux360 for iPad** ($149): It's not cheap—far from it, actually—but this case offers more protection and more functionality than many of its rivals. The case slips fully around the iPad (the original iPad isn't supported), and the keyboard itself closes atop the tablet's display when not in use. It relies on Bluetooth to connect, and it's most useful in Laptop mode. In other words, it props your iPad up in a way that the keyboard is out in front and flat on the table, much like a notebook or netbook. If you're just interested in watching a flick, flip the keyboard backward and use it as a stand.

▶ **ClamCase** ($149): These are available to suit the entire iPad family, and moreover, ship in both black and white hues to match the two available colors for the iPad itself. In many ways, the form and function of this one resembles that found in the Crux360; you can essentially turn your iPad into a netbook. But the 14 shortcut keys allow you to copy, paste, control music, and put your iPad to sleep (among other things) with a single press. If you make an effort to integrate these into your workflow, you'll be richly rewarded with loads of extra time.

▶ **Logitech Tablet Keyboard for iPad** ($69.99): The name's deceiving here. A single purchase actually nets you two products—you get a cover to protect the screen as well as a separate Bluetooth keyboard. (See Figure 15-1.) The former doubles as a kickstand, making it feasible to set your iPad up on a table and then use the keyboard for input. The downside is that you're required to haul around two different products, but the upside is significant. Not only is it half as pricey as competing options, but you can use the standalone Bluetooth keyboard with other tablets, notebooks, and desktops, too. Multimedia short-cuts are included on the keyboard, and the case/kickstand supports both horizontal and vertical orientation.

FIGURE 15-1: Logitech's Tablet Keyboard for iPad.

▶ **Logitech Keyboard Case by ZAGG** ($99.99): Not to be confused with the simi-larly named product I just mentioned, it's one of the few iPad keyboard cases that's one or the other, but never both. In other words, it's a shell that clips over the iPad's display when you're not using the product. When you are, you unclip the case and slot your iPad into it; from there, it's a kickstand and key-board at once. It's also one of the slimmest to be both a case and a keyboard, and models are available to suit different iPad models.

▶ **Solidline RightShift** ($99): Beefy. That's the word that comes to mind when gazing at this one, which wraps fully around one's iPad and unfurls to become a keyboard. That said, it's also far classier than many of the alternatives, and given that you can order it in brown, black, or red, it might be the best option for suit-donned employees who need even their iPad to be businesslike at all times. Per usual, it connects to the iPad via Bluetooth.

▶ **Adonit Writer** ($79.99 to $99.99): In a world of me-too keyboard cases, somehow this one manages to differentiate itself. The keyboard itself is staggeringly small, but it means that the entire cover is far slimmer than most of the other guys. It also triples as a kickstand, and the black and tan motif looks downright sensual.

▶ **Incase Origami Workstation** ($29.99): Already own an Apple Wireless Keyboard? If so, this is probably your least expensive option, as it's primarily a keyboard case that happens to convert into an iPad stand.

The Unorthodox Alternatives

Tired of the traditional? Looking for a keyboard with a pinch of creativity? No sweat. From bendable options to those that fold in half, I'm outlining a few of my favorites in the keyboard realm that generally don't get the attention they deserve. (Wondering what a keyboard looks like rolled up? Have a look at Figure 15-2.)

FIGURE 15-2: Scosche freeKEY, all curled up and ready to roll.

- **Acase Flexible Portable Wireless Bluetooth Keyboard** ($30): Be warned—this one's tiny and cramped—but it's also *flexible*. In other words, you can actually roll this keyboard up in the same way you'd roll a shirt while packing.

- **Menotek Flexible Bluetooth Waterproof Mini Keyboard** ($30): I'll see your flexible keyboard, and raise you a *waterproof* flexible keyboard. It's compact, it's thin and it bends. In fact, you can roll it up tight until you need it. But understand that the lack of rigidity means that the typing experience is far different, and in most ways, subpar compared to a proper keyboard.

- **Scosche freeKEY Flexible Water Resistant Keyboard** ($60): It's twice as expensive as the others, but it's a name I trust. The quality of the materials is also higher, and while it rolls up tight, the keys themselves have an above-average amount of travel. It also supports a USB connection; useful for recharging its batteries while still using it on other USB-equipped products.

- **Matias Bluetooth Folding Keyboard** ($85): The primary benefit of choosing this over one of the more compact keyboards is simple. Folded in half, this keyboard is hardly larger than some of the most diminutive Bluetooth iPad keyboards, but unfurl it and you're presented with a full-size keyboard that's ideal for long typing sessions.

- **HiPPiH iEagle Foldable Wireless Keyboard** ($100): This one is an Apple Store exclusive, and while pricey, provides a bundled carrying case as well as an iPod touch or iPhone stand for those that also own one of Apple's smaller iOS products.

STANDING TALL

Many of the best cases these days have a kickstand function built in, but if you own a case-only affair (or you just want something a little more substantial), I have a few extra recommendations.

- **Belkin Chef Stand + Stylus** ($40): If you're spending entirely too much time in the kitchen, you might consider using your iPad to look up recipes and investigate ingredients on the fly. This sturdy stand holds steady even if bumped, and the easy-to-grip stylus prevents you from having to place your greasy digits on the iPad's panel.

- **Belkin Kitchen Cabinet Mount** ($50): It's another kitchen mount, but it's useful everywhere. The clipping mechanism enables you to hoist your iPad anywhere near a cabinet, so craftspeople in workshops can easily position their guides above 'em while working (as an example).

▸ **HyperJuice Stand** ($130): The HyperJuice brand has been producing killer Mac accessories for years, and this dual-purpose stand is no exception. (See Figure 15-3.) Aside from enabling you to tilt your iPad at varying angles, it also packs a built-in 40Wh battery. In other words, you can tilt your iPad while recharging it, even if you aren't near a power outlet. (Assuming the Hyper-Juice is charged, of course.)

FIGURE 15-3: There's a battery in that stand, believe it or not.

▸ **dzdock** ($30): Handbuilt in America? Check. Machined out of metal? Check. Designed by an 11-year old? Check. It's a simplistic stand, but it's not only beautiful, it's highly functional, easy to travel with and relatively inexpensive.

▸ **Macally ViewStand** ($30): It's machined out of aluminum, so it certainly fits the iPad motif. It's also multifaceted, supporting four different views and serving as a fairly attractive desk ornament even when your iPad isn't onboard.

▸ **Jadu Industries Skadoosh** ($69.95): One of the stranger-looking stands on the market, this sophisticated contraption can grip your iPad and tilt it just enough to make for comfortable typing, or nearly vertical for watching movie clips. If you're aiming for maximum flexibility in terms of angles, this is the one to snag.

IPAD CASES FOR EVERY OCCASION

If you've already wrapped your iPad up in a keyboard case, you can bypass this section. If you're still with me, I'm using this space to showcase some of my recommendations in the booming world of iPad cases. Protecting one's slate is only half of the solution; wrapping it in something that represents you as a person is the other. The iPad exudes style. If you're going to cover any of it up in the effort of protection, you need a case that gives off its own aura of cool.

Stylized Protection

Just because you're in the market for a case doesn't mean you don't appreciate Apple's design. The case market for the iPad is a truly massive one, with everything from understated business options to homegrown fashion statements. I've chosen a few of my favorites that strike a nice balance between adding style and keeping your cargo protected. And, as I mentioned before, each member of the iPad family is a bit different in size. Check with the manufacturer before you buy to make sure the chosen case will fit your device.

- ▶ **Etch A Sketch iPad Case** ($39): It's an Etch A Sketch. But it's an iPad case. I shouldn't have to explain further, but I am going to dash some of your enthusiasm by confirming that you can't actually twist the knobs and make squiggly grey lines appear on your iPad.

- ▶ **BookBook for iPad** ($70): It's simple, yet beautiful. It's also a great way to conceal the fact that you're walking around with an iPad. TwelveSouth's book-themed case zips your iPad within, with the exterior appearing as a well-worn novel. It also folds back on itself to double as a kickstand.

- ▶ **Waterwear for iPad** ($39.95): I'm having a tough time thinking of a scenario where you'd actually need to use your iPad while underwater, but for beach-goers, having it in a dry bag is definitely a great way to guard against mishaps. This case protects the iPad from water (and sand, and who knows what else) while still allowing it to be touched.

- ▶ **Kensington SecureBack** ($79.99): If you frequently use your iPad in an office environment with lots of strangers passing by, it's probably worth strapping one of these on your prized possession. It's one of the few cases that incorporate a trusted locking system, enabling users to tether their iPads to their desks. If you rush off to a meeting and leave it behind, it can only go as far as the cable attached to it.

- **Blythe King's handmade vintage fabric cases** (varies): The major accessory makers have plenty to offer, but as is the case so often, it's the artisans that offer up the most customizable solutions. These handmade cases are a popular on craft-selling site Etsy, and you can rest assured that by purchasing one, you'll have the *only* one. Visit www.etsy.com/shop/blytheking.

- **SkoobaWrap** ($19): It looks more like a colorful napkin than an iPad case, but the Velcro corners come together to completely encase one's iPad. It's a softer option, so it won't protect from serious drops, but the fabric doubles as a polishing cloth.

- **ColcaSac** ($40+): Here's an environmentally friendly option, and a beautiful one to boot. These are colorful, patterned, soft, and handmade in Salt Lake City, Utah. They don't get much more unique than this, as you can see in Figure 15-4.

FIGURE 15-4: ColcaSac's iPad case is downright heartwarming.

The Rest of the Best

The Smart Cover protects your iPad's display, but leaves the rear completely open and susceptible to damage.

If you're craving a healthy dose of minimalism, Apple's own Smart Cover ($39 to $69) is a great option. It's available in a variety of colors, and serves a mind-boggling array of functions for being so simple. For starters, it magnetically affixes itself to the side of your iPad 2 or new iPad, making installation and removal a snap. Furthermore, iOS 5 is designed to recognize when a Smart Cover (shown in Figure 15-5) is open or closed; when you peel it back, your iPad automatically bypasses the Lock Screen. When you shut it, your iPad automatically shuts its screen off. It's worth noting that the Belkin Snap Shield (priced at around $20) is one of the few *rear* iPad covers that is compatible with Apple's Smart Cover; in other words, it allows use of two cases at the same time.

It's worth picking up a screen protector from ZAGG or Griffin, regardless of which case you choose.

The Smart Cover also folds up in a variety of forms, enabling users to create a couple of kickstand arrangements. If you're a woeful iPad 1 owner, there's great news to be had. The Smart Cover—despite being engineered to only work with the newer iPad models—actually fits beautifully on the original with a bit of work. All you need are a couple of $\frac{3}{8}'' \times \frac{3}{16}'' \times \frac{1}{32}''$ block magnets, steady hands, and a pinch of patience. Unfortunately, the Smart Cover unlock feature isn't operational on the original. You can find a full how-to guide here:

```
www.therussiansusedapencil.com/post/4000630884/
smart-cover-for-ipad-1
```

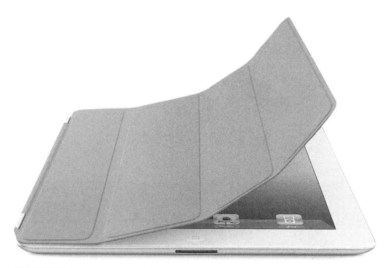

▶ InvisibleShield and NLU (BodyGuardz) sell full-iPad clear wraps that protect your device from scuffs, but they're no match for drops.

FIGURE 15-5: Apple's Smart Cover, looking smart.

As I stated from the start, the accessory market that has emerged around the iPad has led to some pretty astounding pieces of kit, one of which is the simply titled Movie Mount from Makayama (shown in Figure 15-6). At a glance, it's little more than a plastic frame to encase your iPad, but upon closer inspection, you find a pair of hot shoes for connecting lights and microphones and a mount for lenses. The idea here is to provide budding videographers with inexpensive tools to turn the iPad into a capable capturing tool, and at $69.95, all that's missing is a $4.99 download of iMovie in the App Store.

The music industry in particular has gravitated towards the iPad, with a slew of high-end, elaborate docking stations and accessories that enable the iPad to become the brains of many musical operations. Numark's iDJ Live ($100) is assuredly one of the zaniest iPad peripherals on the market, and oddly enough, is still technically a "stand." The "stand" just so happens to be attached to a pair of turntables, a mixer (with crossfader), and a slew of outputs meant to connect it to a professional audio system.

▶ ProRemote, at $100, is one of the more advanced iPad music controller interfaces, functioning with Apple Logic, ProTools, and Ableton Live.

FIGURE 15-6: Makayama's Movie Mount will make a director out of you, yet!

THE *OTHER* MUSIC DOCK

Looking for something truly outrageous? Look no further. Akai's SynthStation49 ($269) might just be the most outrageously wonderful keyboard dock ever invented. Mostly because it's not the "keyboard" you're probably thinking of. In truth, this is a musical keyboard—the "tickling the ivory" kind of keyboard—but it features a dedicated iPad dock where your tablet sits. It acts as the brains of the operation, enabling you to create all sorts of cacophonic tones with the 49 keys that sit in front of it. Learn more at **www.akaipro.com/synthstation49**.

If you're looking for a similar gizmo with a bit less size and functionality, the Ion Piano Apprentice, at $100, is my recommended ticket. Learn more at **www.ionaudio.com/products/details/piano-apprentice**.

BLUETOOTH HEADSETS AND HEADPHONES

The iPad isn't capable of making a conventional cellular call the way an iPhone can, but that doesn't mean that voice communications have been excommunicated entirely. Skype and many other VoIP apps support voice calling, and rather than yelling at your iPad in an effort to speak with someone on the other end, pairing up a Bluetooth headset can make for a far more peaceful experience.

Trouble is, there are literally hundreds of options—all sorts of shapes and sizes, and all sorts of confusion surrounding them. I recommend that you stop fretting and pick either the Samsung HM7000 ($100) or the BlueAnt Q2 ($100). Both of these have exceptional audio quality; I'd suggest picking whichever design floats your boat and calling it a day.

From a listening standpoint, there's AirPlay. But if you're aiming for something a little more personal (yet equally wireless in nature), a set of Bluetooth headphones are your best bet. Jaybird's JF3 Freedom Bluetooth stereo headset ($100) is a lovely option, with outstanding audio quality and a remarkably unobtrusive design. Veho's Bluetooth cans ($110) offer a differently styled solution, and the fold-up design makes them perfect for travel.

▶ The iPad doesn't ship with any headphones—wired or wireless—so you'll be providing your own regardless.

▶ Sadly, the iPad has a tough time syncing with many Bluetooth-enabled car audio systems.

HACKS AND WORKAROUNDS

Although Bluetooth keyboards, headsets, and headphones work without any trickeration, you're probably wondering if the keyboard's best mate—the mouse—has a place in iOS's heart. Unfortunately, it doesn't. Not according to Apple, anyway. iOS was designed to be controlled completely and entirely by touch, and in a touchable world, a mouse cursor just doesn't have a home.

Just because Apple doesn't support Bluetooth mouse input by default, it doesn't mean that all hope is lost. If you're willing to jailbreak your device, search for and install the BTstack Mouse app. When it's installed, your iPad should automatically recognize Apple's Magic Mouse, Magic Trackpad, and pretty much any other Bluetooth mouse you have hanging around. You can find video demonstrations of the hack in action here:

▶ With every successive iOS update, Apple usually thwarts the latest jailbreak; it usually takes a month or so for the jailbreak community to override it.

    www.redmondpie.com/control-ipad-with-magic-mouse-9140743/

NOTE If you'd prefer to use your iPad to control accessories on the other side—yes, even on the *PC*—I have a handful of app downloads that even a non-jailbroken iPad can use. I-Clickr PowerPoint Remote for iPad ($10) is a stellar app for converting your iPad into a presentation remote, while TouchOSC ($5), DiddyMidiDJ ($5), and AC-7 Pro Control Surface ($10) are all useful for controlling audio programs.

Picking up a Bluetooth headset to make Skype calls is ideal, but it's an expensive endeavor. If you also own an iPhone, and you've managed to not lose the stock set of headphones that came with it, you have all you need. That set, with its inline remote and microphone, works just fine when used with Skype on the iPad. Sharing is caring!

UTILIZING THE DOCK CONNECTOR

If you're ambitious, you can find aftermarket versions of this with many more inputs, including video out, micro-USB, and CompactFlash.

The 30-pin Dock Connector situated on the bottom of every iOS device in recent memory has become a commonly accepted protocol. On the iPad, it serves myriad purposes, and Apple's $29 iPad Camera Connection Kit is one of the first apparatuses I'd recommend buying.

Without any trickery at all, the device (see Figure 15-7) allows for images to be instantly loaded into the iPad's photo album off of Secure Digital (SD) cards or USB connections. By default, the adapters support standard photo formats, including JPEG and RAW, along with SD and HD video formats, including H.264 and MPEG-4. By this point, you shouldn't be surprised to hear that Apple's standard functionality is only part of the fun. A (now-aged) hack enables the USB adapter included in the kit to facilitate the connection of an external USB hard drive. You need a jailbroken iPad, a special split-USB cable to provide enough juice to the HDD, and a spare computer to complete the trick. Your miles may vary (much like the creator's ambition to further develop the process), but you can find a full walkthrough at http://time-more.com/ipad.

FIGURE 15-7: The two-piece iPad Camera Connection Kit...not as powerful as it once was.

If you're willing to spend a bit of cash, there's actually a legitimate solution that allows a hard drive to be recognized by an iPad. Sanho's HyperDrive is hailed as "the world's first and only iPad-compatible hard drive," and it's available in a variety of capacities. The basic HyperDrive HDD case—which allows you to install your own 2.5-inch hard drive—costs $90, while 500GB, 750GB, and 1TB versions are available for between $240 and $390. The company also offers the HyperSpace Color; it can also be recognized by the iPad, but has a full-color display integrated into it in order to sift through content without having to connect it to a host device.

Users can load all manners of content—videos, images, and so on—onto these drives, and when you connect them to the iPad's Dock Connector, they're made available and accessible on the iPad. No jailbreaking required; it just works.

> Sanho's HyperDrive iFlashDrive works the same way, but houses up to 32GB on a USB key; it's far more compact.

POWERING DOWN

Prior to the introduction of iOS 4.2, the USB adapter in the bundle supported USB keyboards, microphones, and a whole host of other USB accessories and instruments. For reasons unknown, certain changes in iOS 4.2 forced the adapter to provide only 20mA—down from 100mA. That power reduction made it impossible for most accessories to work as they had in a pre-iOS 4.2 world. For shame.

The SD card adapter has another useful feature. Although it's designed to play back videos shot on your digital camera, you can actually trick the iPad to play back any video file. If you have a DVD, you can rip it and convert it to H.264 (HandBrake works excellently for OS X systems). From there, just drop the resulting video file into the DCIM folder on your SD card. When you plug that SD card into your iPad via the adapter dongle, you're able to play back the video and import it onto your iPad.

The downside, if there is one, is that the adapter assumes this is just a video shot on a camera. Thus, it's stored in the Photos app instead of the Videos app, which means that chapter navigation is lost, and you can't pick up playback where you left off should you exit the video. That said, it's still a fantastic unadvertised feature, and it's a stellar way to load multiple videos for viewing on your iPad if you're running out of storage on the iPad itself.

If you're looking to grab a microphone that connects directly into the iPad's Dock Connector, you have a smattering of great options. Soulo (http://soulo.com/)

is ideal for amateurs looking to engage in digital karaoke, whereas Tascam's iM2 (`http://tascam.com/product/im2/overview/`) is ideal for recording sound checks or live concerts. The upcoming Apogee Mic (`www.apogeedigital.com/products/mic.php`) looks to be perfect for podcasters hoping to record their buttery smooth vocals right on the iPad.

Moving over to video, there are a couple of wired adapters that some may prefer over AirPlay. I've had good luck with it, but as with any wireless technology, dropouts and stutters are more apt to occur with AirPlay than with hardwired solutions. Apple's $39 Digital AV Adapter pipes content over HDMI, while the $29 Apple VGA Adapter lets you output video over a VGA connection, albeit at a lower resolution. If those aren't enough, the $39 Apple Component AV Cable and $39 Apple Composite AV Cable output video from compatible apps.

NEXT-LEVEL ACCESSORIES

Enough with this whole "productivity" thing. At its core, the iPad's all about fun, and there are *plenty* of completely unbelievable, thoroughly amazing accessories to bring out the kid in any owner. If you can dream it up, it probably exists, and I've listed a number of my favorites here:

- **ION Audio iCade** ($99): Regardless of whether you grew up in the age of Pac-Man, this is an absolute must-have for retro gamers. The iCade is a bona fide miniature arcade cabinet that comes to life as soon as your iPad is slapped within, enabling a real-deal joystick and accompanying buttons to control the gameplay of a slew of Atari's Greatest Hits. (See Figure 15-8.)

- **Sonoma GuitarJack** ($149): Plug it into your Dock Connector, and you get an audio interface that plays nice with a wide range of instruments, microphones and other audio via ¼-inch instrument and ⅛-inch stereo mic/line inputs. It's hailed as the first device-powered iOS accessory that offers stereo recording, simultaneous voice and instrument recording, 60 dB of continuous level control, configurable Pad, Lo-Z and Hi-Z modes, and increased drive for headphones.

- **Logitech Joystick for iPad** ($20): It's as simple a peripheral as there ever will be, but it's a huge asset to gamers who play titles with a faux D-pad in either screen corner. You can move this suctioned joystick about to fit the user interface of any game you play, providing a more realistic joystick feel. Just remember to order a pair if you play titles with dual D-pads.

FIGURE 15-8: Your iPad has never looked so comfortable.

▶ **ThinkFlood RedEye mini** ($49): Plug this bantam dongle into your headphone jack, open the RedEye application (free), and you're on your way to controlling every A/V component in your living room via Infrared. The app is powerful enough to control your TV, AV receiver, Blu-ray player, and nearly anything else that supports IR, and the app allows for full customization in order to establish macros and multi-component commands.

▶ **GameChanger game board for iPad** ($80): It's the first game board to integrate the iPad as an integral part of game play; instead of spinning a conventional wheel, you're able to spin a virtual one on the iPad, while the physical component of moving pieces remains. Call it the perfect blend of old school and new.

▶ **Seagate GoFlex Satellite** ($200): It's a 500GB, USB-powered, battery-equipped hard drive, but the internal file system and built-in Wi-Fi module enables the unit to stream videos, music, and photos to your iPad...*sans cabling*. It can stream for up to five hours before needing a recharge; and yes, it works perfectly fine as a traditional hard drive all the while.

SUMMARY

Be it a case, a keyboard, or one of a million things that are meant to be plugged into the iPad's Dock Connector port, you won't have any issues outfitting your tablet with appropriate accessories. Cutting through the noise and finding peripherals as well built as the iPad itself, however, requires a good amount of research. Budgeting for a case and a keyboard makes a lot of sense for those who are aiming to protect their investment and enhance their productivity; and while a part of you may cringe at covering up Apple's own industrial design, there are plenty of covers and sleeves out there that actually make the product more personal.

CHAPTER 16

Troubleshooting and Jailbreaking

Ask twenty people, and you're bound to find one who swears up and down that Apple products simply never have issues. "That's a Windows thing," they'll say. Candidly, Windows has garnered that reputation for a reason, but Apple has most certainly not earned a gold star in Never Failing 101.

In my experience, Apple products have failed (and even faltered) less frequently than their Windows-based counterparts, though I suspect much of that is due to the overwhelming amount of malware that targets the operating system with the lion's share of users. On the tablet side, however, using the iPad is by far a smoother experience than that offered up by Windows-based alternatives. Put simply, Windows isn't engineered for tablets; iOS is.

I say all that to bring into focus just how rare it is for serious problems to arise on the iPad, but to say problems are nonexistent would be fibbing. In this chapter, I walk through some of the most common uncommon issues, as well as how to get around them, through them, or over them. I also discuss recovery and DFU modes (useful for getting yourself out of binds) and the iPad's unique charging requirements. Finally, I talk about the murky, innovative world of jailbreaking—an action not smiled upon by Apple, but one that can be remarkably enlightening if done with precaution and care.

JAILBREAKING

▶ If you're familiar with "rooting" on the Android side, this is the iOS equivalent.

The mere mention of the word sends shudders down the spines of those who've been burnt by hacks gone wrong before, and to everyone else, it just *sounds* illegal. Perhaps it's the unadulterated use of "jail," or maybe it's the allusion to something going wrong— "breaking." Either way, it's a choice word used to describe an admittedly dangerous technique that gives the end user an unprecedented amount of access to an operating system that ships with extremely rigid rules from the factory.

▶ Apple has actually battled this ruling. Meanwhile, rival Microsoft is openly allowing people to hack the Kinect. Clearly, different mindsets.

As it stands, an iPad can only run programs that are deemed fit and not harmful by Apple. There's precisely one place to go to source an app, and that's Apple's own App Store. On one hand, it oozes simplicity. On the other, it makes the pondering man wonder what all he's missing. Turns out, there is a smattering of other app stores in existence—none of which are approved (or even publicly recognized) by the folks in Cupertino. You may feel dirty even reading into this as far as you have, but fret not; under the Digital Millennium Copyright Act, jailbreaking Apple devices is legal in the United States of America, but Apple makes crystal clear that doing so could void your iPad's warranty.

Why Even Bother?

It's a question I get often: "What do I gain from jailbreaking? Is it worth it? Why should I risk it? What's the first thing I should do if I end up going through with it?" The amount of mystery and intrigue surrounding the art of jailbreaking is actually quite impressive. Almost everyone who owns an iOS device has at least heard casual mention of it, but only the brave dare open up the web browser to search for more information on it.

The reality is quite different than the common line that you hear. Much like the term "hacking" gets a sour reputation, there are a great number of positive, non-harmful things that iPad owners can do by jailbreaking. Beyond the whole "additional access to apps" thing—which I dive into shortly—one of the primary reasons for jailbreaking was to unlock iPhone handsets for use on any carrier worldwide. In fact, that tidbit alone was monumental in keeping jailbreaking legal.

> **NOTE** Apple's systems have been historically closed, even when they're "open." Take FaceTime, for example. Apple claims that it's an open standard, but to date, no other company has actually integrated it into a shipping product. iTunes might sell DRM-free music, but unless you procure your tunes directly from Apple's music shop, iTunes in the Cloud won't do you any good. (Without paying $24.99 per year for iTunes Match, anyway.) iOS is pretty well sealed, but a rabid community of jailbreakers somehow manages to tear through its seams like clockwork, opening access to uncertified stores and wild applications that most common consumers don't even know exist. It's an underground world, but one worth exploring given the right preparations.

Of course, the iPad isn't capable of making voice calls, and moreover, doesn't suffer the same carrier-locked fate as U.S.-bound iPhones. All members of the iPad family are sold sans carrier lock; that means that the AT&T iPad Wi-Fi + 3G/4G can have its SIM card removed, a T-Mobile SIM card inserted and it still connects to the latter's EDGE data network (provided that the SIM is provisioned for data access).

> Why just EDGE? AT&T 3G/4G products don't support T-Mobile U.S.'s 3G/4G frequencies.

The more useful reason for jailbreaking, however, is the fact that you can take your iPad Wi-Fi + 3G/4G to any civilized nation, pick up a rental Micro SIM, and surf away on a local cellular data network—all without roaming or hacking. It's important to note that all iPads with built-in 3G/4G modules use Micro SIM cards rather than full-size SIM cards. Even if you arrive in a locale that only sells the latter, you can still get it to work with your cellular-enabled iPad. All you need is a pair of scissors, a steady hand, and access to the following tutorial:

www.engadget.com/2010/07/09/how-to-resize-your-sim-and-drink-the-sweet-nectar-of-mobile-fre/

As for owners of the Verizon Wireless model? Unfortunately, there's no SIM card at all in the VZW model. That one relies on a CDMA cellular network, which doesn't use the conventional SIM card.

Beyond all the wireless network talk, there's a very real (and growing) desire to access more applications than the ones Apple lets through its doors. Programmers are capable of producing applications that do far more complex tasks than Apple allows out and in the open. But if an app submitted to the App Store violates any of the company's polices—however questionable those policies might be—that app receives a rejection from the company. The bubbling desire to truly unlock the potential of Apple's iOS

> Some jailbroken apps, like Wi-Fi Sync, eventually become adopted by Apple for use in its App Store or the core of iOS.

devices (the iPad included) has helped spur a litany of applications that aren't welcome in the App Store visited by many millions each day. But they're *more* than welcome in a place called *Cydia*.

Cydia acts as a tool to search for and install applications that are stored in a great many repositories. All of these, of course, require a jailbroken device to access. Apps within jailbreaking stores can be free or costly; it's just another market entirely outside of Apple's purview. To give you an idea of what you can find in here that you won't find in the *actual* App Store, the MyWi application enables jailbroken devices with a 3G/4G radio to share their data signal over Wi-Fi, with no monthly fees raining down from associated carriers. That's usually all I have to mention before people become emphatically interested in the jailbreaking scene. Take a look at a few jailbroken apps within iOS in Figure 16-1.

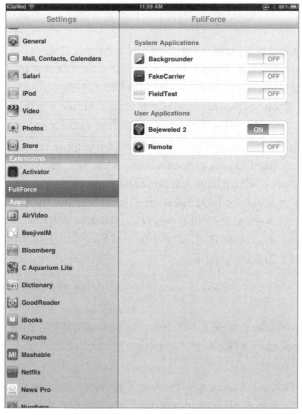

FIGURE 16-1: See Activator? That's a tell-tale sign that jailbreaking is active.

To recap, the two *primary* reasons people take an interest in jailbreaking are to free their iPhones from carrier locks (not applicable to the iPad, of course), and to have access to a nearly limitless number of apps without having to wait for Apple's golden gates to open and allow them onto the official App Store.

What's the Downside?

With every successive release of iOS, Apple seems to make it more and more difficult for jailbreakers to gain access. It's a cold war, of sorts. Apple knows it can't stop jailbreaking from a legal standpoint, but it certainly does everything it can to wrap its code in a shatterproof layer. iOS 5 itself *has* been jailbroken, but it took a lot longer than prior iterations of the operating system. There are also no guarantees with any jailbreak; the iPad may be supported, while the iPad 2 or new iPad may not be. The jailbreaking scene is one that changes and evolves rapidly, with compatibilities changing by the hour some weeks.

The other important tidbit here is the recognition of two major kinds of jailbreaks. There's tethered, and then there's untethered. Both give hints at what they are, but neither just come right out and say it. History has shown that the former nearly always comes before the latter, and I've also found that patience is not only a virtue at the DMV, but in the world of jailbreaking, too. Tethered jailbreaks are easiest for hackers to accomplish, but you're forced to have your iPad plugged into your computer's USB port for the jailbreak to complete. The first time around, it's not so bad; the problem arises when your iPad decides to lock up, freeze, or otherwise go on the fritz while you're away from your machine.

A tethered jailbreak requires the assistance of a computer to boot up every single time. In other words, if you power down your iPad and attempt to turn it back on, you're greeted with an unusable product until you can re-tether it to your host computer and try again. If you're constantly carrying around a notebook computer that you can use to revitalize your jailbroken iPad should it require a reboot, tethered jailbreaks are worth installing. Otherwise, you'd be well advised to hold off until the untethered counterpart arises.

That variant, predictably, doesn't require the assistance of a connected computer in order to start up or reboot. You can simply use your iPad as you normally would, without fear of rebooting into a "bricked" state.

▶ To keep up with the changes, follow @MuscleNerd and @comex on Twitter. They're tightly involved with the evolution of jailbreaks.

▶ Many people jailbreak older devices to add functionality that Apple removes; for example, adding MMS capability to the original iPhone via jailbreak.

DEFINING A BRICK

Bricked is a term thrown around quite often, and it usually refers to an iOS device being unusable for one reason or another. If you attempt to reboot an iPad using a tethered jailbreak, but there's no computer nearby to tether it to, you boot into a black screen that's completely impassable without a partner machine. Some jailbreaks and hacks have been known to brick iPhones, rendering them useless when attempting to make phone calls. And I've personally seen my own iPad bricked when the installation of an iOS 5 beta went awry due to the use of an outdated iTunes build. If you monkey around with your iPad and eventually reboot into a black screen of hopelessness, you can consider yourself bricked.

The good news, however, is that not all bricks remain as such. *True* bricking requires that your iOS device never actually returns to life. In effect, it becomes only marginally more useful than an item used by a common mason. Whenever you jailbreak, bricking is a real possibility. It doesn't happen frequently, but it does happen, and you should be well aware of those consequences before you ever take a single peek down the rabbit hole.

Okay, So How Do I Do It?

One of the reasons that jailbreaking remains a relatively underground activity is the natural fear that a voided warranty could lead to an unwanted repair bill. But perhaps even more significant is just how difficult it is to understand the process, implement the changes and track the updates. While the jailbreaking community is as fervent as ever, the lack of standards has led to a fragmented release schedule, non-uniform labeling, and a situation where there are a couple of leaders instead of one common company overseeing things. The "do as you will" mentality that makes the jailbreaking scene so vibrant and innovative is also a pitfall when it comes to actually understanding it.

There's an unhealthy amount of jargon surrounding the entire scene, so I've done my best to break it down.

- ▶ **Jailbreaking:** The art of running a software package to unlock your iPad for use with unauthorized applications.

- ▶ **Tethered jailbreak:** A jailbreak that requires a host computer to facilitate the iPad boot process.

- ▶ **Untethered jailbreak**: A jailbreak that *doesn't* require a host computer to facilitate the iPad boot process.

- ▶ **Cydia** (`cydia.saurik.com`): An app that runs on jailbroken devices; used to find and install unauthorized software packages, including apps, system extensions, and interface tweaks.

- ▶ **Dev-Team** (`blog.iphone-dev.org`): A few dedicated hackers that should be followed for the latest in jailbreaking news.

- ▶ **Ultrasn0w**: An unlocking program designed by the Dev-Team to break carrier-locked iPhones from their shackles, and give them the ability to function with international SIM cards.

- ▶ **Redsn0w**: This unlocking program enables jailbreaking in the greater sense, opening up the ability to install unauthorized apps on your iPad, iPhone, or iPod touch.

When Apple releases a new iOS build, there's precisely one way to acquire it, and one way to install it, regardless of whether you use a Mac or Windows-based machine. You open up iTunes, you download the new version, and you wait for the magic to happen. The situation described here couldn't be further from the situation found in the jail-breaking world. Oftentimes, Windows and Mac tools arrive at different times. Moreover, jailbreak tools are typically released in beta (or alpha) form and then new builds are released in quick succession after early adopters report back with bugs and issues.

> **WARNING** As with any alpha or beta software, you should take *great* caution in installing pre-release jailbreaking programs. Untested and unproven jailbreaks, particularly those in beta form, can potentially damage your iPad beyond repair. Furthermore, Apple will simply turn the other cheek if you show up for tech support with a jailbroken device. Your only technicians to consult are others in the jailbreaking community, and while it's an admittedly tight-knit crew that has shown to be exceptionally helpful, it's far from a guaranteed fix.

These days, jailbreaks are mostly software-based. That's to say, you simply download the most recent Redsn0w software package (naming conventions can, and usually do, change over time), plug in your iPad, and let the software run. Instructions on usage typically arrive either within the software package or on the forum post announcing the new version. You'll be quickly overwhelmed if you rely on an Internet search to find jailbreaks. There *are* a few legitimate alternative sites out there that offer jailbreaks for a fee, but I'd recommend steering clear. Authentic jailbreaks from the Dev-Team are always made available for free, and you can find them at `blog.iphone-dev.org`. Check out a shot of the Dev-Team site in Figure 16-2.

FIGURE 16-2: The Dev-Team's site isn't flashy, but it's chock-full of information.

The exception to this rule is JailbreakMe (www.jailbreakme.com), which is shown in Figure 16-3. Designed by @comex, this is a simplistic website that enables users of iOS devices to surf to the site, press a button, and have the product jailbroken. It's far and away the easiest method, but it also tends to lag behind software jailbreaks in terms of release. If you're looking for simplicity, though, it's probably worth waiting for JailbreakMe to be compatible with your product and iOS build.

▶ On a jailbroken iPad, Cydia is your go-to app store. It's hardly elegant, but it serves the purpose.

It should be obvious, but I can't stress this enough: Back up your iPad to iTunes before applying a jailbreak. If anything goes awry, you can plug your iPad into your computer, select the Restore option (see Figure 16-4), allow iTunes to reformat your tablet, reinstall the latest legitimate iOS build, and then add your backed up music, apps, documents, and photos. If you forget to back things up (or just opt out), you're stuck starting over if ever your jailbreak renders your iPad useless.

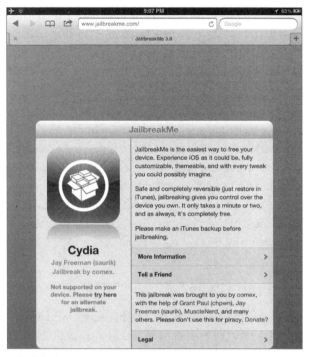

FIGURE 16-3: If you have a compatible device, surfing to this site initiates the jailbreak process.

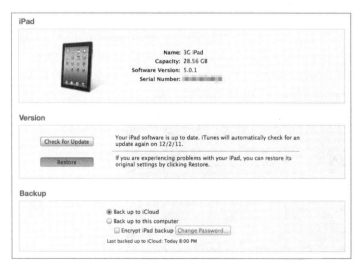

FIGURE 16-4: Clicking Restore gives you the option to Back Up (take it!) or opt out of backing up (don't do it!).

▶ Believe it or not, the standard APP Store still functions on jailbroken devices.

▶ No need to seek Cydia separately; it's included with every jailbreak.

Furthermore, there may end up being a need for you to lose your jailbreak. It's not unfathomable to run into sluggish performance (or worse) when heedlessly installing uncertified apps, and while the aforementioned method "unjailbreaks" your iPad and restores it as it came from the factory, you need that backup if you're looking to avoid duplicate transfers.

Rather than being a store in and of itself, Cydia is simply a universally accepted tool that provides access to apps and extensions that are hosted elsewhere. You *can* install new "sources" in Cydia that search repositories of existing apps, but I confess that most of those are designed to encourage and facilitate piracy. In my mind, jailbreaking should be approached by those who simply want access to creatively and passionately designed apps that—for whatever reason—can't find a home in the App Store. Given that Apple's own App Store still functions on jailbroken devices, users should still head there in order to purchase apps that made it in.

The Best Apps for Jailbroken iPads

If you go through the trouble of jailbreaking your iPad, be it tethered or untethered, you sell yourself short if you don't dive into the bucket of apps that is unavailable to those who are living on the tame side. The options here are even more unlimited than the conventional App Store, but the following list breaks down a few of my suggestions:

▶ **Activator** (free; see Figure 16-5): If you've grown frustrated by the limited multi-touch gesture support on the iPad, here's your extension. It's a beautifully designed, highly practical tool that enables users to customize what gestures do what, and considering that many jailbreak apps require this to be installed, it's a good foundation to have around.

FIGURE 16-5: Activator opens up an entirely new world of control possibilities on the iPad.

- ▶ **OpenSSH** (free): Tired of moving things around the Apple-approved way? This app enables users to SSH into their iPad from a computer in order to edit, move, or change files.

- ▶ **SBSettings** (free): Similar to the settings drop-down menu found on many Android devices, this provides quick and easy access to toggling many settings and services. Furthermore, an Activator gesture can be programmed to pull this up, tossing one shortcut on top of another.

- ▶ **CyDelete** (free): On a non-jailbroken iPad, if you long-press on an app you see a small X appear over it—Apple's built-in core apps notwithstanding. Cydia apps lack this feature, but by downloading this, they gain the easy delete feature.

- ▶ **RetinaPad** ($2.99): One of the more frustrating things on the iPad is downloading an app you're excited about, only to find that it's not optimized for the iPad's enlarged display. Some apps, such as Foursquare, aren't apt to ever support the iPad's display. This app manages to not only enlarge iPhone apps, but actually upscale them to take advantage of the resolution.

- ▶ **Action Menu** (free): It took Apple the better part of eternity to add basic copy and paste functionality to iOS, but the jailbreak community still thinks they can do the company one better. This adds more customizations to handling and moving text, and the (worthwhile) $2.99 Action Menu Plus Pack adds six more actions, including History, Lookup, and the option to instantly tweet text you've selected.

- ▶ **QuickGoogle** (free): If you have Activator installed, just assign a single gesture to bring up a box, which enables you to peck in any search term and have it immediately sent to Google.

- ▶ **Infiniapps** ($0.99 each): This suite of apps enables mega multi-taskers to shove as many apps as they want into a folder and as many apps as they want into the Dock, and place icons vertically, as well as horizontally.

To say that this is just the tip of the iceberg would be understating things tremendously. The amount of customizations available in the Cydia app store is staggering, and the only way to truly stay on top of what's out there is by following the beat in related forums and message boards. I recommend heading to TiPb.com, ModMyi.com, iPadForums.net, MacRumors.com, iPadHelp.com, and iFans.com. These sites provide active, informative user forums, and most of them also provide frequently updated tips, tricks, and hacks related to the iPad and iOS as a whole.

A LOOK AT RECOVERY MODE

Recovery mode is a completely natural mode of operation for the iPad. Although the title could lead you to believe that it's reserved for situations where your iPad is in a real pickle, it's actually the state the iPad slips into whenever a user initiates a standard iOS upgrade or restore. If you've seen the screen in Figure 16-6, you know your iPad is in recovery mode.

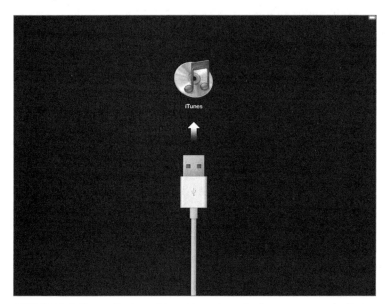

FIGURE 16-6: If your iPad panel has this on it, you're in recovery mode. Godspeed.

Every so often, however, recovery mode decides to take on a life of its own. Although uncommon, I've seen iPads continually restart but never display the Home screen. In the case of an update or restoration being cut short by a yanked cable, a power outage, or a computer freeze, your iPad may sink into a deep sleep that it simply can't exit. If you're looking to force your seemingly bricked iPad into a *workable* recovery mode, you can follow the steps below:

1. Disconnect the USB cable from the iPad, but leave the other end of the cable connected to your computer's USB port.

2. Press and hold the Sleep/Wake button for a few seconds until the red slider appears and then slide the slider and wait for your iPad to turn off.

3. If you're having trouble turning the device off using the above mentioned method, press and hold the Sleep/Wake and Home buttons at the same time; after it turns off, release them both immediately.

4. Now that it's off, press *only* the Home button and reconnect the USB cable to iPad. If you're on the right track, your device starts to turn on. (If your iPad is extremely low on battery life, you may see a red charging screen; let it proceed to charge and check back in about five minutes.)

5. Continue holding the Home button until you see the Connect to iTunes screen; after you spot that, you should release the Home button.

6. Open iTunes, tap OK on any recovery mode alerts, and use iTunes to restore iPad.

Remember, when using recovery mode, you can only *restore* the iPad. All user content is erased, but if you had previously synced with iTunes on your computer, you can restore from a previous backup—that brings your multimedia, contacts, documents, and so on back to where they belong. If you still need further assistance, give this article a peek: support.apple.com/kb/TS1538.

> **TIP** If you get stuck in recovery mode and *really* don't want to complete a restore or firmware update, you can look to TinyUmbrella (thefirmwareumbrella.blogspot.com) or RecBoot as an alternate way to escape.

A LOOK AT DFU (DEVICE FIRMWARE UPDATE) MODE

To put it bluntly, Device Firmware Update (DFU) is recovery mode on steroids. It's the next level of recovery, with the primary difference being the ability to interface with iTunes *without* loading the iPad operating system or boot loader. Technobabble got you down? Look at it this way—entering DFU mode (as seen in Figure 16-7) enables you to override Apple's mandate that the latest official iOS build be the one applied within iTunes. Recovery mode allows an iPad to have the same iOS build reinstalled, or it allows a newer *official* build to be applied (that is, going from iOS 5.0 to iOS 5.0.1). With DFU mode, users are able to change the firmware in either direction, enabling an iPad running iOS 5.0.1 to be downgraded to iOS 5.0.

Rather than just using whatever the most recent build is downloaded to iTunes, you can manually choose an .ipsw file saved to your computer by pressing the Alt/Option key while clicking the Restore button in iTunes. There are myriad reasons why you'd want to manually choose an iOS version to install on your iPad. In some cases, new iOS builds kill compatibility with iOS-friendly car audio interfaces. Perhaps you'd like to manually install an iOS beta before you're actually supposed to. On occasion, new iOS builds break compatibility with select apps. And, of course, if

▶ Wondering how to gain access to older versions of iOS? You can find a monstrous library at www.felixbruns.de/iPod/firmware.

you accidentally let your jailbroken iPad update to the newest official iOS build, your jailbreak—and all associated apps—are evaporated.

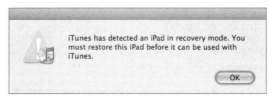

FIGURE 16-7: If you see this pop up in iTunes, it's safe to assume your iPad is in recovery mode...unless the screen is black, meaning it's in DFU mode.

▶ Remember, all new Apple-approved iOS builds usually kill preexisting jailbreaks.

If you place your iPad into DFU mode, you can install any firmware you want, provided that you have two things. First, you need the desired .ipsw file, which you can download from www.felixbruns.de/iPod/firmware. Second, you need the version of iTunes that was out when the matching iOS build was out. You can find a fantastic archive of old iTunes versions at www.oldapps.com/itunes.php.

But here's the thing—you can't easily put two iTunes versions on a single machine. The libraries conflict, your playlists could be overwritten, and in general, I just don't recommend trying it. Whenever I need to downgrade with an older version of iTunes, I use an older PC that I keep around for hacking tasks such as these. If you've a spare machine, I highly recommend using that. Trying to run two copies of iTunes on a single machine is a recipe for disaster (and tears).

Furthermore, you need saved SHSH blobs from an old iOS version in order to install that old version on an iPad. With that, you also need to bypass Apple's firmware signing security model, which is the final hurdle to getting an iOS build to function with iTunes. You can find an entire how-to guide that explains the ins and outs of SHSH blobs at:

www.ipadforums.net/ipad-hacking/24323-shsh-blobs-frequently-asked-questions-updated.html

Without further ado, here's a guide to getting your iPad into DFU mode:

1. Connect your iPad to your iTunes-equipped machine.

2. Turn your iPad completely off (hold down the top Sleep/Wake button, then slide to shut down).

3. Hold down the Sleep/Wake button *and* the Home button for ten seconds and then release only the top Sleep/Wake button.

4. Continue to hold down the Home button until you see an iTunes dialog box informing you that an iPad in recovery mode has been found.

If you've done this correctly, your iPad's display remains solid black. If you see any graphic at all, you're actually in recovery mode.

If you're looking to install a very specific firmware or iOS build on your iPad, or otherwise gain access to portions of the iPad that are generally locked down, DFU mode is your access point. Be warned, however, that modifying files on your iPad could indeed result in a bricked device. And if it's bricked, no Apple warranty applies.

> **TIP** DFU mode can be a last resort for iPads that are corrupt or stuck for any number of reasons. I've seen an iPad that refused to accept a restoration attempt from iTunes while in recovery mode, but by booting it into DFU, the restoration attempt was successful. In theory, the existence of DFU mode should make it impossible to brick your iPad beyond repair via software. Hardware hacks are another matter, though.

CHALLENGING CHARGING REQUIREMENTS

Due to the years of iPhone and iPod touch dominance before the iPad ever surfaced, a great many products emerged with charging support for the aforementioned Apple devices. Everything from speaker systems to charging stations to automotive adapters were engineered to charge iPod touch and iPhone units, but those weren't designed to output enough power to charge the iPad. You see, high power USB devices are defined as those that draw more than 100mA from the USB power line; low power devices are ones that draw 100mA or less.

No, you can't charge the iPad over FireWire. I tried.

The 10W power adapter that ships with the iPad outputs significantly more power than the smaller USB power plug that ships with the iPhone. But beyond that, many USB ports or docking accessories built *pre*-iPad were designed to energize "low-power" USB products. Not surprisingly, the iPad is most certainly not one of those. If you attempt to charge your iPad with one of those antediluvian solutions, you'll probably see a message like the one shown in Figure 16-8.

The only surefire solutions for charging the iPad are the 10W power plug that it ships with, a USB port on a relatively new Mac (2008 or newer should be fine), or a USB power adapter that ships with the iPhone. It's worth noting, however, that the latter two rejuvenate the iPad at a slower rate than the proper 10W adapter. These days, a slew of peripherals and accessories go out of their way to ensure iPad charging support; given that the device has such a huge amount of market share, it's obviously vital to provide charging support whenever possible.

FIGURE 16-8: This is what you see when you try to charge the iPad over FireWire, for example.

FIGURE 16-9: Quite possibly the most annoying error an iPad owner can see. Plugged in, but not enough oomph to charge.

If ever you connect it to a strange USB port, you can immediately see if it's receiving enough power to charge by looking at the top right corner. If you see a Not Charging message (see the upper-right corner of Figure 16-9), then you'll know that the port you're using isn't providing enough power.

TIP Before tossing your PC notebook in the rubbish after it refuses to charge your iPad, try this. Take a look at the current battery percentage and then press the Sleep/Wake button at the top to turn the display off. Leave the iPad plugged in for five to ten minutes and then check the battery percentage once more. I've found that many underpowered USB ports do charge the iPad if the power-draining display is switched off, but as soon as it's toggled back on, the Not Charging message reappears.

TAKING YOUR IPAD IN FOR SERVICE

If you steer clear of jailbreaking, iPads are generally reliable. But of course, as with any monolithic consumer electronics company, problems can and do arise. Dealing with Apple's phone support (www.apple.com/contact) is about like dealing with any-one's phone support—it's not exactly something anyone wakes up looking forward to. But unlike most rival companies, Apple has a massive advantage when it comes to customer support: Apple Stores and Apple Specialist resellers.

LOCATING HELP

You can find your nearest Apple Store at www.apple.com/buy/locator. Locate your nearest Apple Specialist—authorized by Apple to deem themselves "in-dependent Dealers and Service Providers"—at channelprograms.apple.com/Specialist.

If you're within driving distance of an Apple Store, your best bet is to set up a Genius Bar appointment. Each Apple Store has a Genius Bar stocked with trained employees that do nothing but service Macs, iPads, and Apple products. They aren't there to sell you product protection plans you'll never need or a set of orange head-phones that your son "would just love"—they're there to fix your gear, period.

Best of all, *it's absolutely free to make a Genius Bar appointment.* Yes, free. Even if your product is out of warranty. Most people find this arrangement truly unfathom-able, but by placing trained professionals in front of Apple customers at no charge, the company has created a significant competitive advantage that I've yet to see matched by a rival.

There's no need to pick up the phone to make an appointment. Just point your web browser to www.apple.com/retail/geniusbar, select the locale nearest you, and choose an available date and time for your appointment. A few clicks later, you have an e-mail confirmation and the ability to change or modify it at any time prior. I advise arriving approximately ten minutes early on your appointment day, but be prepared to wait another half-hour beyond your scheduled time. They aren't late often, but I've seen it happen.

You should also make every effort to bring *everything* remotely related to your issue. Bring your iPad, your charger, a USB cable, any accessories that have been

▶ Try not to book the final Genius Bar appointment for the day. (Unless you know you'll be brief!)

▶ When you arrive for your appointment, just notify any employee that you're "here for your Genius Bar appointment." They'll sign you in.

giving you issues, and even your computer that you use to sync it with (assuming it's portable enough to make the trip). The more you bring, the more likely the experts are to solve what's ailing your poor tablet. If the problem isn't abuse, and your iPad's under warranty, you can have it fixed either on the spot or in-store, depending on how serious the issue is. Even if it costs you, the Genius walks you through everything before providing you with an estimate—all for free.

> **NOTE** If you live in a more rural or remote area, accessing an Apple Store might not be feasible. Apple Specialist resellers act as extensions to those core stores, and in all of my experiences, they have been more than willing to help. The people that run these shops are your neighbors—locals who have a passion for Apple and technology in general. In fact, those preferring a personal touch may want to aim first at a Specialist.
>
> They're authorized to do the same repairs that bona fide Apple Stores can do, and they generally do it with a far bigger smile. As an anecdote, an Apple Specialist in Maine let me borrow a FireWire cable to rescue data from an older MacBook Pro while I was on vacation. *At no charge.* That's the kind of attitudes these resellers carry.

SUMMARY

Apple deliberately kept a lot of doors closed in iOS and iTunes, likely to improve the overall experience for the masses and prevent too much tinkering. That tinkering, however, can lead to all sorts of beautifully innovative apps and extensions, all of which can be found and utilized on a jailbroken iPad. Tapping into Cydia allows new potential to be unlocked on your device, but it also opens it for malware and unoptimized applications to mar the experience.

Dipping one's toes into the jailbreaking world while being prudent is something that I highly recommend, but only for users who are well versed in backups and not averse to having to restore the iPad in case things go awry. There's a certain level of risk associated with deviating from Apple's predefined iOS path, but, as with most risk, this too brings about great reward.

In the case that something goes south, you have options for getting back on track. Understanding recovery and DFU modes is vital to keeping your nerves calm and your iPad in service. For times when you just need to see the expert, Apple's envious Genius Bar and network of authorized specialists are there to investigate and solve issues.

Index

S

S/MIME, 63

Safari
  Add to Home Screen, 274
  keyboard shortcuts, 96
  pinching, 107

Samsung HM7000, 305

Samsung SCH-LC11 Mobile Hotpot, 12

Sanho HyperDrive, 307

SBSettings, 321

ScoreCenter XL, 236

Scoshe freeKEY, 298–299

screen captures, 87, 89

screen orientation
  GMail views, 49–51
  locking, 88–89

ScreenChomp, 123

SD (Secure Digital) card adapters/slots, 10, 307

SD TV shows, data plan requirements, 14

Seagate GoFlex Satellite, 161, 310

Search Web, 44

Search Wikipedia, 44

searches
  apps, 217–220
  Game Center games, 182
  search engines, changing, 105
  Search Web, 44
  Search Wikipedia, 44
  Spotlight, 104–105
  Universal Search, 42–44

secondary dock bar, 88–89, 107

secondary menu bar, 91–92

secondary monitors, 165–167

setting up
  3G, 11–18
  AirPlay, 127–128, 133–134
  AirPort Express, 129–130
  FaceTime, 110–111
  Find My iPad, 20–21
  Game Center, 173–174
  iCloud, 281–284
  iMessage, 248–250
  Twitter integration, 260–262

ShairPort, 144

Shairport4w, 134

SharePod, 79

shortcuts, 86–92
  auto-correction, 95
  hard reboots, 87
  Home button, 87
  keyboard shortcuts, 94–98
  locking screen orientation, 88
  muting volume, 88–88
  Power button, 87
  screen captures, 87
  secondary dock bar, 88–89
  secondary menu bar, 91–92

Showyou, 264

SHSH blobs, 324

Shuttersnitch, 162

SkoobaWrap, 302

Skyfire, 18, 212–214

Skype, 118–123
  call forwarding, 123
  calling plans, 120
  instant messages, 123
  Online Number, 122
  receiving calls, 122
  Skype Credits, 120–122
  SMS messages, 123
  syncing contacts, 71

Slacker Radio, 232

Slide to Power Off option, 87

Smart Cover, 302–303

SMS messages. *See also* iMessage
  Skype, 123

social networking
  apps, 267–269
  Facebook, 264–267
  location-based networking, 269–273
  Twitter, 260–264

software updates, 24

Solidline RightShift, 298

Songkick Concerts, 231

Soulo microphones, 307–308

speakers
  AirPlay-enabled, 135–137
  USB speakers and AirPort Express, 129